'Part festschrift, part eulogy, part love letter, Art
with John Bowlby – and his own journey to
theoretical exposition with vivid anecdote in ways that are readable, personal, engaging
and very real. Like Bowlby himself, his story brings much-needed fresh air into the
sometimes stale world of psychoanalytic discourse. Strongly recommended for all practitioners and students, who will find here a rare amalgam of common sense and
inspiration.'

Prof Jeremy Holmes, MD, FRCPsych, University of Exeter, UK. Author,
John Bowlby and Attachment Theory, and *The Search for the Secure Base*

'Arturo Ezquerro brings a contagious enthusiasm for life and relationships which makes
Attachment Theory more real, attractive and palatable. My father would have been
deeply moved by it.'

Sir Richard Bowlby, medical and scientific photographer,
and eldest son of John Bowlby

'A labour of love which gives a fascinating insight into the mind and ideas of the father
of Attachment Theory.'

Dr Colin Murray Parkes, OBE, MD, FRCPsych, DL. Author,
Bereavement: Studies of Grief in Adult Life

'This marvellous book weaves the author's professional journey into an account of his
six years of affectionate supervision with one of the great developmental scientists of the
twentieth century. Bowlby's own biographical journey, and his single-minded determination to define "the nature of the bond" move the narrative along, and move the
reader too. The volume also gives compelling narratives on the history of psychoanalysis
and the post-war Tavistock Clinic.'

Dr Sebastian Kraemer, FRCPsych. Honorary consultant child and adolescent
psychiatrist, Tavistock Clinic. Family therapist. Co-editor,
The Politics of Attachment: Towards a Secure Society

'Reading this book has been a great pleasure and has taken me back 45 years to when
John Bowlby was my tutor at the Tavistock Clinic. I soon realised his warmth and
thoughtful passion... The volume is a warm and faithful tribute to Bowlby's life's work
and to all those touched by the grip of attachment and separation.'

Dr Marcus Johns, FRCPsych. Psychoanalyst, former Tavistock Clinic's
consultant, director of the London Child Guidance Training Centre and
editor of the Bulletin of the British Psychoanalytical Society.

'Arturo Ezquerro has written an eloquent and moving account of the life and thought
of John Bowlby whose recognition of the importance of childhood attachment has now
become common wisdom, after being met initially with strong resistance in the psychoanalytic profession. Of all the fields of scientific enquiry, psychoanalytic theory is
perhaps the one most affected by the personality and experience of the propounder, and

one of the merits of this study is to place Bowlby's thought intimately within its biographical and professional contexts. The latter appropriately include the author's personal testimony to the quality of Bowlby's mentorship and, if the most touching moments in the book are judiciously chosen quotations from patients, this seems very apt to its subject's evident ability to listen.'

Prof Michael Bell, English and Comparative Literary Studies, University of Warwick, UK. Author, *The Sentiment of Reality: Truth of Feeling in the European Novel* and *H. D. Lawrence: Language and Being*

'This volume brings to life a great man and his ideas in a way that the best of biographies can. And while the book is at it, we learn as much about Bowlby's ideas as about his warmth and passionate nature, to which so many of his students and co-workers became personally attached.'

Prof Bob Hinshelwood, MD, FRCPsych, Centre for Psychoanalytic Studies, University of Essex, UK. Author, *What Happens in Groups*, *Research on the Couch* and *Psychoanalysis and History*

'A book that, uniquely, combines scholarly erudition with passion; wisdom with compassion. It teaches us about the dehumanising effects of dogma and systems and the healing potential of attachment.'

Dr Paul Mallett, consultant psychiatrist and former Medical Director, Central and North-West London NHS Foundation Trust

'A vivid, original and personal account of a great man. John Bowlby's attachment theory is now widely known and accepted. What is less well known is the intense struggle Bowlby had to convince his critics, especially the psychoanalytical establishment, and the hurt this occasioned him. This book gives a highly readable account of the group and institutional politics surrounding the emergence of the theory, alongside Bowlby's own personal relationships and his profound influence on the author. In all our work, we strive to achieve some form of psychological integration. This book pulsates with that striving – and achieves it, with respect and love for its subject.'

Dr Morris Nitsun, PhD. Consultant psychologist, and training analyst, Institute of Group Analysis. Author, *The Anti-Group, The Group as an Object of Desire* and *Beyond the Anti-Group*

'Arturo Ezquerro has meticulously researched the origins of Attachment Theory and tracked the course of its development with the same qualities of persistence and rigour that he learned from John Bowlby, his much-loved mentor. Ezquerro leaves no stone unturned in an almost detective-like investigation of Bowlby's biography and sources of influence, resulting in a story of the first order in which all the pieces eventually come together. This book transforms a "theory" into a lived experience that is comprehensively informative and a pleasure to read.'

Liza Glenn, consultant psychologist, Jungian analyst and senior trainer, Institute of Group Analysis

'This book is a masterpiece of clarity: a most readable scholarly exposition of Bowlby and his works. I can strongly recommend it to general practitioners and all professionals in primary care.'

Dr Clare Gerada, director of clinical governance for Primary Care; medical director, NHS Practitioners Health Programme; and former president, Royal College of General Practitioners

'A lovely blend of a personal reminiscence of John Bowlby and a history of how attachment theory developed. Arturo Ezquerro gives rich and privileged memories from Bowlby's family and close colleagues, as well as vivid illustrations from his work as a child and adolescent psychiatrist and group analyst. The volume raises key questions about psychoanalysis and its development as a theory of the mind and as a treatment method. I really did enjoy reading this unique book.'

Dr Gwen Adshead, FRCPsych. Consultant forensic psychiatrist and group analyst. Co-author, *A Matter of Security: Attachment Theory, Psychiatry and Psychotherapy*

'This wonderful book is essential reading for everyone whose work is involved with families. John Bowlby's attachment theory is portrayed in a very real, moving and sensitive way. I found it pivotal to my role in understanding the grief of parents when a child died.'

Jenni Thomas, OBE. Founder, Child Bereavement Trust. Awarded for lifetime achievement and educational merit, British Medical Association

'A touching, beautifully crafted, new biographical profile of John Bowlby – inspiring, eloquent and powerful.'

Carlos Durán, linguist and author

'A great reading experience which has brought the figure and work of John Bowlby alive and real in a way I can use in my work. This is a book that no one interested in Bowlby and attachment will want to be without.'

Dr Ray Haddock, MB ChB, MMedSc, FRCPsych. Consultant medical psychotherapist, group analyst and systems-centered practitioner and consultant

'An eminently readable and captivating journey into John Bowlby and the entire field of attachment – a huge learning experience.'

Jacqueline Fogden, group analyst, psychotherapist and former head-teacher

'Shrink unwrapped: A telling yet affectionate portrait of John Bowlby, the man – a joy to read.'

Bryan Rimmer, Fleet Street writer

'I couldn't stop reading... This book is an encouragement to become attached, to grow and to love – a truly uplifting experience.'

Anthony Stone, consultant psychotherapist

'*Encounters with John Bowlby* brings to life the context, development and applications of attachment theory, in a way that is accessible, enjoyable and enlivening.'

Kate **White**, senior supervisor and teacher, The Bowlby Centre. Editor, *Attachment: New Directions in Psychotherapy and Relational Psychoanalysis*

'This very special book covering Bowlby's life and work is a timely and delightfully clear reminder of how crucial attachment research is to both our understanding of ourselves and the care of future generations. Highly recommended to all professionals and public, and to those in positions of authority.'

Dr **Felicity de Zulueta**, FRCPsych. Emeritus consultant psychiatrist in psychotherapy, former director of the Trauma Unit, South London and Maudsley NHS Foundation Trust and senior clinical lecturer, King's College London

ENCOUNTERS WITH JOHN BOWLBY

Encounters with John Bowlby: Tales of Attachment is an insightful, heartfelt and faithful homage to John Bowlby (1907–1990), the 'father' of Attachment Theory. The book unfolds as a touching and absorbing biographical journey into his life and work, where Bowlby is portrayed vividly through his individual, family and group attachment history, as well as his personal and professional development.

This is a thoroughly researched and unique volume: a creative hybrid of scholarly erudition and passionately delivered real-life experiences covering the entire field of attachment. The work is co-constructed from the privileged position of sitting at the feet of the founder of the theory, drawing on his lifelong research and knowledge. The reader can learn from and identify with stirring, true stories that illustrate the struggle to become attached, to survive and to grow.

Encounters with John Bowlby will appeal to anyone who is interested in personal development and relationships. It will be of special interest to mental health and other healthcare professionals, as well as students undertaking doctoral courses or attending other courses related to attachment and John Bowlby.

Dr Arturo Ezquerro, a consultant psychiatrist, psychoanalytic psychotherapist and group analyst, is senior lecturer, assessor and trainer at the Institute of Group Analysis, and former Head of NHS Medical Psychotherapy Services in Brent, London. He was supervised by John Bowlby at the Tavistock Clinic (1984–1990) and has published over 60 articles and book chapters in five languages.

ENCOUNTERS WITH JOHN BOWLBY

Tales of Attachment

Arturo Ezquerro

Routledge
Taylor & Francis Group

LONDON AND NEW YORK

First published 2017
by Routledge
2 Park Square, Milton Park, Abingdon, Oxon OX14 4RN

and by Routledge
711 Third Avenue, New York, NY 10017

Routledge is an imprint of the Taylor & Francis Group, an informa business

British Library Cataloguing in Publication Data
A catalogue record for this book is available from the British Library

Library of Congress Cataloging in Publication Data
Names: Ezquerro, Arturo, author.
Title: Encounters with John Bowlby : tales of attachment / Arturo Ezquerro.
Description: 1 Edition. | New York : Routledge, 2017. | Includes bibliographical references and index.
Identifiers: LCCN 2016017838| ISBN 9781138667631 (hardback) | ISBN 9781138667648 (pbk.) | ISBN 9781315545554 (ebook)
Subjects: LCSH: Bowlby, John. | Psychologists--Great Britain--Biography. | Attachment behavior.
Classification: LCC BF109.B69 E97 2017 | DDC 150.92 [B]--dc23
LC record available at https://lccn.loc.gov/2016017838

ISBN: 978-1-138-66763-1 (hbk)
ISBN: 978-1-138-66764-8 (pbk)
ISBN: 978-1-315-54555-4 (ebk)

Typeset in Bembo
by Taylor & Francis Books

Dear Tamsin,
I hope you find this
slice of history interesting
lots of love
Fabian

PS. I enjoyed his teaching

To María, to Arturo and to Ignacio – for making life more meaningful.

CONTENTS

FIGURES

ABOUT THE AUTHOR

FIGURE 0.1 A recent picture of the author.

Dr Arturo Ezquerro (MB BS, MRCPsych, TCAPsych, MSPsych, MIntsGA), a consultant psychiatrist, psychoanalytic psychotherapist, and group analyst, is senior lecturer, assessor and trainer at the Institute of Group Analysis, and former Head of NHS Medical Psychotherapy Services in Brent, London. He was supervised by John Bowlby at the Tavistock Clinic (1984–1990), and has published over 60 articles and book chapters in five languages (English, Spanish, Dutch, Italian and German). Author's email: arturo.ezquerro@ntlworld.com

ACKNOWLEDGEMENT

John Bowlby has been present in my mind throughout the writing of *Tales of Attachment*. He is a large part of my world: six years of mentorship with him at the Tavistock Clinic have become a truly timeless experience. I am deeply grateful to him and to his wife Ursula who survived him by ten years, during which she wrote to me regularly with her warm and delightful reminiscence of John. They were a loving and inspirational couple; their relationship is an important part of the book.

I am most grateful for the help I have received from members of the Bowlby family: Xenia and Richard Bowlby, Pia and Carlos Durán, Sophie Barnard and Juliet Hopkins. I have much enjoyed each and every one of my meetings with them. They have given me a special window of memories into their relationship with their father, father-in-law, grandfather and uncle. I particularly value the support and enthusiasm of Richard Bowlby, as vividly portrayed in his foreword, and of Carlos Durán who provided precise and helpful observations on the text.

I very much appreciate the encouragement and backing that I have received from Peter Bruggen and Anton Obholzer with the book project. They were my research and clinical tutors at the time when I was supervised by Bowlby and Bruggen became my mentor after Bowlby's death. My relationship with them played a significant part in my development; they remain a motivating force.

While working on the book, I have also felt stimulated by what I learned from Caroline Garland, Sandy Bourne, Sue Reid and Dick Bird, my other main Tavistock supervisors, as well as from Harold Behr, Adele Mitwoch, Earl Hopper and Malcolm Pines, my chief trainers at the Institute of Group Analysis.

Tales of Attachment: Encounters with John Bowlby has in fact been a group experience. I have been inspired by key authors who have written about Bowlby's journey, principally by Jeremy Holmes, Suzan Van Dijken, Robert Karen, Mario Marrone, Mary Ainsworth, Inge Bretherton, Frank Van der Horst, and John Byng-Hall. I have also felt connected with John Bowlby through my contacts and conversations with colleagues from the International Attachment Network and the Bowlby Centre, including John Southgate, Colin Murray Parkes, Tirril Harris, Felicity de Zulueta, Gwen Adshead, Maite Pi, Liza Glenn, Mark Linington and Kate White.

My extended thanks go to many other colleagues and friends, as well as to members of the Tavistock Clinic, past and present. Among them Margaret Rustin, Sebastian Kraemer, Domenico Di Ceglie, Pat Land, Louise Lyon, Margot Waddell, Amanda Hawke, Gill Bryant, Jacqui Dillon, Alice Byrnes, Tony Jaffa, Tony Kaplan, Paul Mallett, Jan Wise, Rizkar Amin, Nicolás Caparrós, Isabel Sanfeliu, Maureen Kendal, Peter Wilson, Rosalyn Mayho, Chris Ridley, Susannah Kahtan, Morris Nitsun, John Schlapobersky, Bob Hinshelwood, Michael Bell, Clare Gerada, Belinda and David Chalom, Jenni Thomas, Ray Haddock, Likda Morash, and Emilio Butragueño are all noteworthy. They have read parts of the manuscript, made helpful suggestions, provided lovely anecdotes, or reassuringly discussed with me different aspects of the project. Within this group I am especially grateful to Jacqui Dillon for trusting me and sharing painful memories about her traumatic past and her recovery.

I wish to acknowledge the help received in obtaining much valued material from Karnac, the Wellcome Trust, the Tavistock & Portman NHS Foundation Trust Library, and the King's Fund, Institute of Group Analysis & Group-Analytic Society Joint Library. The guidance received from Elizabeth Nokes in particular has made my job considerably easier.

I am always going to be indebted to three friends for their generous and invaluable aid with the book's editing and polishing up. My relationship with them has been a much appreciated and enjoyable learning process. Jacqueline Fogden has given a consistently sensitive, maternal quality to the work and lots of common sense. Marcus Johns has provided a caring and reliable paternal perspective, together with excellent psychoanalytic tweaks to the latent content and structure of the book. Bryan Rimmer has helped me make the text jargon-free and has coloured it with a wonderful sense of humour.

The completion of the work also owes a good deal to colleagues who have played a supportive and enabling role in my life, at times when I have felt lost or vulnerable: Vicente Madoz, Barbara Frosh, Tony Garelick, Richard Caplan, Jane Marshall and Anthony Stone.

Finally, I could not have written this book without María Cañete – not without her love, understanding, patience, and companionship.

FOREWORD

Arturo Ezquerro brings a contagious enthusiasm for life and relationships to *Encounters with John Bowlby: Tales of Attachment* – he is truly passionate about attachments. My father, John Bowlby, was passionate about helping vulnerable people to enjoy close, intimate and mutually satisfying relationships – especially children and their families. He tried all his life to improve children's mental health, with the hope of a happier and more peaceful society in the future.

My father's childhood was grossly disrupted by the First World War, particularly his relationship with his father. After being abroad for five years as a senior military surgeon at the Front, my grandfather returned home 'a changed man' – I assume he suffered from post-traumatic stress. I was born during the Second World War in 1941, and my father was serving at the War Office Selection Board so as a young child I saw very little of him. But I was fortunate to be raised by a devoted and caring mother within her large extended family.

As a small child, it was difficult for me to form a close bond with my father. This was partly due to his war-time absences, and partly due to his own attachment history of losing a loving nanny who raised him, and who left him when he was about four. After the War my father liked to explore the natural world with the family and to spend time with the children. He and I gradually developed a close companionship bond, but he continued to find it difficult to express affection openly to those he loved. He was more able to show his feelings towards his colleagues, students, patients, and especially to his much loved grandchildren. During the last twenty years of his life, he and I had many discussions about his ideas on *attachment theory* – something that I have increasingly learned to treasure, and to share.

My father believed passionately in the value to society of devoted and sensitive parents. He recognised the huge commitment that it takes to do the job well. It is more than the countless hours of hard work; it is about the quality of the relationship. He wrote in 1953:

> The provision of mothering cannot be considered in terms of hours per day, but only in terms of the enjoyment of each other's company which mother and child obtain. Such enjoyment and close identification of feeling is possible for either party only if the relationship is continuous.... Just as a baby needs to feel that he belongs to his mother, a mother needs to feel that she belongs to her child, and it is only when she has the satisfaction of this feeling, that it is easy for her to devote herself to him.

My father did not define his use of the term 'continuous' when describing an attachment relationship and this has led to a long-standing confusion. I feel confident that he meant an enduring relationship lasting many years, where periods of separation are shorter than those that would cause the child major distress or trauma. The length of these periods will depend on the age of the child, with whom they are left, where they are left, how often they are left, the child's temperament and the quality of their relationship with their primary attachment figure (PAF) – the person who is raising them, usually but not necessarily the birth mother.

Following my father's presentation of his paper "The Nature of the Child's Tie to his Mother" in 1957 at the British psychoanalytical society, I witnessed his struggle to get his attachment theory more widely accepted. I was struck by the great resistance he met from many (but not all) of his professional colleagues, and the dismissive and aggressive tactics used by some sections of the general public. I fear that similar attitudes have emerged in some sectors of society in recent years. There is now a culture of long working hours, of putting financial profit before people and relationships, coupled with the impact of excessive use of computer games, social media and other technology that deprive many children and adults of opportunities for intimate human contact – and it is the children who are paying the highest price.

Creating and maintaining secure attachment relationships is becoming more and more difficult, and the mental health of children does not seem to be improving as my father had hoped. Our DNA has not changed significantly in the past 200,000 years, so what are the experiences that our children are having (or not having) that could account for this lack of improvement in their mental health? Studies in developmental neurobiology and epigenetics have been focussing on the first three years of life – a particularly sensitive period of child development. Some of these studies have looked at stressful experiences in early life that can adversely affect the rapidly developing brain of babies and toddlers, with reports of varying degrees of negative associations. I am very concerned that our society has developed a culture that pushes the stress experienced by babies and toddlers close to dangerously high levels. In too many cases the stresses have been pushed so far as to be overwhelming, and have become a risk factor contributing to future mental health problems.

Attachment theory is now one of the foremost paradigms for understanding human development and relationships, and a constantly increasing number of health and care professionals across the world use attachment principles in their daily practice. However, for many members of the general public who are raising babies and toddlers, attachment theory remains largely unknown or has become misunderstood and distorted. With the internet now being the first source of information for many new parents, it is not surprising that much of this confusion is the result of changes in the meaning of important terminology used in attachment theory.

I have no qualifications in psychotherapy – my work was in scientific and medical photography – but after my father's death in 1990 I was encouraged to give talks about his work to special interest groups in the health and care professions. The people who most encouraged me included Mario Marrone, John Southgate and Arturo Ezquerro, all of whom had been supervised by my father. In my talks I sometimes use a quote of his, published in the Boston Globe in 1987 (when he was eighty): "What most astonishes me about family life in the United States is that mothers tell me they can't afford to look after their own babies, in the richest country in the world!" He felt that Western Societies often denied the enormous amount of time, care and attention that emotionally enriching parenting demands. In 1951 my father had written: "If we value our children, we must cherish their parents".

Throughout the millions of years of human evolution, parents have been cherished by others and supported in raising their babies. Much of this support would have been to help care for their babies and toddlers – but what would have been the quality of the baby's relationship with the substitute carers, before the baby was left with them? In my view, the baby would typically have been left in the care of a trusted family member to whom the baby had already developed a secondary attachment. They would have been a familiar person, not an unknown care provider – and the care would have been in a familiar location (the environment of evolutionary adaptedness).

Many of the talks I am asked to give about my father's work on attachment theory are for childcare organisations, and I am a supporter of childcare providers who actively promote personal continuity of care and the development of a stable secondary attachment with each baby and toddler they care for. The term 'child care' has undergone a complete change of meaning over recent years and this has led to further confusion. In 1951 my father published a monograph for the World Health Organization titled "Maternal Care and Mental Health", which was republished in 1953 as *Child Care and the Growth of Love*. In the early 1950s, *maternal care* and *child care* were interchangeable and both referred to care provided by mother. However, over the intervening years, the meaning of *child care* has changed and it now means care of a child by anyone other than mother.

There are some other terms that cause confusion, but first it is worth outlining the healthy cycle of *attachment seeking behaviour*. During a typical day in the life of a securely attached toddler at home with their primary attachment figure (PAF), the toddler will spend much time exploring. Although there is significant variation, typical exploration behaviour involves venturing away from the immediate proximity of the PAF and then returning at regular intervals for reassurance before venturing off once more. However, if the toddler becomes aware that their PAF is not where they expect them to be and is therefore not immediately accessible, the toddler's attachment seeking response will be triggered and they will usually protest very loudly and start to search for their PAF.

Typically the PAF will hear the cries of protest and call out reassuringly and then return to the toddler within a few moments. Upon reunion with the PAF the toddler's attachment seeking responses will be satisfied, their cries of protest will stop and the toddler will soon resume exploration. My father called this sequence of events 'maintenance of proximity' and it is a typical cycle of healthy exploration with brief periods of attachment seeking behaviour and the occasional urgent reunion between the toddler and their PAF whenever called for. This seemingly unremarkable behaviour has protected babies and toddlers for millions of years; it is central to the formation of childhood attachments and family bonds today, and is at the very heart of attachment theory. However, 'maintenance of proximity' is now being called 'separation anxiety'.

During my talks I am frequently asked about 'separation anxiety' and this is another term that causes confusion. In the second volume of my father's trilogy on *Attachment and Loss: Separation, Anxiety and Anger*, he addresses the consequences to babies and toddlers of varying degrees of temporary separation from their PAF. My father used the term 'separation anxiety' to describe only the very disturbed behaviour and serious long term consequences to a toddler of experiencing several days or weeks of separation in hospital or residential care-home without access to their PAF. However, this level of psychopathology is now termed 'separation anxiety *disorder*', and all other protests of babies and toddlers when separated from their PAF are now referred to as 'separation anxiety'.

The term 'separation anxiety' does not distinguish between different degrees of separation distress. This one term now covers the whole range of distress from the briefest moment during 'maintenance of proximity', up to prolonged and often intense levels of distress when separated from their PAF for several hours. To add to the confusion, the name for the developmental stage that starts at five or six months old (when protest at separation becomes apparent) is also being called 'separation anxiety' and it is often not clear whether it is the behaviour or the developmental stage that is being referred to. This already confused situation is further compounded by the term 'normal'. A typical behaviour associated with an age-appropriate stage of infant development is described as being normal behaviour (such as in maintenance of proximity), but the word 'normal' is now being taken to mean healthy. Normal is being used to describe *all* levels of separation protest that are now *all* being described as healthy – while very often they are not. A baby or toddler's distress at being separated may well be a *predictable* behaviour, but just because distress at separation is predictable. It must not be assumed that distress is a healthy experience.

A further confusion I have noticed concerns 'easy' babies who can be left with anyone without protesting. 'Easy' babies and toddlers who do not protest when left by their PAF with an unfamiliar care provider in unfamiliar surroundings are thought to have adjusted quickly and settled in well to the new situation. Many such babies and toddlers develop the habit of coping with the pain of separation in this unfamiliar situation by shutting down their attachment seeking response, and some of these babies have periods when they activate their emergency defences and they cope with the fear of separation by dissociating.

This is a serious problem that can occur when babies and toddlers have not been given the opportunity to form a secondary attachment (in the presence of the PAF) to one familiar day-care provider (their *key person*) by having regular and frequent visits for some weeks before being gradually transitioned into day-care. Developing and maintaining a secondary attachment to one key person can present problems in day-care settings where the importance of secondary attachments is not given sufficient priority and where high staff turnover prevents continuity of care by the key person. Leaving babies and toddlers without a secondary attachment figure significantly increases their levels of stress – during this very sensitive period of brain development.

My father and Arturo had a continuous working relationship over six years of fortnightly mentorship meetings. The narrative of their warm, affectionate and mutually fulfilling relationship is touching. The book clearly shows that attachment is about proximity-seeking (physical and emotional), as well as exploration and growth; it is about regulating the distance from and to a secure base. By reporting, jargon-free, captivating stories of attachment in my father's life and in the lives of other people who were significant to him, the book is accessible to professionals, students and public. I think it makes attachment theory more real, attractive and palatable. This book gives a very personal image of my father and I have no doubt that he would have been deeply moved by it.

Sir Richard Bowlby, London 2015

PREFACE

Reading *Tales of Attachment* has been a great pleasure and has taken me back 45 years to when I started training in Child Psychiatry at the Tavistock Clinic, where John Bowlby was my clinical tutor and Hyla Holden was my supervising consultant. As a junior and inexperienced psychiatrist I was in awe of John Bowlby and at first, unnecessarily, somewhat frightened of him, imagining him as a rather gruff ex-Army officer dealing with a new recruit.

I was soon to realise Bowlby's warmth and thoughtful passion for the children and families that came to us for help, and the care he put into thinking about what was the most effective intervention that could be made which could restore the child back onto the path of healthy development. Careful not to do anything that might make life worse for the child and if the possibility of moving the child to a specialised boarding school was being considered, then it was important to visit the school oneself and to be as sure as possible that one was not disrupting an attachment that would place the child in a worse situation.

It was mandatory for us to see all the Robertson's films on childhood separation and to know that they could move us to tears and that this was not unexpected. The Director of the Clinic at that time told us how he had 'blubbed' and that some managers had to walk out because it was too anguishing. We were aware that it was this pain of separation which could lead to the denial of the importance of secure long-term attachment so that children in their environments, at home and in institutions such as hospitals, children's homes, boarding schools and residential nurseries, might receive repetitive staff changes that were heartbreaking for the children and often for their carers.

This is part of Arturo Ezquerro's *Tales of Attachment*, which describes the developments and changes that have occurred over the last 45 years and the appropriate trainings that are now available. But though things have improved in understanding and, more importantly, acknowledging the needs for young children, it is important not to become complacent, as the strains of caring for the young and vulnerable, both in peacetime and in conflict zones, can lead to denial or burnout and consequent damage or cruelty to the child.

It is difficult for me at this distance from my training to separate out all the various ideas that became part of me as being identified with particular attachments to tutors and consultants. I was fortunate to have had contact with many thoughtful and compassionate men and women, but I was pleased to find that in remembering John Bowlby I was also thinking of Hyla Holden and what I had absorbed from him. It was no surprise to find that his daughter, Katherine Holden, a historian, has written *Nanny Knows Best: The History of the British Nanny.*

Tales of Attachment is a warm and faithful tribute to John Bowlby's life's work, and to all those touched by the grip of attachment and separation.

Dr Marcus Johns, London 2015

INTRODUCTION

John Bowlby (1907–1990) is the 'father' of *attachment theory* and one of the sharpest British thinkers of the twentieth century. His formidable intellect and will, together with the development and integration of his multiple identities (as a doctor, psychologist, psychoanalyst, child psychiatrist, teacher, scientist and theoretician) built an outstanding man – as Parkes (1995) put it, a truly exceptional character.

Bowlby had a desire, a dream, a vision. He regarded the wellbeing of children and families as a long-term investment in the mental health of future generations, which in turn would contribute to a more humane, egalitarian and democratic society. Bowlby's message was deceptively simple: we need our mothers ... and fathers ... and groups; we need one another. He was no doubt a group person, a man who conceived the human mind as a social phenomenon and collaborated with others throughout his life. And he wrote about group attachments:

> During adolescence and adult life a measure of attachment behaviour is commonly directed not only towards persons outside the family but also towards groups and institutions other than the family. A school or college, a work group, a religious group or a political group can come to constitute for many a subordinate attachment 'figure'. In such cases, it seems probable, the development of attachment to a group is mediated, at least initially, by attachment to a person holding a prominent position within the group.
>
> *(Bowlby, 1969, p. 207)*

This book is above all a heartfelt and faithful homage to John Bowlby, the real man; to his gentleness, compassion and encouragement; to his humanity; to the clarity of his thinking; to his perseverance; to his genius. The book is, also, a deep expression of gratitude for the gift of six years (1984–1990) of fortnightly mentorship he gave me.

I was privileged to be with Bowlby in the last part of his journey, a time when he had gathered most resources and experience to draw from. He was happy, confident, actively creative and well prepared to face the end of his life. His late years were integral to his pilgrimage. My impression is that he grew happier as he was getting older. The many battles of his working life were over; he had done his job; he was satisfied that his message had been delivered and finally appreciated.

Bowlby was a passionate, honest and sensitive clinician. He genuinely believed in his patients and in their capacity to use their own resources to recover from real life traumatic experiences, which he thought of as *mental fractures* – no more no less:

> the human psyche, like human bones, is strongly inclined towards self-healing. The psychotherapist's job, like that of the orthopaedic surgeon's, is to provide the conditions in which self-healing can best take place.
>
> *(Bowlby, 1988a, p. 152)*

This medical analogy is a powerful injection of hope. It is also a compliment to his own father, a caring physician and competent surgeon who, paradoxically, was largely absent from his life.

As an enthusiastic, inspiring teacher and trainer, Bowlby was respectful of the work and contributions of his colleagues. He provided a reliable secure base from which it was easier to explore new territories and integrate diverse sources of knowledge. He was supportive, encouraging, and stimulated open-ended personal and professional development. As my mentor, at no point did he criticise the work of my other supervisors who were mainly of different theoretical orientations. He in fact alerted me to publications, often not his own, which would assist me in dealing with problematical situations. And he offered suggestions that would help me understand and value the work of others.

As a remarkable scientist and theoretician, Bowlby (1974, 1978, 1991b) was precise and rigorous. He recognised that a good theory must not only make sense in terms of the validity of its formulations but it should also be capable of guiding clinicians to improve their practice, as well as mapping new directions for future research and validation. He emphasised that such a theory should be open to revision, expansion and refinement, in order to accommodate itself to the new data obtained via new observations or explorations.

Bowlby's attachment theory is no longer a theory but a fact. Although there is plenty of room for an ongoing search into optimal relationships, there can be no doubt that we are born with a basic instinctual necessity for attachment – a need to be meaningfully connected with other people for our survival and creativity. Indeed, there is no such thing as an instinct, but an instinctual substrate interacting with a constantly evolving environment. Attachment needs stay with us across the life cycle.

John Nash, one of the most successful mathematicians of the twentieth century, had a psychotic breakdown in 1959 – at the time his wife Alicia Lardé was pregnant with their first child. Nash felt a sense of rejection by his wife for she now had his rival, the baby, in her womb. He was diagnosed with 'paranoid schizophrenia'.

The story was dramatically personified in the film *A Beautiful Mind*, directed by Ron Howard, in 2001.

Nash's illness put such a strain on the marriage that Lardé was unable to cope with it; she divorced him in 1963. Since then Nash had a large number of psychiatric hospital admissions, until 1970 when Lardé allowed him to live in her house as a lodger. This new home base, where Nash was neither too close nor too distant from Lardé, helped him to gradually develop resilience, as well as a reasonable level of emotional security and stability.

Nash's previous highly anxious and ambivalent attachment with Lardé eventually became secure enough. He was able to get rid of his paranoid delusions and won his battle against psychosis, some 20 years after his first breakdown. In 1994, Nash received the Nobel Memorial Prize in Economic Sciences and put meaningful human connection before accurate theorising (Welsh, 2013). In his speech, as reported by Magagna and Jackson (2015, p. 126), he said:

> I've always believed in numbers and the equations and logics that lead to reason. But after a lifetime of such pursuits, I ask: What is truly logic? Who decides reason? And I have made the most important discovery of my career, the most important discovery of my life: It is only in the mysterious equations of love that any logic or reasons can be found....

Looking into Alicia's eyes, Nash continued: "I am only here tonight because of you. You are the reason I am".

We are shaped by our attachments; we are social creatures who depend entirely on each other. The sociability within us and around us, our solidarity, is the essence of our humanity. Our ancestors of East Africa could not have survived one night alone. And attachment relationships are as essential as ever in a rapidly changing digital world (Cundy, 2015).

Yes, of course, the internet has helped us overcome geographical hurdles and has made various aspects of our lives easier. However, it has significantly reduced the time we spend together and has created an illusion of intimacy. Digital gadgets are good for making contact, for sharing information and for commercial transactions, but not so good for deepening intimate relationships. Susan Pinker reported in *The Guardian*, on 21 March 2015, that British people of all ages now devote more time to digital devices and screens than to any other activity except sleeping. A quarter of Britons say they feel emotionally unconnected to others, and a third do not feel connected to the wider community. (And, on 23 June 2016, 51.9% voted to disconnect from Europe.)

If Bowlby were alive today, I suspect he would have welcomed the benefits of modern technology – which in a number of ways is supporting our wellbeing and communication with others. But he would have been cautious about the risk that our lives might be undermined by an affectionless virtual environment. He would have probably said that we need more than pixelated electronic ties – and that we in fact need more secure attachments to create a more secure society in which we can nurture communities of diverse, person-to-person relationships.

The warm, affectionate, mutually fulfilling, person-to-person relationship that Bowlby and I developed over the years is the guiding thread throughout the Encounters' volume. The main part (eight of the twelve chapters) consists of an inclusive biographical journey into Bowlby's life and work. He is portrayed vividly trough his individual, family and group attachment history; his mixed feelings towards a largely absent father and emotionally distant mother; his turbulent youth; his personal and professional development; his battles with psychoanalytic colleagues; his caring leadership; his loving relationship with Ursula (wife and secure base); his insecurities as a parent; his enjoyment as a grandparent; his warmth as a teacher; his loyalty as a friend.

The personal is political. Bowlby grew up in a British upper-middle class family where the principles of 'King, Country and Empire' were cultivated. Although he did not criticise his parents, his evolving views could be seen as an indictment of the type of upbringing to which he had been subjected and to the culture that had fostered it. His change in political persuasions before the Second World War, from his family's right-wing Tory tradition to his own left-wing Labour choice, can be understood in the light of his commitment to help vulnerable children and families – which in turn contributed to his growing social consciousness.

Bowlby, and members of his Tavistock research team, had to challenge prejudices and policies which in the culture of psychoanalysis, psychiatry and the wider healthcare economy were dominating thinking and practice. His huge efforts at theory building were chiefly in the service of social change. As I perceived him in his work he was impeccably reliable, eager to learn, unashamedly inclusive and undogmatic – as well as able to cultivate systemic awareness, sensitivity to diversity, openness to different perspectives and refined ethical principles.

The filter of time, 25 years after his death, has given me a valuable historical perspective – which enabled me to agglutinate a range of key 'post-Bowlby' contributions. I believe I have provided a comprehensive synthesis of these important accounts of his life and work, connecting them up with my first-hand experience of Bowlby, his family and his thinking. Mary Ainsworth, John Byng-Hall, Jeremy Holmes, Robert Karen, Sebastian Kraemer, Mario Marrone, Colin Murray Parkes, Frank Van der Horst, and Susan Van Dijken, have been a particularly great influence.

The research into the genesis and development of attachment theory has been thorough and academic; yet I have meant to deliver it in a jargon-free, palatable way. Like Bowlby, I think that history and context are crucial for understanding. Lorna Wing put it this way: "Nothing is totally original. Everyone is influenced by what's gone before" (quoted in Feinstein, 2010, p. 9). So I have included wide-ranging historical accounts of the Tavistock Clinic and the British Psychoanalytical Society, their origins and evolution. These two bodies played a significant part in Bowlby's development – and he made outstanding contributions to both institutions.

While the bulk of the volume is a relational biography of Bowlby, I have taken the liberty of exploring some topics and themes that, through our mentorship, I realised interested him or generated some discomfort in the last part of his life.

These explorations I have done in the four other chapters. They reflect important aspects of my relationship with him and my own professional growth. I shall outline the rationale behind it.

Bowlby stimulated my interest in group psychotherapy with children, adolescents and adults. A less known part of his work is that he had in fact conducted a weekly therapy group for mothers and their babies or young children, which he extended over three decades. This was a slow-open group which people joined and left when ready, enabling new members to join. He welcomed discussions of my group work with enthusiasm and encouraged me to train as a group analyst.

Bowlby valued a great deal the crucial influence that siblings and peers have in our development. Attachment to a peer group is a powerful bond in its own right and plays an especially major role in adolescence. This will be illustrated in one of these four chapters, which is devoted to the therapeutic work with young people and their families in an innovative in-patient adolescent unit.

But peer group attachments are present well before adolescence, and can develop exceptionally early under extremely traumatic circumstances. I was captivated and moved by an astonishing paper, "An Experiment in Group Upbringing" (Freud & Dann, 1967), which Bowlby handed to me as if wanting to say: go on, explore this further. The paper reveals the tragic story of six children who were orphaned during the first year of their lives, as their parents were murdered by the Nazis in the gas chambers. Forming a peer group attachment helped them survive.

In addition, Bowlby told me that he had been largely unaware of the huge prevalence of child sexual abuse until the late 1970s. He added that during most of his career child sexual abuse was rarely referred to by anyone and that, on those rare occasions, the abuse was considered to be the product of the patient's fantasies and not a real episode. According to him, this denial contributed to a dreadfully ignorant clinical practice with the victims and delayed a much needed social awareness of the problem for more than half a century.

With his commendable trustworthiness and humility, Bowlby further intimated to me that he felt he had not been adequately trained so as to develop enough expertise to treat survivors of child sexual abuse. But he joined the voices that denounce the high incidence of incest and its damaging effects on children – and he unequivocally referred to this as sexual exploitation of the children (Bowlby, 1979a). He subsequently became conversant with the literature on the subject and challenged colleagues who denied that the abuse had taken place (Hunter, 2015). My expedition into this had the additional motive of giving hope to the victims, as movingly illustrated in the story of a survivor who recovered from the abuse through attachment-based psychotherapy.

I think there is a parallel between child sexual abuse and professional sexual abuse. Bowlby at one point had described this problem as a "hot potato" (quoted in Hunter, 2015, p. 154). He was most concerned about the unethical behaviour of some of his colleagues. He was not totally against occasional and gentle physical touch as a gesture of support, because in certain circumstances it can have therapeutic value. However, he told me that touch has to be used with much care and discretion as there is a risk that it can be taken as sexual. And he emphasised that therapists have a special duty to protect vulnerable patients and to help them feel safe – for which reason it is crucial to understand the strength of unmet attachment needs that these patients often bring to therapy.

As he referred to in the first volume on *Attachment and Loss*, Bowlby also told me in supervision that it was most unfortunate that Freud had been unable to grasp the centrality of attachment – both in our development and in the patient–therapist relationship. Not understanding properly the strong unmet attachment needs that patients often bring to the consulting room may increase the risk of sexual boundary violations. That is, sexual exploitation of a vulnerable person by someone who is in a position of power. Not long ago, I was disturbed to learn that a close colleague of mine had abused one of his adult patients who had herself been abused as a child. This reinforced my determination to advocate for the victims. We should not turn a blind eye!

Bowlby, I believe, would have been pleased to see the four diverging chapters included in this new biographical profile. They are integral to his thinking and ingrained in our working relationship – which holds these chapters together. My memories of his teaching and therapeutic attitude inspired me to write in support of survivors of abuse. Bowlby's approach was one of commitment, outspokenness and compassion for vulnerable people suffering or trapped in vicious cycles of anxiety, anger and depression. He taught me to see these problems in the light of disruptions of attachment bonds and adverse, traumatic real life events.

In several passages I have offered reflections on Bowlby's outstanding capacity for an unreserved self-examination of his own beliefs, biases and preferences. These considerations contain multi-layered thought processes, feelings and experiences through which his ideas (as well as mine and those of other colleagues) came to emerge, changed and evolved over time. He had a decisive impact on the development of many people who worked with him, including myself.

It is not possible to write (or read?) a book like this without thinking about one's own life, work and relationships. We have all at some point struggled to become attached, to survive, and to develop in our families, groups and work settings. So, I think the reader will be able to identify with and learn from one or another of the attachment stories narrated.

I have aimed to provide a reasoned integration of theory, research, training and clinical practice – with a view to making the volume useful, attractive and stimulating to mental health and other healthcare professionals and students. I have also intended to write in a forthright, caring manner and in plain English, hoping that the book will equally appeal to anyone who is interested in relationships and personal development; or who has ever been a patient.

Finally, writing *Encounters with John Bowlby: Tales of Attachment* has been in a way a cathartic journey – and I can imagine that much of Bowlby's writings had a cathartic element too. But a book like this is much more than a catharsis. It is a form of relational exploration and, as such, an opportunity to be creative and to grow: a therapeutic experience in its own right!

1

AN ENCOUNTER WITH JOHN BOWLBY

The call came from Skye. It was the voice of John Bowlby's younger daughter, Pia Durán, with the news I had been dreading. Earlier in the day, her father had died peacefully at the age of 83 following two strokes. He was surrounded by his widow, Ursula, with eight close family members. I felt hugely sad; but also experienced a powerful sense of closeness with him. I had a strange thought that, in dying, he had given me a gentle push to grow as a full professional adult. I felt increasingly able to explore uncharted territory in a foreign land and, soon after his death, I became a consultant psychiatrist in psychotherapy, working in the National Health Service (NHS) – the largest provider of healthcare in Europe.

Bowlby died on 2 September 1990, but he still is very much alive in my mind. I held my first one-to-one meeting with him in his office at the Tavistock Clinic on 17 January 1985. We arranged hour-long individual supervision on a fortnightly basis, which he provided until he died. I had met him at the beginning of October 1984 at the seminar on attachment theory that he conducted at the Tavistock. This was attended by some twelve trainees in child and adolescent psychiatry.

Despite my appalling English and my poor knowledge of the theory, I took an active part in the seminar; I sometimes asked silly questions, which exposed my ignorance. Quite a few times I saw him smiling spontaneously after my questions. However, he never made me feel stupid or inadequate. Being the only foreign student in this group, I was able to have the naturalness or impudence that my British peers felt unable to display. They were all senior registrars on their way to becoming consultants and could not really afford the luxury of formulating silly questions in public. Anyway, they appeared to be more knowledgeable than I was.

Bowlby was going through his very creative, late golden years. At the seminar, I was haunted by the strangely precise and transparent nature of his thinking, as well as his gentleness and encouragement to us all in the group to develop our own ideas. The way he formulated the concept of a *secure base*, and its link to the quality of exploration, had a strong impact on me: it made a lot of sense. When the seminar came to an end, just before Christmas, I approached him in the group room and said that I wanted to know more about attachment theory. I was expecting that he would provide me with a reading list. But he gave me the gift of an appointment to meet him in the New Year, he said: "For a chat".

Retrospectively, I realise that my rather bold approach and his more than positive response were to make one of the most significant happenings in my life; certainly the most important of my professional life. As his mentorship developed, he gradually became a secure base for me. Now that, in retiring from the NHS I have started my own golden years, I feel able to tell a story about Bowlby's life and work, and about the impact he had on me and many other people. I hope to involve you, the reader, in this journey of exploration.

At a mentoring session, in April 1990, Bowlby told me that he would soon need to have bowel cancer surgery. He was reasonably relaxed and added that he was hoping to resume our supervision shortly after. During his hospital stay, I sent him a bunch of flowers with a message: "John, I hope you score one hundred". This was the first and only time I addressed him by his forename. During the brief separation, I was sensing his mentorship might soon come to an end. Part of me was anxious about it, but a larger part of me was feeling confident that no one could take away what I had learned from him in the previous six years. Our relationship had become a big part of my world. Bowlby belonged to my grandparents' generation; my relationship with him was frank, painless and conflict-free.

At the Tavistock's book launch of *Charles Darwin: A New Biography*, Bowlby's (1990) last book, he was in a wheelchair recovering from his recent operation. It was May 1990. I looked for him and smiled into his eyes; he smiled back with warmth and pleasure, while saying: "Thank you, Arturo, for the beautiful flowers". He was physically frail and pallid, though full of contagious vitality. Paradoxically, I could still perceive him as stronger, wiser and more able to cope with the world; a firm and caring secure base, which would stay with me after his departure. From this base, I was able to safely explore and navigate through feelings of frustration, even anger, and love towards both my patients and colleagues.

I knew his time would come at one point in the not-so-distant future, but I could also see that he was larger than life. In the next couple of months he continued supervising me at his London home until his last trip to Skye.

The supra-vision of supervision

An encounter between one of the most creative thinkers of the twentieth century and a rather undeveloped, although eager, foreign student was an unlikely occurrence. Why it did happen and how it was sustained open-ended, I do not know. At first, I thought that the calibre and breadth of Bowlby's work would intimidate me. But I was surprised by his warmth and naturalness. I felt at home.

I was interested to learn that, in the last few years of his life, Bowlby was very enthusiastic about teaching and supervision. He gave many papers, lectures and seminars to a large number of professional audiences, in many different settings. Indeed, he was not in retirement. He was especially pleased to be the 1981 Freud Memorial Visiting Professor of Psychoanalysis at University College London; a place that brought back memories of his own time there as a student.

Bowlby made clear his devotion to new generations of trainees: "Invitations from students' societies always got priority since students are likely to be less committed to traditional ideas than their elders and, in any case, theirs is the future" (Bowlby, 1991a, p. 30). Domenico Di Ceglie (a consultant child and adolescent psychiatrist who came from Italy and trained at the Tavistock some 10 years earlier than I) recently told me that Bowlby was inclusive and welcoming, with a contagious enthusiasm for teaching, which made him feel at home. That I can strongly identify with.

At our first individual supervision, Bowlby gave me a present: a paperback copy of the first popular edition of *Child Care and the Growth of Love* (Bowlby, 1953a). I understood that he wanted to start his teaching with a basic, very readable book. I also wondered if his choice might have been conditioned by the naive questions that I had asked at the seminar the previous academic term. I must confess that reading the book was a disturbing experience. It pushed me to think about the quality of care I may have received during my early life in La Rioja, deep at the heart of unknown Spain (except for the wine), where the provincial greyness of the post-Civil War years was atrocious and oppression was at its peak.

I was the first-born child of my parents. During my early childhood, the family suffered a number of major losses in short succession. I was one year old when my mother gave birth to my brother, but his twin died. That coincided with my maternal grandfather being diagnosed with terminal cancer. He passed away within a year. Ten months later my sister was severely brain damaged at birth. The following year my mother had a stillborn baby. I do not know how my parents were able to survive. Coping with the loss of a parent is hard enough but, at least, the grieving process can be a natural one. Losing a child is something for which our minds are not and cannot be fully prepared; children are supposed to survive their parents, which makes it much harder for the parents to grieve the loss.

In the case of a stillborn baby, birth and death are fused – which brings bewildering contradictions. When one twin dies and the other survives, the parents face very difficult clashing tasks: celebrating and nurturing the newborn living baby, whilst needing to grieve the loss of their dead baby. Bowlby's expertise on childhood mourning gradually helped me understand the complexity of these traumatic experiences. In the following years, I was also fortunate to work at the Tavistock with Sandy Bourne – a Kleinian psychoanalyst who supervised a number of psychotherapy groups for bereaved parents that I co-conducted with Jenni Thomas (Officer of the Order of the British Empire for her work on neonatal bereavement). Bourne pioneered analytic understanding of perinatal grief, in which thinking can be disturbed or hindered: a 'stillborn thought' (Bourne & Lewis, 1984, 1991a, 1991b).

I can imagine the pain and sadness my parents went through. Mourning must have been extremely difficult for them, surely, overwhelming at times. My brother and I must have been confused and bewildered. I can now understand better the nervous and fluctuating quality of the attachment with my mother. But in the circumstances I cannot blame her for not being optimally available.

I never talked to Bowlby about this, nor did he talk to me about personal matters. Of course not – he and I were mindful of professional boundaries. I was grateful to him for the book. Indirectly, I gained new awareness about my childhood trauma. I knew I had to do something about it in my own personal therapy: the best way of protecting my patients from the risk that their trauma would become mixed with my own pain. My past trauma did not belong to the supervision space; this territory was protected for the benefit of the patients I cared for.

Only on one occasion in the nearly six years of our work together, Bowlby extended the professional boundary beyond the full 60-minute hour of his supervision. On 15 December 1988, my brother telephoned me to break the sad news: our father had been diagnosed with terminal cancer. The doctors had said that his life expectancy was less than one year. That was cruel on him: he had just retired the previous month and was going to be deprived of *his* golden years. I was shocked and wanted to travel to Spain immediately to be with Dad.

But I had a psychotherapy patient waiting and another booked straight after the customary 10-minute break in between analytic therapy sessions. This tradition had started with Freud, as he had felt more comfortable seeing his patients for 50 minutes on the clock, rather than a full hour, so he could spend the remaining 10 minutes writing some clinical notes. This timing became a norm for psychoanalysts across the world; except the French, who offer 45 minutes to their patients.

María, my wife, had given birth to Arturo, our first son, a couple of months earlier. I was distressed by contradictory, confusing feelings. I did not want to abandon María and the baby, but I felt most concerned about losing my father and said to my brother that I would travel home as soon as possible. After the telephone call, I was in pain and my mind was clouded: I could not think clearly and just followed my instincts. I decided to see the two patients in succession. That was not easy. I could hardly talk during the sessions. My minimum goal was making an effort to be able to listen to each patient as sensitively as possible, while containing my distress.

I do not know how, but I managed to keep my emotions to myself. During the 10-minute break in between the two patients I had to go to the toilet, where I could contain my tears no longer. It was a time when quite a few psychotherapists were having their mini break. Some six or seven colleagues came in and out while I was trying to recompose myself in the mirror. They clearly saw me and I saw them. No one paid much attention, and each one of them turned their eyes away quite rapidly. This was a culture shock for me, despite the fact that I had already been in London for more than four years.

I think that in Spain this might not have occurred. At the very least, someone would have asked me if I was alright and, quite likely, would have tapped me on the shoulder for warm comfort. Here, I had to survive with the cold comfort of an emotionally empty toilet. I lost my appetite and could not eat any lunch. Early in the afternoon, I held the last supervision with Bowlby prior to the Christmas break. I was feeling internally restless but, I thought, I presented myself with reasonable external composure. I started reporting on one of my patients. Within less than one minute, Bowlby said: "You do not seem to be your usual self today, what's the matter?" I briefly shared my preoccupation with him, to which he spontaneously responded: "I am very sorry to hear the painful news".

Bowlby was kind and especially attentive. I explained that I would be travelling to Spain on my own the following evening, and added that I would return to be with María and our baby son Arturo for Christmas. At the end of the session he gave me a warm and long handshake while saying: "I feel for you. I hope that things do not turn out to be as bad as you fear". The next day, I was surprised to receive a telephone call at home from Carlos Durán (Bowlby's Spanish son-in-law) to invite María, the baby and I for supper with him and his wife Pia, on Christmas Eve. It was a lovely gesture. I was deeply touched by it.

My mentorship arrangement with Bowlby was unusual: it remained independent from the Tavistock Clinic's statutory training structure. Anton Obholzer (Chairman of the Tavistock) was my boss and clinical tutor. Peter Bruggen was my research tutor, a family therapy expert (Bruggen & O'Brian, 1986, 1987), and consultant in charge at Hill End Adolescent Unit – which I shall describe in Chapter 8. Near the end of his prolific career, Bruggen was appointed medical director in one of a new wave of NHS Trusts, when major reforms were introduced in 1991. He thought that public health services needed a good shaking, tougher management, proper costing and better accountability structures. Things turned out differently from what he had expected and he retired in 1994. At the point of his retirement, I asked Bruggen to be my mentor and we agreed to meet monthly. I enjoyed his wisdom until my own retirement from the NHS three years ago, after 33 years work in the public sector.

But, hang on a minute! As a matter of fact, I am not in total retirement and, like Bowlby, Bruggen and Obholzer, I may never quit: I currently enjoy teaching, researching, supervising, writing and helping patients. Since I became a consultant in the early 1990s, I had no formal need for mentorship. However, Bowlby had taught me that learning is an open-ended task and that in looking after myself I was also working for the benefit of my patients. Bruggen made creative use of his own golden years. Earlier in his career, he had been inspired by Bowlby's (1949) landmark paper "The Study and Reduction of Group Tensions in the Family" – a pioneering publication on family therapy.

Following his retirement from the public sector, Bruggen continued teaching and supervising junior colleagues. He also reported many stories of the NHS reforms in a book (Bruggen, 1997). This is a cathartic testimony of about 100 health professionals and managers caught up in the dehumanising culture change of the NHS: a species that used to be the jewel in the crown of British healthcare, but which now appears to be facing extinction. Over the last 20 or so years, public health services in England have been insidiously privatised by the back door. I believe that neoliberalism is gradually eroding the welfare system: the rich can have good access to private medical services, while the needs of the poor and disadvantaged are neglected – and the middle classes are not sure about where they should go.

I suspect that if Bowlby were alive today, he would have felt disappointed by the new health economy inequalities and would have made his voice heard. Very loudly.

Real Madrid: the ups and downs of life

At the age of 59, I can now reflect on personal development with more mature confidence. I was 27 when I arrived in London from Madrid to undergo training at the Tavistock, but felt I was not yet a full adult. My self-esteem was reasonable. I had been told that I was intelligent, good at sports and handsome. I held a good record of honours and distinctions at school and university. I was a thriving junior psychiatrist. But, emotionally, I was largely undeveloped: yes, my personal growth had been arrested under General Francisco Franco's dictatorship.

As a child, I had learned that the General had put many people in jail for so-called indecent behaviour. Every matter seemed to be externally watched and controlled. There was no unanimity, but the uniformity and colourlessness in the country were simply atrocious. There was not even black and white; everything came across as grey, the colour of the dictator's paramilitary forces. Against that background, at the tender age of eight or nine, my imagination was captured by *Real Madrid yé-yé*: a group of young football players, who wore immaculate white shirts and longer hair than was normally accepted in Spain at the time. To my young mind, the whiteness of their shirt was as colourful as that of bright stars in the firmament. It was an antidote to the greyness of Franco's oppressed *Big Brother* society. The name *yé-yé* came from the *yeah, yeah, yeah* chorus in the Beatles' song *She Loves You*.

As an adolescent, maybe, I unconsciously sublimated my developing sexual urges by playing football and trying to score as many goals as possible. It was not as thrilling as a good orgasm but it became a more than stimulating enough experience. I *did* identify with Bob Marley's public statement that football was an important part of himself, and that when he played the world woke up around him. And I was reassured by Albert Camus (1996) who confessed that he owed to football much of what he knew about morality and obligations. On the other hand, Franco did not really give a damn about football; his real interests were fishing and hunting. Tragically, he did not seem to distinguish between the human species and other animal species: many people were drowned or buried in mass graves, in a most brutal manner, just for daring to think differently.

I still feel passionately for Real Madrid, so far the most successful sports club in football history across the world. This is a loyalty of five decades. Considering that I did not have the chance to choose my family of origin, Real Madrid is the longest *love* for which I have made a choice. This relationship (based on role modelling, hard work and achievement) has been a relaxing and motivating experience for me – often mitigating the pain of traumatic events. In fact, Real

Madrid was one of the very few *secure attachments* I had when I left Spain for the British Isles in December 1983. In the early years in London, Real helped me to be connected with my country of birth.

For those interested in a deeper understanding of this *madness*, I recommend the book *Football Delirium* by British psychoanalyst Chris Oakley (2007). It makes good reading for a festive season or long weekend. As you immerse yourself in the book chapters, you will be surprised to find dreams, the social unconscious and sex in the stadium, as well as a special section on *football as therapy*.

I let Bowlby know about my passion. He smiled and intimated to me that he had very much enjoyed sport and physical activity during his youth. In fact, he excelled at sports during his adolescence at the Royal Naval College in Dartmouth (see Chapter 2). Although as an adult he gave priority to flexing his intellectual muscles, over the years he saw many children and young people learning through sport to cope with the emotional ups and downs of defeat and victory, failure and success, anger and love.

In the annual *News and Events* issue of the Institute of Psychoanalysis, the former President of the British Psychoanalytical Society and past Captain of the England Cricket Team, Michael Brearley (2014, p. 2) touched upon some sporting qualities: "For many people otherwise inclined to be inhibited or self-conscious, sport offers a unique opportunity for self-expression and spontaneity. Within a framework of rules and acceptable behaviour, sports people can be whole-hearted".

In normal development, indeed, children achieve a degree of physical coordination and mastery. Walking, running, jumping, climbing, kicking, catching, splashing and dancing can all give a sense of satisfaction and achievement. Sport grows out of the pleasure in such activities. Moreover, "this development in co-ordination is part of the development of a more unified self" (Brearley, 2014, p. 1). Of course, there is fierce competition and rivalry in sports. Interestingly, to 'compete' comes from the Latin *competens* meaning agreeing or striving together. Similarly, 'rival' comes from the Latin *rivalis*, meaning sharing the same river bank or stream.

However, team or individual sports would have not come into existence without group co-operation. Sport "involves ordinary civilities that oil the wheels of relationships and collegial activities, including consideration, respect, and the recognition of limit.... Sport calls too for a subtle balancing of planning and spontaneity, of calculation and letting go, of discipline and freedom" (Brearley, 2014, p. 3). In those rare states of peak performance, when body and mind are at one, life feels harmonious – akin to the experience of being in love.

Regrettably, like other dictators, Franco abused sporting generosity and creativity. He presented sport success as his own achievement and propaganda for his regime to enhance the chance of survival in the international arena. This he did, for example, with what he considered his 'triumph over communism' in the 1964 European Nations Football Cup Final when Spain won over the Soviet Union at the Bernabéu Stadium in Madrid.

Additionally, psychoanalysis had been banned by Franco's Home Office and by the Church as a dangerous and obscene ideology. I had to take a few risks in the black markets of Madrid to buy psychoanalytic books, which I read from cover to cover. That was a breath of fresh air for me, and good food for thought. The books contained intriguing, exciting and captivating ideas about the internal world, dreams and unconscious fantasies. They were also full of sexual symbols – of which more in Chapter 11.

I was actually looking for sex between two consenting adults and that was hard. According to Spanish law at the time, you did not become officially an adult until aged 21. In the circumstances, I decided to hold a moratorium on my psycho-sexual development but my wait to take and give sex was a rather anxious one. Fortunately, Franco died in 1975 before I became too old for the business. I was 19 in fact, but had no right to vote yet. I decided to leave the country for a little while.

The anger expressed by the Military following Franco's death worried me a great deal. The Spanish people seemed to be divided into three main groups: the mourners, the triumphant and a large silent majority. We initially needed to be cautious and temperate. Spain was not yet a democracy. The uncertainty was very intense for three years until the citizens approved the new Constitution in a referendum, in December 1978. However, the equilibrium was rather precarious for several more years. There was in fact an infamous attempted *coup d'état* in February 1981. Democracy was not consolidated until the election of the Socialist Party in October 1982.

I had temporarily moved to Paris in the summer of 1975. I needed to put behind the teachings and metaphors of the Church and the State. During my formative years, the Church had dominated primary school education and corporal punishment was the norm. We received a rather peculiar sexual education: it was full of metaphors and fairy tales. We were told that when mothers and fathers had true love for one another, they would write to God to let Him know (gender taken for granted). God would be happy with the hot news and would send a Holy Spirit to Paris with a new baby.

The Holy Spirit would look for a suitable female stork and ask her to deliver the baby to the home of the lovingly expectant parents. The stork would fly day and night, and would softly drop the baby in the cradle (blue for boys and pink for girls). For as long as I can remember, the story was so fascinating to my infantile mind that I couldn't wait to grow up and go to Paris, the city of light … and that was it.

Here I am, at 19, doing a crash course in French, the language of love. For the next eight years I indeed learned quite a lot of French, I grew my hair and visited hippy communes. I had a number of reasonably rewarding and open relationships. However, I was not an adult yet. I then tried to settle down. I committed myself to a four-year-long relationship with a young woman of about my chronological age, but I was still not sure of my personal identity. What would complete me as a person?

Uncertainty at the Tavistock Clinic

To seek an answer, I decided to come to London to read psychoanalysis. One of my senior Spanish colleagues said to me before departure: "You are an embarrassingly enthusiastic psychiatrist, your career is thriving and you do not need the English!" With some hesitation, I responded: "Child and adolescent psychiatry is not a recognised medical specialty in Spain. I want to train for four years in London and, then, return home to help with the development of mental health services for young people". I consciously thought that this was the main reason why I had separated from my country of birth. But Bowlby and my Tavistock tutors made me think otherwise.

When I told my boss, Obholzer, that I had arranged to see Bowlby for additional supervision, he raised his eyebrows while asking: "Have you been seduced by a great man?" I was taken by surprise and responded as spontaneously as I could in the circumstances: "No, Bowlby did not seduce me; I just want to learn more about attachment theory". Obholzer smiled with a gesture of incredulity and after a pause said: "Well ..., your Spanish charm is helping you to get away with murder!"

I wonder if he might have been indirectly referring to the fact that my role as a foreign, supernumerary, senior registrar in child and adolescent psychiatry was somehow unusual. I had to endure that part of the British medical establishment that at the time described people like me, somewhat dismissively, as 'trainees from overseas' in the purest style of the British Empire – no matter that I had qualified and already worked as a specialist in adult psychiatry in Spain.

Obholzer was a pioneer and created a workshop on institutional processes. I understood that he wanted to warn me about important unconscious forces operating in the workplace, of which I was not aware. His contributions to organisational consultancy have been seminal (Obholzer & Roberts, 1994; Obholzer, 2001). I felt privileged that he involved me in two group relations events at the Tavistock and in the renowned Leicester Conference on institutional group dynamics. Obholzer accepted my mentorship with Bowlby and appreciated its merits as complementary to the statutory supervision I had at the time. I thanked them both for that.

Looking back, after 36 years in the field of mental health and human development, it is my view that in order to help patients to become full grownups psychotherapists need to be adults themselves. There are different pathways to achieve this. Creative supervision and balanced training can certainly help with the task.

I started clinical tutorials with Obholzer in September 1984. That was during the second week of my placement. The first week had been devoted to an induction course for all new staff and trainees. It was here that I met Caroline Garland, a trauma expert and a psychoanalytic group therapist, who made major contributions in the field (Garland, 1998, 2010). She had originally trained, as I also did at a later stage, in the group-analytic tradition – where group analysis is seen as the therapy of the group, by the group, including the conductor (Foulkes, 1946, 1948, 1964, 1975; Ezquerro, 1996a, 1996b, 1997b, 1998b, 1998c, 2004b; Nitsun, 1996, 2015; Dalal, 1998, 2011; Schlapobersky, 2016). Garland was now growing healthily as one of the new generation of influential psychoanalysts at the Tavistock.

Garland became in 1985 the first supervisor of my group psychotherapy practice. She taught me how to fall in love with what I initially understood would be a 'whole group'. She soon clarified that she had actually meant falling in love with the 'group-as-a-whole'. Digesting that concept was a challenging exercise for me, at a time when I was yearning for new adventures. My body was crying out for human contact and sympathetic, friendly voices; my lungs were seeking fresh, democratic air; my lips longing for intimacy; my eyes searching to see a future path more clearly. I needed to mitigate the disquiet of having lost my Spanish base, to which I had been insecurely attached, while not being able to establish a secure base at the Tavistock, yet: I was in no-man's land.

Obholzer was a giant of a man at the peak of his career and Head of the Adolescent Department. His dynamism was such that within a year of my arrival he became Chairman of the Tavistock Clinic, and a major political player. I had spent so much time learning French, and unlearning Spanish, that I honestly considered my English not yet good enough to treat mentally ill patients. When I conveyed my doubts to Obholzer, he pulled my leg: "Come on! You are Spanish, talented and charming; surely, you can take the bull by the horns".

I thought that the metaphor was intentional: Obholzer had already booked an appointment for me to see my first psychotherapy patient and I could not possibly use my French. To make things worse, there were expectations that I should be able to provide a psychoanalytic formulation of the patient's problems. The *Unconscious* was a fourth language for me, about which I am still basically ignorant. Yes, I continue exposing the limitations of my consciousness. For instance, I have just realised that *my* unconscious has played yet another trick on me: the day I started to write this chapter I was totally unaware that it was the 25th anniversary of my father's death. (It also happened that I finished writing the book in the year of the 25th anniversary of John Bowlby's death – something that had not been planned originally.)

My simultaneous exposure to the teachings of Bowlby and Obholzer, to the language of attachment and psychoanalysis, made me dig deeper into my background. I needed to understand where I was coming from before sorting out where I might want to go. And in my work with vulnerable patients it was essential to disentangle what belonged to them and what belonged to me.

My father and my mother had wanted me to play a safe card and become a pharmacist, like themselves. They both had an encyclopaedic knowledge of every illness and every medicine for it. However, for me, being a pharmacist was not a cool-enough job. In fact, I thought that putting tablets in bottles for a living, after five years of in-depth clinical and scientific training, would be such a waste that I felt unable to fulfil my parents' wish – despite my respect and admiration for them. Isn't it ironic that I developed a career as a medical psychoanalytic psychotherapist? If every doctor had prescribed as few medicines as I have done since I qualified, my parents and many of their pharmaceutical colleagues, including my brother, would soon have been made redundant.

My maternal grandparents came from the rural part of La Rioja. At a young age they emigrated from their village to the city of Logroño, the regional capital where my parents and I were born. The country's rural areas had been particularly hit by the poverty backlash that followed the collapse of the Spanish Empire at the end of the nineteenth century. Spain had become a backward country, with a high level of illiteracy. In the region of La Rioja the culture of wine-making contributed to a relative level of prosperity when compared with other Spanish regions. Unlike the atheist or agnostic background in my paternal family and their left-wing ideology, my maternal family had strong religious beliefs and gave in to the Church's propaganda that the Civil War was a crusade to liberate Christian Spain from communism.

During my upbringing, I often had conflictive feelings about two opposing forces around me. The attachment with my mother, in particular, had a decidedly anxious and ambivalent quality. The attachment with my father was not so uneasy but I would not describe it as secure either – in spite of the fact that it was more stable and less conflictive than the attachment with my mother. Overall, the connection with my family and country of birth was insecure and ambivalent; from an early age, I was trapped in a dilemma. As I was becoming a young man, I increasingly felt a need to create an emotional distance from my origins. The need to separate from my mother was particularly intense. But it was not a straightforward move.

I had read that the British were particularly good with the management of boundaries; otherwise, they would not have been able to run such a vast empire. Some 300 years previously, the Spanish themselves had ruled over very large territories extending through all continents across the Globe. But they did not develop effective ways to administer so many lands. Their empire gradually declined and eventually collapsed in 1898. Some unwise politicians decided to go to war against the USA, an emerging superpower, over the sovereignty of Cuba, Puerto Rico and the Philippines. The result was disastrous and the costs incalculable. A number of family members in my great grandparents' generation were killed during this crazy conflict.

Two generations later, I learned from my father that decision-making based on national pride is an absurdity. He himself was a survivor, who had nearly died as a baby and polio left him crippled. He needed to develop survival strategies during the dictatorship due to his family's communist ideology and their support for the left-wing Spanish Republic before the Civil War – which had forced my paternal uncles and grandfather to flee Spain for the relative safety of Spanish-speaking Latin America, after the war.

In the months before cancer killed him, my father told me that he had learned to use his disability to reassure the General that he would not be dangerous: "Having only one normal leg I could not really go very far…" But he had a fine brain. When he saw me using a head-on approach, he would say: "You need to pick your battles; fight only when you are sure you can win". A few days before his death on 22 December 1989, he gave me a big hug while saying: "I am proud of you, Arturo. I love you". I shed a tear and said: "I am proud of you too. I love you, Dad. Very much".

Beginnings and endings

I was expecting my first psychotherapy patient at the Tavistock at 8.00 am on 26 September 1984. Henry was a 19-year-old late adolescent from a traditional

English family. I have never known if Obholzer deliberately chose someone around my emotional age, or if it just was serendipity. I did not dare to ask him anyway. Franco's death when I was 19 had given me a new opportunity to grow, and I thought that Henry was also facing an opportunity for a new beginning. In view of his Britishness, I was surprised that he arrived 15 minutes late. I collected him from the waiting room and said: "Good morning, I am Arturo Ezquerro. Welcome!" Although he could hardly keep eye contact, following my invitation, we did shake hands (his hand was sweating quite profusely). I was not sweating myself but certainly felt some degree of apprehension.

As we walked along the corridor, I asked: "How was your trip to the Clinic?" Henry replied: "Traffic was pretty bad". When I reported this in supervision, Obholzer exclaimed: "Arturo! What have you done? You accused your patient of being late". I immediately replied: "I accused him of what?" Part of me wanted to argue, but I remembered what my father had taught me. I could not possibly win this battle and decided to join the *enemy*. I had not realised at the time that talking in the corridor may become material for analysis. Obholzer was spot on. Of course, I was not consciously accusing Henry of anything but I *had been* slightly irritated by his lateness. After all, I had thought, my success or otherwise would depend on the quality of care that I might be able to provide – for which I needed the patient to turn up on time and engage in meaningful therapy with me.

Yes, my unconscious was letting me down and Obholzer picked it up quickly. He was a fast driver. His thinking was sharp and stimulating; his approach direct and honest – which I appreciated very much. I thanked him again and said: "It seems that I have to learn two new languages with only one shot: English and the language of the Unconscious". He smiled and lit a cigar in a most Freudian-like fashion: "Surely, you can kill two birds with one stone". Obholzer was giving me permission to learn from my mistakes – something that Bion (1962) had called 'learning from experience'.

The Tavistock's environment was a fertile soil for learning. It also created conditions of possibility in my own life, with unexpected consequences. In the Clinic's canteen I met a fellow student, María, Paraguayan born, of Spanish descendants who had left Europe for South America in the sixteenth century. She was easy on the eye, had her own knowledge of French and a beautiful, balanced personality.

I was also haunted by the ancient quality of her Spanish – the language that my ancestors had spoken some 400 years earlier – the time when her own Spanish ancestors had moved to the New World. I sensed the recovery of a lost part of myself and suggested to her that we could be happy living together in a commune. María responded that she would prefer to settle for something more conventional, like getting married. Well ..., I surrendered. But it was a sweet surrender!

Some 16 months after Bowlby's death, his widow Ursula sent a letter with a picture of his gravestone:

Dear María and Arturo,
    It was good to hear from you, from La Rioja.

Please keep the enclosed: I haven't seen it yet (I am due back in Skye at the beginning of May), but our elder son Richard and I planned it carefully. The stone has to be granite, to withstand the wild weather in the Hebrides – it is of a very pale grey Aberdeen granite.

"To be a Pilgrim" is a famous quotation from the 17th century poet and writer John Bunyan (who wrote that classic, "The Pilgrim's Progress"). I didn't want to have anything too thumping obvious, and I hope people will use their imagination about this. To my mind, a pilgrim doesn't meander about aimlessly – he has a definite objective, and if anyone had this, John had.

I'm not sure if you see the Bulletin of the British Psychoanalytical Society, but if not, and if you would like to read the commemorative number about John – including the papers read at the memorial-meeting for him on Oct. 16, 1991 by Pearl King, Eric Rayner (the key paper) and Isabel Menzies – I could lend you the set …

Also contained is an article John wrote himself (in 1985), really for the Psycho-Analytic archives. He called it: 'The Role of the Psychotherapist's Personal Resources in the Treatment Situation', but this is misleading. Only at the very end does he deal with this. The rest (five pages) is about how he came to hold the views he did, starting in 1929, when he was 22.

Yours,
Ursula
[8th January 1992].

I did not ask Ursula about what she meant by 'misleading'. I am aware that Bowlby talked little about himself at a personal level. But I do think that, over the years, he developed an outstanding 'trained intuition'. Parkes (1995, pp. 247–248) superbly formulated one key question for us all:

> Bowlby stands as one of the most brilliant and intrepid thinkers of his time and those who knew him well found loyalty and warmth behind his reserved behaviour. Perhaps the question we need to ask is how the many influences of his life converged to influence the formation of his truly exceptional character.

I shall in this book endeavour to explore Bowlby's pilgrimage, while also accepting that I cannot possibly be entirely fair to his colossal legacy. His journey proved to be not an easy one but he was tremendously consistent with his principles and never surrendered. For seven decades, many of the people who were emotionally close to him or who worked closely with him (whether patients, students or colleagues) experienced the beauty of loving him and being loved by him.

Bowlby's body rests in a serene and quietly unspoilt grave place close to the cliffs of the Waternish Peninsula. That is on the Scottish Isle of Skye, looking west to the Atlantic where there are new landscapes to explore, in the uncertainty of a never-ending horizon. The stone reads: "*John Bowlby (1907–1990). To be a pilgrim*".

FIGURE 1.1 Bowlby's gravestone on the Isle of Skye.

Note

Small portions of this chapter have been published by Karnac in *John Bowlby: The Timeless Supervisor* (Ezquerro, 2015). This was part of a special issue of the journal *Attachment* to commemorate the 25th anniversary of Bowlby's death.

2

AN OUTLINE OF JOHN BOWLBY'S PILGRIMAGE

Edward John Mostyn Bowlby was born in London on 26 February 1907, only six years after the death of Queen Victoria. He was brought up in an upper-middle-class family where Victorian tradition was the norm. His father, Sir Anthony Alfred Bowlby, had worked his way through the ranks to become a Major General in the Royal Army Medical Corps. He developed into a renowned Royal Physician and military surgeon. During the First World War, Sir Anthony was distinguished for his bravery treating wounded soldiers at the Front. However, on his return home, he was a changed person in the eyes of his family and did not work again as a surgeon. It seems likely that he might have suffered from post-traumatic stress.

As a child, Sir Anthony had to endure a major traumatic experience. He was only five when his father (a journalist who covered the British–Chinese Opium War) was captured and tortured to death. As a young man, he decided to delay his marriage in order take care of his widowed mother until her death. A caring son and doctor, he was portrayed as a remote, intimidating, hard-working and for-midable person. Despite being admired by his six children (three girls and three boys) he was often inaccessible to them. It would appear he could not express affection for them openly, nor could they for him.

Bowlby, the fourth child and second boy, loved and was loved by his mother, Lady Mary Bridget Mostyn Bowlby (known as Lady May). She was the eldest daughter of a gentle and easy-going clergyman who, despite his grand origins, was happy to live in a small English village during his entire working life. Like her husband, she was rarely able to openly communicate affection to her children, but was more accessible to them than he was.

Suzan Van Dijken (1998, p. 25) refers to an interview in which, at the age of 80, Bowlby described his mother as a very stable, capable and sensible (rather than sensitive) person. Like many parents of her generation and class, she held the view that it was dangerous to respond promptly to the children's bids for attention and affection, as this would spoil them.

The children's main daily contact with their mother took place when Minnie, the nursemaid, brought them to the family's drawing room for one hour between tea and bedtime. Bowlby developed a close attachment to Minnie, whom he described as his primary care-giver. Her departure, before his fourth birthday, was a major loss for him. He later wrote: "for a child to be looked after by a loving nanny and then for her to leave when he is two or three, or even four or five, can be almost as tragic as the loss of a mother" (Bowlby, 1958b, p. 7).

After Minnie left, the main responsibility for his care and education was transferred to Nanny Friend. She was a disciplinarian and, at times, sarcastic person; which Bowlby resented, particularly as he was trying to come to terms with his loss. However, she was a good story-teller who introduced Charles Dickens' novels to him, including Oliver Twist. This masterpiece is particularly sharp in exposing the misery of London's orphans during the Dickensian era. The poignant and sordid way these children were led into criminality may have had some influence on Bowlby's later interest in child welfare.

Interestingly, one of his first publications was *Forty-four Juvenile Thieves: Their Characters and Home Life* (Bowlby, 1944). Within the family context, he was emotionally close to his maternal grandfather, who taught him swimming, fishing, riding and shooting during the long summer holidays in Skye. It was at this time when the mother freed herself, to some extent, from the constraints of the rigid family routines in London. Van Dijken (1998) reports that she tried to pass on her love for nature to her children, through long walks with them. She taught them how to identify flowers, birds, trees and butterflies.

Bowlby and his older brother Tony appeared to be the mother's favourite children. They were close in age (only 13 months apart) and character. In many ways they were treated as twins: put in the same clothes and in the same class at school. They developed a strong sibling rivalry, although they became good friends. Bowlby had to stretch himself to overtake his brother, who was similarly keen to keep his seniority. At the age of 15, Bowlby physically fought and defeated Tony for the first time. That happened when he discovered that Tony had spoiled a picture that Jim (their younger brother with learning difficulties) had made out of dried flowers (Holmes, 1993).

Bowlby had always been very protective of his brother Jim. This combination of fierce competitiveness, on the one hand, and his concern for children with special needs and the disadvantaged, on the other, became prominent features to his personality. He was a caring and compassionate person throughout his life. In 1961, he set up a Benevolent Fund Committee at the British Psychoanalytical Society to help members who, through illness or ageing, had gotten into financial or other difficulties.

The war years and beyond

Bowlby was only seven when the First World War erupted. His father, Sir Anthony, was immediately sent off to the Front. Bowlby and his brother Tony were later dispatched to boarding school because of the danger of air raids on London, they were told. He retrospectively maintained that "this was just an excuse, being merely the traditional step in the time-honoured barbarism required to produce English gentlemen" (Holmes, 1993, p. 17). The English preparatory school system took its toll and he became the recipient of corporal punishment. During a geography lesson one of his teachers beat him up for making a simple mistake – describing a cape as a cloak rather than a promontory.

Bowlby naturally disliked this treatment, which contributed to an overall feeling of unhappiness when he looked back to his school days. It is quite significant that he started *Separation: Anxiety and Anger*, the second volume of his trilogy on attachment, with a quote from Graham Green: "Unhappiness in a child accumulates because he sees no end to the dark tunnel. The thirteen weeks of a term might just as well be thirteen years" (Bowlby, 1973, p. 21).

I can imagine that he missed the daily contact with his mother, siblings, nanny and nursemaids a great deal. Van Dijken (1998, p. 27) refers to a personal reflection of the adult Bowlby who said that he had been sufficiently *hurt* but not sufficiently *damaged*, as a result of his childhood experiences. He had in fact survived his childhood adversities to become a sufficiently resilient and self-assured adolescent.

The young Bowlby soon developed an interest in deep waters. At the age of 14, he was sent to the Royal Naval College, Dartmouth, in 1921, where he excelled at sports and became top of his academic group. His father saw it as best for him to become a sailor in the Navy. In spite of his outstanding record at the Naval College and a prestigious posting to HMS Royal Oak, a ship of the Atlantic Fleet, in May 1924, he found life in the armed services dull and useless. He also suffered badly from seasickness. However, while in the Navy, he learned organisational skills and discipline – which lasted a lifetime (Holmes, 1993, p. 17).

On 19 July 1924, Bowlby wrote to his mother to let her know that he wanted to look for a more satisfactory job which "would improve the community as a whole" (quoted in Van Dijken, 1998, p. 46). That was a manifestation of his youthful idealism at the age of 17. With the help of a friend, who was on the same ship, he persuaded his father to buy him out for a total of £440. There was a rule that if cadets left before they were 21, their parents had to pay the Admiralty £40 for each term that their son had passed at Dartmouth (Bush, 1935).

After leaving HMS Royal Oak, Bowlby spent a year at University College London learning Latin and other subjects necessary for admission to Cambridge, the second largest University in the UK. In 1925, he joined Trinity College as an 18-year-old student of pre-clinical medicine – something that his father had considered as the second best option after the Navy. He excelled at Cambridge, where he won several prizes and obtained a first class degree in psychology (a subject that his father disliked) and pre-clinical sciences, in 1928.

Bowlby was particularly interested in developmental psychology. He also did a considerable amount of work in evolutionary biology. He was just 22 when his father died in April 1929; but, according to Parkes (1995), it would appear that he found the loss 'un-traumatic' – on the surface, at least. In some way, the end of his father's life was the beginning of a new stage in Bowlby's life. He gradually felt freer to pursue his own rather than his father's interests. He soon gained a reputation of being an independently minded person, with a powerful and contagious inner calm.

Before his father's death Bowlby had chosen an unconventional path and went to work for a year at a couple of progressive schools rather than going straight on to clinical medicine. He wanted to learn more about child development. One of the schools, Priory Gate, was for *maladjusted* children – as they were then called. It made a strong impression on him.

Bowlby had powerful encounters with these unhappy and disturbed children, with whom he was able to communicate well. He was particularly struck by two of the youngsters. An eight-year-old boy was desperate to make a direct close contact with him and followed him as his shadow. In contrast to that, a fifteen-year-old adolescent was very emotionally shut-up (see Chapter 5).

The climate in the institution was one of seeing the children's emotional and behavioural problems in the light of their difficult background. At the school, Bowlby also met a senior colleague, John Alford, who advised him to train as a child psychiatrist and psychoanalyst. He followed this advice and came to London in the autumn of 1929 to study clinical medicine at University College Hospital. Concurrently, he went into personal analysis with Joan Riviere, a committed follower of Melanie Klein.

The training of the young Bowlby

Bowlby qualified as a doctor in 1933 and went to the Maudsley Hospital to train in adult psychiatry for three years. During this training he developed a scientific mentality under the influence of Aubrey Lewis, who was an open-minded, middle of the road psychiatrist with a background in medical psychology. Lewis was particularly sceptical about dogmatic beliefs and became a good role model. In an autobiographical article published posthumously, Bowlby (1991a) referred to Lewis's influence on him and to Riviere's complaint that, as a result, he was trying to think everything out from scratch – taking nothing for granted! His attitude was one of suspending judgement until he would be able to gain more experience.

During most of his psychoanalytic training from 1929 to 1937, Bowlby followed Kleinian directives and concentrated on the interpretation of 'unconscious transference' (see Chapter 9). That is, feelings that the patient may experience towards the analyst without being aware of – which usually relate to unresolved and largely repressed past experiences. He often felt uneasy, but had to compromise in order to qualify. He did not get on with the first supervisor but felt better about the second one, Ella Sharpe. She was a Kleinian at the time. Later, following the controversies between the Kleinians and the Freudians, she joined the new Middle or Independent Group that was formed at the British Psychoanalytical Society (see Chapter 3).

Bowlby also joined the Independent Group and remained in it until the end of his life. He perceived Sharpe as a warm-hearted person, with a good understanding of human nature and a sense of humour, which helped him to treat patients with sympathy as fellow human beings (Bowlby, 1991a). In 1936, after completion of his adult psychiatric training at the Maudsley, he obtained a job at the London Child Guidance Clinic: he was keen to develop a career as a child psychiatrist. What he learned at the Clinic changed his way of formulating emotional problems. He could see more clearly how adverse childhood experiences and family events contributed to the adult's vulnerability to psychopathology.

Bowlby became more confident in treating his adult patients by inviting them to explore and talk to him about their real life experiences during childhood and adolescence. He continued using the transference in Kleinian terms, though doing so less often, while also helping patients put into words difficult or conflictive feelings towards their parents and other significant figures in their lives. When the material reported by the patient indicated that there were good grounds to believe that he or she had been rejected or unwanted, Bowlby (1991a, p. 26) may say: "It sounds to me as though your mother never really wanted you".

Bowlby was able to be openly self-critical too. He reviewed the treatment of patients who had made little progress in terms of what he himself might have missed as therapist, rather than in terms of the patient's defensiveness:

> My first patient, a woman in her late thirties in an acutely anxious and agitated state, was, I can now see, in a condition of seriously disturbed mourning following the death of her mother with whom she had had a pathogenic relationship. Neither I nor my supervisor were in any way aware of that.
>
> *(ibid., p. 26)*

As he talked to his analyst about his new conceptions, following what he was learning at the Child Guidance Clinic, she became overcautious about giving the *green light* for his qualification. Indeed, Riviere realised that her analysand's ideas were following a path different from that of prevalent Kleinian thinking, and she considered that giving attention to real life experiences was a distraction from what matters most: the internal world. For Bowlby, also, the internal world was very important. However, he was coming to the conclusion that

> one can only understand a person's internal world, and thus see his current situation through his own spectacles, if one can see how his internal world has come to be constructed from the real-life events and situations to which he has been exposed.
>
> *(ibid., p. 27)*

It is interesting that, in spite of her emphasis on *unconscious phantasies*, Bowlby's analyst strongly believed in relationships. She made clear her underlying thinking that each personality is formed out of countless, never-ending, influences and exchanges between ourselves and other people. In her view, these other human beings are a part of us; inevitably, we are members of one another. She put it succinctly: "the inner world is exclusively one of personal relations" (Riviere, 1952, p. 162).

Despite their differences, the relational connection between Bowlby and Riviere was solid enough for him to become an Associate Member of the British Psychoanalytical Society in the summer of 1937, after eight years of personal analysis – which was to continue for a further couple of years.

Bowlby's next steps were to prepare the dissertation required for full membership of the Society, with voting rights, and to undertake further training in child analysis under the direct supervision of Melanie Klein herself. His first child patient was a highly restless, hyperactive and aggressive three-year-old boy, who was brought to therapy by an anxious and distressed mother. Bowlby wanted to see the mother as well, as he suspected that the child's problems might be connected to the difficult relationship the child had with her. However, Klein considered that the mother–child relationship was irrelevant and instructed Bowlby not to see the mother – something that was difficult for him to bear.

Within a few months he was sorry to learn that the mother had been admitted as an inpatient to a psychiatric hospital and the treatment of the child could no longer carry on. Bowlby was left with the impression that, in the prohibition to see the mother, both the needs of the child's family and the needs of the child had been neglected. Klein was mainly concerned with the unconscious phantasies of the child as determinant to his psychopathology. The differences in supervision continued with the handling of the next patient, but the training was interrupted with the outbreak of the Second World War.

Bowlby did not want to have an open clash with Klein and decided not to continue his training in child analysis after the war. Just before the war, in June 1939, he had presented a ground-breaking paper for his full membership of the British Psychoanalytical Society: "The Influence of Early Environment in the Development of Neurosis and Neurotic Character" (Bowlby, 1940). Criticism by Klein and others was not a surprise for him; he had received a privileged communication: "Beforehand, I had been warned by Mrs Klein's daughter, Melitta Schmideberg, who was a friend and well-disposed to my thesis, that it would meet with much criticism" (Bowlby, 1991a, p. 27).

Bowlby's ideas were still in an embryonic form and he did not defend them aggressively, but was sufficiently assertive to pursue them in spite of the obstacles. He had enough confidence to suggest that the analyst should study not only the patient but also the environment where the patient was brought up, and the interaction between the two, in a way similar to how nurserymen need to analyse the nature of the plant, the properties of the soil and the relationship between both.

In his dissertation, Bowlby also recommended therapeutic work for those parents who had themselves experienced problems in parenting. He postulated that the recognition of the difficult feelings that they would have had as children would help them to be in a better position to understand and tolerate similar feelings in their own children. The bottom line was to prevent the trans-generational transmission of problems.

Bowlby's approach was loyal to psychoanalysis while applying the new methods that he was acquiring as a child psychiatrist in his work with parents: "A weekly interview in which their problems are approached analytically and traced back to childhood has sometimes been remarkably effective" (Bowlby, 1940, p. 176). In spite of challenging Klein's emphasis on the child's fantasy world and proposing attention to actual events, he received enough support from senior members, particularly from Susan Isaacs, and the dissertation was accepted. The following year it was published by the *International Journal of Psychoanalysis* (Bowlby, 1940).

Power differential was a prominent feature of the British Psychoanalytical Society at the time. Paula Heimann (1899–1982), a German psychiatrist and psychoanalyst who would become Melanie Klein's secretary, noted the sharp contrast between the atmosphere in the Berlin Psychoanalytic Society and the atmosphere in London:

> Oh, how awesome and foreboding! The wearing of hats by respectable ladies was the rule, and the more dignified you were the bigger the hat … . And no sitting round the table here. There was a formal rostrum with rows in order of seniority; old at the front and small at the rear, terrified of the long walk up to the front if you dared to speak.
>
> *(quoted in Van Dijken, 1998, p. 96)*

Personal and family developments

While in Cambridge, the young Bowlby was introduced to Evan Durbin by his brother Tony. Durbin was an academic and politician whom the historian David Kynaston described as the Labour Party's most interesting thinker of the 1940s, and arguably of the twentieth century. Durbin turned out to be an MP for Edmonton and served as Minister of Works in the post-war Attlee's Cabinet. Durbin and Bowlby gradually became close friends. In 1933, with the purpose of helping one of Bowlby's former colleagues at Priory Gate School, they set up a sandwich bar in London with the name of Bogey's Bar. Bogey was one of Bowlby's nicknames (Van Dijken, 1998, p. 167).

Durbin and Bowlby spent a great deal of time thinking, talking and walking together: "It was hard to keep up with them as they strode rapidly through the Cotswolds, deep in conversation" (Holmes, 1993, p. 22). Like Lewis at the Maudsley, Durbin challenged his friend's incipient psychoanalytic ideas. This in fact stimulated and sharpened Bowlby's intellectual development. Their friendship grew. He was best man at Durbin's wedding with Marjorie, and moved in with them in 1934. They shared a house for four years until Bowlby's wedding with Ursula Longstaff in 1938, where Durbin was best man.

In the pre-war years, Bowlby and Durbin became very concerned with the rise of fascism, and decided to jointly write a book: *Personal Aggressiveness and War* (Bowlby & Durbin, 1939). While his friend studied the socio-economic factors that may contribute to the war machine, Bowlby concentrated on the psychological factors that may lead to aggression. As a scientist rooted in Darwin's theory of evolution, he surveyed the literature on aggression in apes and other higher mammals, drawing parallels with human behaviour. As a newly qualified psychoanalyst, he lucidly explored the concept of unconscious aggression.

In a well-balanced paper, "Between Love and Aggression: The Politics of John Bowlby", Mayhew (2006, p. 19) gives a broader historical and social perspective of the creative influence brought about by the relationship of these two altruistic friends:

> Bowlby's collaboration with Evan Durbin, a little-known but important economist and political philosopher, was underpinned by a belief that social responsibility was an evolved psychological potentiality that could be actualised in the mother–child bonding process. This reflected and reinforced their democratic socialist vision. Furthermore, their work helped usher in a new technological framework for conceiving of social policy, a framework that would dominate British politics after the Second World War.

On 3 September 1948, aged 42, Durbin died as he drowned while rescuing two children, including one of his daughters, whose boat had capsized. This tragic event came to pass at Strangles Beach on the coast of Cornwall. Bowlby, on holiday nearby, was devastated by this untimely loss but he immediately reacted with his compassionate and caring heart. He organised, together with Durbin's close parliamentary colleagues, a trust fund to support the Durbin's children through their education (Holmes, 1993, p. 22). I cannot help thinking it eerie that the deaths of two such close friends should occur just one day apart – though Bowlby's was 42 years later. Durbin's premature death was a massive loss for Bowlby and, no doubt, contributed to his growing concern for the study of human grief and loss.

In her compelling comparison of attachment theory with Mahler's separation-individuation theory, Coates (2004, p. 575) described Bowlby as "a socially very shy student". In his early adulthood, he appeared to have had difficulties in relating to women, let alone forming lasting romantic relationships with them. That was not unusual in young men who had grown up in a man's world. In an interview on 11 May 1991, his brother Tony reported: "He went through a period of being unable really to latch onto a proper relationship with a girlfriend" (quoted in Van Dijken, 1998, p. 80).

During the time of his psychoanalytic training, Bowlby had a number of short-lived and, at times, tempestuous liaisons with several girlfriends. In the mid-1930s, he was all but formally engaged to Lady Prudence Pelham. His mother had been consulted and she was delighted about this aristocratic woman. Bowlby, according to his brother Tony, spoilt this relationship "by having an affair with Lady Pelham's sister". Soon after this, Bowlby had a relationship with Rose Montague who would later marry Charles Elton, a close friend of Ursula's family. In the same interview, Tony reported that Rose had been a girlfriend of his and Durbin's back in their University days (Van Dijken, 1998, p. 81). Of course, that had nothing to do with sibling rivalry!

Much later, in an interview at 80, Bowlby described his relationship with his brother Tony as follows:

> We were intense rivals [laughs] and I believe that my brother being the eldest son was rather more favoured than the younger son. Well the younger son wasn't in the mood to accept that [laughs] and so this rivalry was nothing if not intense. I may say we were very close companions at the same time and … very similar in character.
>
> *(in Byng-Hall, 1987, pp. 18–19)*

Conversely, as reported by Van Dijken (1998, p. 19), Tony talked about the same two aspects of their relationship: "the friendship depended upon his accepting that I was his senior. Once he tried to push me into a junior position, I fought like a little tiger. It was horrible".

Van Dijken (1998, p. 81) also referred to a suggestion made by Riviere that Bowlby went through a period of depression while in training analysis, and that this could have made it difficult for him to establish and sustain loving relationships with women. It might have also been the other way around that his relationship difficulties with women perhaps contributed to his depression. I wonder about Riviere's perception of the confidentiality due to her patient at the time.

Bowlby, at one point, considered changing analysts. However, his senior colleague Susan Isaacs (a fellow analysand of Riviere) persuaded him not to do so (see Chapter 12). In the last period of his psychoanalytic treatment, around the age of 30, he clearly wanted to settle down in his personal life – which indeed he did. Interestingly, he was introduced to the Longstaff family by Rose Montague who was also a close friend of Ursula's eldest sister. This was at a shooting holiday in Hampshire's New Forest in 1937.

At the time Bowlby met Ursula, the Longstaffs were a family of seven attractive daughters living with their pipe-smoking mother whose father, a physician, had given up medicine for mountaineering and had abandoned his wife for a younger woman. "Ursula, the third daughter, intelligent and beautiful but more diffident than her older sisters, attracted his [Bowlby's] interest" (Holmes, 1993, p. 22). That was well timed; he and Ursula fell for one another. They married in 1938 and had four children: Mary Ignatia (born in 1939), Richard (born in 1941), Pia (born in 1945) and Robert (born in 1948). Bowlby would later joke that by the time of his marriage he had spent all his money on his training analysis (Marrone, 1998).

Initially, the Bowlbys lived with friends, partly to share costs and partly to enjoy the comradeship they all felt as middle of the road socialists. During the war, the Bowlbys and the Durbins shared a house in York Terrace, London, where a number of famous psychoanalysts had their consulting rooms. These included Ernest Jones who was Freud's official biographer, President of the British and International Psychoanalytic Associations, and the first English-speaking person to practice psychoanalysis.

The pattern of sharing accommodation continued for a number of years after the war. This was largely based on Bowlby's recognition of the benefits of an extended network of friends and family when bringing up small children. Ursula called this the 'tribal area', a version of the extended family, which she felt sure "is repeated countless times all over the world, though less so in Britain" (Marrone, 1998, p. 18).

For several years after the war, the Bowlbys house-shared in Hampstead, North West London with Jock Sutherland, his wife Molly and their child. Sutherland was a distinguished Scottish psychiatrist who was Medical Director of the Tavistock Clinic from 1947 to 1968; that is, the first 20 years of the Clinic under the umbrella of the newly created National Health Service. Bowlby was Deputy Director of the Tavistock and Director of the Children and Parents' Department (see Chapter 4).

The Bowlbys were destined to stay in their Hampstead home for the rest of their lives. It was here that I said goodbye to John Bowlby, both as mentor and fellow human being, at the conclusion of our last meeting in his garden on 26 July 1990, one month to the end of his pilgrimage (see Chapter 12).

Some free associations

It is strange, somehow, that I have just jumped from Bowlby's early days as a family man to our goodbye. I can remember well the last day with him; so well that, unless I am hit by dementia, when my time comes I might still recall this day. A few months earlier, in May 1990 when he had surgery for his bowel cancer, I had realised that he would be departing soon. In view of my history of anxious attachments, it may not have been surprising to experience some separation anxiety; but no, it did not happen. As I was anticipating our ultimate separation, a powerful feeling of peaceful sadness filled me up – sadness without depression.

Bowlby had given me a gentle, caring warning that his time would come before long. Internally, I started to mourn him. When he left for good, I hugely missed him. But my tears, in a way, were happy tears. I had met Bowlby at a critical point when I was a foreigner, like *L'Étranger* of Albert Camus (1983), in no-man's land. Right from the outset, I felt at home with him. Over the months and years, I developed a trusting and secure attachment with him. He came across as someone happy with himself and at peace with the world.

I had been in Skye with María in the summer of 1985, without knowing that the Bowlbys had their second home there. We felt welcomed by the local people and very much enjoyed our stay. I would describe it as a timeless experience, which is also how I would describe my attachment with Bowlby. His death was a great loss and a reminder of our mortality. But he stayed. Our mutually fulfilling relationship is an important part of my internal world, as he and his Kleinian analyst had put it: a world of inter-personal relations.

Of course, Bowlby stayed in the internal world of Ursula with whom I enjoyed a lovely and ongoing epistolary contact until her own death on 3 February 2000. She sent me, in 1991, a copy of what she had written following his death:

I had not anticipated how I should feel. If I had imagined this, I am sure I should have believed myself totally shattered. He was my Rock of Gibraltar ... . Instead of being shattered, I felt suddenly comforted. He seemed secure in my heart and I knew I would carry him about with me for the rest of my life. I have this sense of continuous companionship. I am never lonely ... I can't understand the 'how' or 'why' but I accept it as a wonderful gift from God.... I feel that John had both expanded – into a world of total freedom, together with the winds, the sea, the hills, the flowers – and contracted, into my heart.

I did share my mourning with John Southgate. He had started supervision with Bowlby in 1987, in the same room and at the same time and day I was having mine, so we alternated fortnightly for the next three years having a feeling of being 'twin' supervisees. He gave me a copy of the obituary he wrote, which would later be published in *The Guardian*:

I was shocked and saddened today to learn of the death of John Bowlby.... Many people in older age rest upon their laurels and cease to be creative. Not so with him ... even when in a wheel chair, recovering from an operation, he apologized for not being able to work the next week. Our debt to him is enormous.

(Southgate, 1990, p. 11)

Some weeks later, Southgate visited Bowlby's grave and shared with me the experience of his journey:

Driving through snow and blizzards, blocked roads, floods and perils, then onto Skye where the gulf stream warms the snowy mountains ... curtains of showers, curlew and kestrels.... Discover a plot of flowers and a tree ... John Bowlby is dead but his spirit lives on in his work and ideas, in our work, and in the people who knew him.... I thought of the old socialist Joe Hill, whose saying was 'do not mourn, organise'. A more fitting epitaph for John Bowlby would be: do mourn, then organise.

(Southgate, 1990, p. 11)

I could not have put it better. In a number of ways, during his childhood and adolescence, Bowlby may have developed an avoidant pattern of attachment that he carried into his adult life (Holmes, 1993). This is consistent with the view of family members like his niece, Juliet Hopkins, and his eldest son, Sir Richard Bowlby, who reported that his father displayed an "avoidant attachment style" (quoted in Issroff, 2005, p. 16). People employ avoidant coping strategies as a defence when their natural needs for emotional connectedness and affection are repeatedly not met, so they *protect* themselves from further disappointment because of their needs not being met.

There was no avoidance in Bowlby's approach with me and this experience is shared by my peer group. Among the older generation of colleagues, Sutherland

(1990) knew him particularly well and suggested that he may have developed a protective shell for not showing his feelings as readily as other people do (see Chapter 12). However, Sutherland was convinced that Bowlby was the possessor of a deep and powerful fund of affection, which translated into a caring concern for those who worked with him. That was certainly true in the six years of fortnightly mentorship I had with him.

Like his father, Bowlby was some 10 years older than his bride. Jeremy Holmes (1993) wrote about the Bowlby family being affected by dyslexia, a condition unrecognised at the time. The children's academic difficulties were a source of some sorrow and frustration for Bowlby who found parenting a difficult role. He would be renowned in the family for resisting his children's clamouring demands with the phrase: "Now, don't bully me, don't bully me" (quoted in Holmes, 1993, p. 15). By contrast, his eldest daughter, Mary considered that he was a brilliant grandfather. Maybe he was slightly remote as a father and followed his own father's tradition of hard work and long holidays – to partly compensate for not having a close contact with his children when they were young.

There is an amusing anecdote about the eldest son, Richard, at around the age of seven, asking: "Is Daddy a burglar? He always comes home after dark and never talks about his work" (quoted in Holmes, 1993, p. 25). During the holidays in Skye, Bowlby and his family did enjoy walking, bird-watching, boating, fishing and shooting together – something that he had enjoyed doing as a child with his parents and siblings. In London, Bowlby's favourite family outing was a first-class ballet performance at the Royal Opera House or at the English National Opera.

Bowlby (1988a, p. 11) had postulated that fathers may be filling a role that resembles and is close to that filled by mothers. But, he believed, in most families the role of the father is different from that of the mother. The father is more likely to engage in physically active and novel play than the mother and, especially for boys, he may become the child's preferred play companion. Overall, however, Bowlby did not write much about the highly significant bond that children have with their fathers. This might be partly explained by his experience with his own father, Sir Anthony, who was largely absent for him: away for nearly five years during the war and otherwise rarely available, due to his extremely hard-working schedule.

In the summer 1989, María and I invited Bowlby, his wife Ursula, their daughter Pia and her husband Carlos Durán for a meal in our London home. The gathering was warm, relaxed and thoroughly enjoyable. They all made positive comments about the food. María explained that I had done the cooking. Bowlby showed a big surprise on his face, as if he believed that a man's role in the family would not include cooking.

One day in the spring of 2014, María and I went to see one of Lope de Vega's plays with Pia and Carlos. Pia commented that there was a clear division of parental roles in her parent's family home, and that it was her mother who took most of the responsibilities for bringing up the four children. Pia recalled that her mother persuaded her father to keep two evenings free for family life with the children.

FIGURE 2.1 Bowlby's visit to the author's family, summer 1989.

Some 22 years earlier, I had sent to Ursula a paper on group-analytic therapy and attachment (Ezquerro, 1991). That was my theoretical dissertation for membership of the Institute of Group Analysis, in which I explored an idea that a sense of belonging may help members to experience a therapy group as a secure base. This had previously been suggested by Liza Glenn (1987), a Jungian and group analyst who had also been supervised by Bowlby. Ursula responded promptly:

Dear Arturo,
    I found that I could read most of your paper without difficulty, though some of the technical parts are over my head.... What I write now was suggested to me by reading your paper, but they are just my amateur free associations ... I think you should insert a sentence or two, following your list of 'modern predators', pointing out that, as with animal predators, BEING ALONE makes one much more vulnerable. Hence keeping proximity, as an insurance against disaster. (Especially if this is so of a child, who is without an adult companion).
    As regards finding one's Secure Base in a group, I think this is a masculine possibility. Personally I have never felt any group, except my own family, gave me a sense of security. My family was large – seven sisters, all now grandmothers, all still extremely close and supportive. But I do think men are different, and they value – and find useful – what I call 'the hunting band'. This consists of a feeling of kinship brought about by enthusiasm about doing the same thing, whether it is hunting or mounting-climbing or collecting butterflies. But it is something outside oneself.
    When my two sons were children I noticed that they did not really care what the boys they played with were like, so long as they enjoyed doing the same thing as themselves (tinkering about with cars, for instance).

Our two daughters were much more discriminating about personality, however, and chose as their playmates the girls whom they liked as people. You see the difference?

Yours,

Ursula

P. S. My flu is on the wane; I am recovering, I'm glad to say

[25th January 1992].

So, what was Bowlby like? Holmes (1993) thinks that he had an extraordinary capacity to reconcile divergent features of his personality. He describes these elements as contradictory although, I believe, they in fact were complementary to one another – and came together to build a truly exceptional character:

> reserved, yet capable of inspiring great affection, quintessentially 'English' and yet thoroughly cosmopolitan in outlook; conventional in manner yet revolutionary in spirit; equally at home with the sophistication of Hampstead and in the wilds of Skye; ... a man of action who devoted his life to the inner world; determined in his convictions and yet without overt aggression; ... someone who believed passionately in the importance of expressing emotion, whose own feelings were an enigma.
>
> *(Holmes, 1993, p. 30)*

The months following Bowlby's death gave rise to massive expressions of love and gratitude by many colleagues from the Tavistock Clinic and the mental health world at home and abroad (see Chapter 12), in addition to those from his family:

Dear María and Arturo,

I have run out of Christmas cards – everyone in the world has sent me them – but anyway I think you will prefer this photograph of John, taken by our son Richard (medical photographer at the Royal Free Hospital). He is coping with details of John's memorial-service. Richard and Xenia live next door to me ...

Pia's godmother – a very old friend – wrote to sympathise on John's death, and Pia replied to her – that he had left "a lot of love and strength behind". I'm sure this is true ...

We are having a memorial-service for him on Jan. 8th. I need to warn you that parking is nil, but London Bridge Tube Station is only four minutes' walk from the cathedral, and this is the route we shall take (I and the rest of the family).

I don't know if you have seen the current 'Tavistock Gazette', which has 22 riveting pages about John. You need to send the editors (Susanne Griffin and Gill Stern) £1 + postage (50 p), as they are in deep debt ... but move fast, as not many copies are left. They really are a mémoire in themselves, and I feel sure you will like to read them.

Yours,

Ursula

P. S. The Tavi Library has a very good obituary of John, by Rudolph Schaffer (ex-Tavi). I do recommend it. If not, let me know and I will send you a photocopy. It's really brilliant.

[19th December 1990].

In the Appendix, I shall provide an abridged chronology and a list of authors who have written about Bowlby's personal and professional journey. His pilgrimage.

3

JOHN BOWLBY AT WAR AND THE PSYCHOANALYTIC CONTROVERSIAL DISCUSSIONS

By the end of the First World War it was becoming clear that its devastating effects were contributing to psychological distress and mental illness. This was particularly so for the soldiers who had survived but suffered major physical and emotional wounds. What nowadays is clearly documented as post-traumatic stress disorder had not yet been recognised, let alone conceptualised. However, some doctors were beginning to categorise the war's psychiatric casualties in terms of suffering from *shell shock* or *war neurosis*.

In this post-war context, a small group of psychiatrists under the leadership of Hugh Crichton-Miller opened the Tavistock Clinic in 1920. It was originally known as the Tavistock Institute of Medical Psychology. The founder members worked hard to create informed public opinion and concern, which could drive reforms in the direction of mental health provision and training.

In the early days, the Tavistock developed psychological treatments for shell-shocked soldiers. From the outset, clinical services were for both adults and children. The Clinic's first patient was in fact a child, although a proper Children's Department did not open until 1926. From the beginning, it was clear that offering free treatment meant that the training of a new generation of professionals would have to be essential, in order to maximise resources. At the time, among the roughly 80 Tavistock physicians who contributed around six hours a week, many had little or no psychiatric training.

The impact of bereavement was enormous: roughly three-quarters of a million Britons died in the war, leaving around a quarter of a million widows and nearly four hundred thousand fatherless children. It was in the other foremost psychiatric institution in Britain, the Maudsley Hospital, where mental health professionals became aware of the fact that complex bereavement was a risk factor in the development of psychosis. It was during his psychiatric training at the Maudsley Hospital, from 1933 to 1936, that Bowlby became conversant with the link between bereavement and psychotic illness.

Ernest Jones, who had founded the British Psychoanalytical Society in 1913, was reluctant to allow psychoanalysts to work at the Tavistock Clinic. He saw it as a dilution of the *pure gold* of psychoanalysis and officially banned the Clinic for members of the Society. In 1933, John Rees took over the Tavistock's leadership from Crichton-Miller. From then until 1939, in spite of Jones' interdiction, the Clinic proportionally had the period of greatest expansion in treatment, training, external lectures and courses, as well as numbers of staff and trainees.

The Tavistock became the main centre for psychotherapeutically based psychiatry in the United Kingdom, and well known throughout the world. It attained international standing through the development of links with organisations in the main Commonwealth countries and the United States. It also started to undertake systematic research. In September 1939, at the outbreak of the Second World War, Rees was invited to take command of British Army psychiatry. He assembled a team of psychiatrists who co-operated with the military hierarchy in the rehabilitation of psychiatric casualties and the maintenance of good morale.

Tavistock Clinic staff organised psychosocial interventions in the selection and allocation of officers and soldiers, in order for them to work adequately to their personality and level of skills; Bowlby was to join this team. Members of the Tavistock were also helping with the treatment of the civilian population, traumatised by the bombing of cities, the evacuation of children and the shock of bereavement.

The experience of massive human relations problems, under stress and dislocation, strongly influenced the thinking and practice of the Clinic after the war. As we will see in more detail in Chapter 4, psychodynamic social psychiatry and psychology, group psychotherapy and research developed: "So once again war was the stimulus of the 'second birth' of the Tavistock Clinic" (Dicks, 1970, p. 7).

Concerns for children and soldiers

At the beginning of the war, Bowlby tried every available channel to voice his concerns about the dangers of evacuating young children for long periods of time without their mothers or close relatives. In total, almost one and a half million people were evacuated from the big cities. He and Evan Durbin wrote to *The Times*, and collected signatures from influential people like Rees – the Tavistock Clinic's Medical Director. The letter was ignored, which disappointed Bowlby a great deal. He wrote to his wife Ursula on 19 November 1939: "The letter to 'The Times' seems to have been sabotaged which is annoying" (quoted in Van Dijken, 1998, p. 108).

However, on 16 December 1939, the *British Medical Journal* published a letter in which it was stated that such separations could lead to a severe disruption in the healthy development of the child's personality and the capacity for social relationships, with long-lasting effects: "For instance, it can lead to a big increase in juvenile delinquency in the next decade" (Bowlby, Miller, & Winnicott, 1939, in Winnicott, 1990, p. 14). The warning proved to be prophetic!

In his final report to the National Trust, Hyla Holden (2009) described some after-effects on children evacuated to war-time residential nurseries. For the majority, their early lives were twice disrupted by separation from those whom they loved: first, from their own families and, later, from their nurse-carers. Holden, a close friend who worked with Bowlby at the Tavistock, remarked on a recurring theme: many of these children had expressed the feeling they were always 'the odd one out' after having returned home. They frequently fell into despair when separated from those to whom they were attached. They did not know whom to blame and often ended blaming themselves.

If they felt unloved, it could be hard for these children to hold onto the possibility that they were lovable. Travelling in war time was difficult; many children received only a few visits and some none at all. Anna Freud and Dorothy Burlingham established a residential nursery in Hampstead for children evacuated from other bombed areas of London. They set new therapeutic standards in child care. In the nursery the children were divided into small, family style groups each under the care of one or two individual carers.

The importance of family visiting was emphasised, so that the children did not think that they had been abandoned. These visits enabled them to feel that they were worth visiting (Freud & Burlingham, 1944). James Robertson was one of the social workers at this residential nursery. (In the next chapter, I shall give details of his work with Bowlby at the Tavistock after the war.)

With the outbreak of the war, Bowlby joined the Emergency Medical Service. After the Dunkirk evacuation he had to help with military psychiatric casualties. He initially worked at an ex-infirmary in Lancashire, but was shocked by the dreadful conditions under which the patients were treated. He made a complaint but, as his concerns were ignored, he resigned from the service. He was later invited to join the Royal Army Medical Corps. Here, he had a prominent role in the newly created War Office Selection Boards (WOSB) and he met colleagues from the Tavistock. These included John Rees, Ronald Hargreaves, Wilfred Bion, John Rickman, Jock Sutherland, Harold Bridger, Eric Trist, Henry Dicks and others.

This group was portrayed as the 'invisible college', in that they maintained collegial links with each other throughout the war years. The group successfully contributed to what has been described as 'psychosocial model building', which included a number of tasks such as: (1) to identify problems; (2) to look for new solutions when old ones had failed; (3) to collaborate with military personnel in the structure of the models; and (4) to hand back the innovations to the military (Pines, 1991).

At one point in our supervision, Bowlby portrayed Bion as a creative man and a charismatic figure who had had a significant influence on him during the war and in his early days at the Tavistock following the war. Bowlby also commented that he felt Bion had been significantly traumatised by witnessing the brutal death of his friends and comrades at the Front during the First World War. Bowlby was impressed by Bion's intellectual calibre but gradually lost interest in Bionian theorising, as he felt that it was becoming too speculative.

Bion, an analysand of John Rickman and later of Melanie Klein, was apparently uninterested in Bowlby's work. In 1942, while serving at the Army Medical Corps, he and Rickman started what has been called the *First Northfield Experiment*. Rickman was deeply interested in anthropology and sociological phenomena. Northfield was a psychiatric military hospital, near Birmingham, in the heart of England. The Hospital had been reorganised in order to help the Army with the identification and treatment of recoverable cases of mental breakdown and the discharge of the unrecoverable.

Bion and Rickman were put in charge of the training and rehabilitation wing at Northfield. They introduced a radical treatment regime in which the main technique adopted was one of group discussion and the study of group dynamics (Bion & Rickman, 1943). Neurosis was seen as the *enemy*; soldiers had to learn to face this enemy and to develop the courage to do so without retreating again. Bion's experience as a young tank commander in the First World War stood him in good stead. He was a fully-fledged fighting man himself.

However, the project had to close after only six weeks – a decision delivered by Rees, Medical Director of the Tavistock Clinic. Bion was furious (Kraemer, 2011, p. 90). The military authorities had not been included in the venture; they were uncertain about the novelty of the method and puzzled by the disturbance caused in the wider hospital environment. Although the experiment was in some way a manifestation of creative genius, Bion and Rickman were unable to anticipate the far-reaching consequences that such drastic change could have on a whole social system. Harold Bridger (1990, p. 73) believed that Bion was not trusted because he aimed to return most of the men to active service rather than getting them invalidated out.

An effort like this was unprecedented in the British armed services. Bion and Rickman turned the notion of authority on its head by distancing themselves from a traditional position of authority in order to push the soldiers to have to find their own. While soldiers in groups can be moved by elementary forces that undermine judgement and thought, they can also develop real authority under stress through their attentiveness to one another. In spite of the premature closure of their project, Bion and Rickman laid the theoretical foundations upon which others were to build. The first section of Bion's (1961) *Experiences in Groups* remains a seminal piece of work about how to set up a therapeutic community for traumatised patients.

The *Second Northfield Experiment* was indeed based on the ideas of Bion and Rickman. However, it used group psychotherapy more specifically for the well-being of the soldiers rather than the demands of the Army. It started in 1943 and was led by S. H. Foulkes. He was a Freudian psychoanalyst who, in 1933, had to flee Nazi Germany into the relative safety of England. It was safe no longer, but he was able to navigate through the pressure he was under. In contrast to Bion, his approach was gentler. Bowlby's (1946a, 1947) therapeutic values in war and peace were closer to Foulkes' than to Bion's.

Foulkes' attitude was so *benign* that he often started a therapy session at the Hospital saying: "while we are in this group, we are not at war" (quoted in

Ezquerro, 2004a, p. 203). An enthusiastic and innovative group of psychiatrists was formed: Foulkes (1946) worked closely with Main (1946), Bridger (1946, 1985) and others. Despite their caring approach (or perhaps because of it) as distinct from martial attitude, they were more successful than Bion and Rickman at gaining the support of the military authorities. Although the two experiments differed in pace, technique and effectiveness, they shared many underlying concepts such as social responsibility and the therapeutic use of the 'milieu'; that is, the hospital as a whole community.

The *Northfield Experiments* are considered to be an important landmark in the world of mental health and in sociology. The experiments were fundamental in the creation of the therapeutic community movement, as well as the development of group psychotherapy, social psychiatry and organisational consultancy. Lessons learned at Northfield still remain relevant to the practice of psychiatry and psychotherapy, as well as the study of institutional group relations and processes.

Bowlby was more than receptive to the clinical application of the new developments. He used group principles and methodology in his therapeutic work with families; something that he called 'joint interview technique':

> This technique stems directly from techniques used by Bion and Rickman in adult group therapy and by members of the Tavistock Institute of Human Relations for dealing with tensions in social groups.... It is a technique whereby the real tensions existing between individuals in the group are dealt with freely and openly in the group, much as, in an individual analysis, the tensions existing between different psychic systems within the individual are dealt with freely and openly with the analyst.
>
> *(Bowlby, 1949, p. 126)*

Was Bowlby a fighter or a peace-maker?

Early on in his work, immediately prior to the war, Bowlby showed a keen interest in the search for the causes of human aggression, particularly in the early years of life. He realised that most of the adult patients he had seen with a history of violence had displayed marked aggressiveness during childhood. On the other hand, he was appreciating that a stable emotional bond with the mother helped children to regulate their aggressive impulses. It might be of relevance that his early publications related in fact to the theme of aggression in childhood.

Bowlby's (1938) first paper, "The Abnormally Aggressive Child", was soon followed by "Jealous and Spiteful Children" (Bowlby, 1939). Through his work at the London Child Guidance Clinic, he was learning that the problematical child of today was vulnerable to becoming the neurotic or psychopathic grown-up of tomorrow. He conceptualised psychotherapy as preventative medicine, which could help change not only individual people but also families and society as a whole.

The war had a strong impact on Bowlby's professional and personal life. Before its outbreak, he was involved in pacifists movements that tried to prevent what appeared to be an impending military conflict. Together with Durbin, he actively participated in the Symposium on *War and Democracy*, organised by young Labour politicians in 1938. As we saw in the previous chapter, their contributions were published as a book with a clear message: "war is due to the expression in and through group life of the transformed aggressiveness of individuals" (Bowlby & Durbin, 1939, p. 41).

It might also be of interest to note that the book highlighted deprivation or threatened deprivation as "one of the chief sources of hatred and aggression" (Bowlby & Durbin, 1939, p. 67). Feelings of hatred and aggression can be projected onto members of other groups. Other people then become scapegoats and are punished or persecuted: "it is basically along these lines that Bowlby explained the Nazi's use of the Jews as scapegoats and Hitler's urge to make war with the other European states" (Van Dijken, 1998, p. 107).

Bowlby had been very concerned for a number of years about the ascendancy of fascism in Europe; particularly the growing threat of Nazi Germany. He had been politically active in an attempt to influence the British Government to deal with such a threat by diplomatic means. However, when the war started he volunteered to fight for his country and, also, for the freedom of the European countries that had been subjugated by Hitler's abominable machinery of hatred and destruction. He was not called up to go to the Front, but served actively using his knowledge as a psychoanalyst, psychologist and psychiatrist to support soldiers and civilians.

In October 1939, Bowlby began to do some part-time work at the Child Guidance Clinic in Cambridge. He wrote to Ursula: "I can't tell you how pleased I am to be a free man again and able to divide my time between genuine work and weekends with you" (quoted in Van Dijken, 1998, p. 112). He was in direct contact with children who were separated from their parents through evacuation.

Together with Susan Isaacs, who had supported him with his psychoanalytic membership dissertation, Bowlby conducted a survey on evacuated children. As a result, the Government was criticised because there was a realisation that the human element in the evacuation process had not been worked out carefully: "In time of danger and uncertainty individuals have even greater need for unity and for the reassurance provided by the familiar background of their lives" (Isaacs, 1941, p. 154).

Additionally, Bowlby complained that the Government did not employ enough experienced social workers to help with the process of placing children in suitable foster homes. He later told a *Sunday Times* journalist: "Evacuation was a bad mistake and it was the child guidance people who had to pick up the pieces" (quoted in Inglis, 1990, p. 154). In 1948, the British Minister of Health retrospectively accepted the negative effects that the evacuation had had on children's mental health. He produced a statement that was reported in the WHO's monograph (Bowlby, 1951, p. 70):

One point which all experience in the evacuation scheme has emphasised is the importance of the family in a child's development, and the impossibility of

> providing children with any completely adequate substitute for the care of their own parents.

The damage caused by the many deaths, separations and losses during the war made Bowlby even more determined to realise his plan: devoting his life to the prevention of mental health problems being transmitted from one generation to the next. He was hoping that this could contribute to less violent societies and, also, to the prevention of war. During most of his professional life he propagated fiercely to make people aware of his reforming views. He had a strong drive for putting his ideas across.

In an interview, aged 80, Bowlby still felt that the ideological battle was not won: "I often see this in terms of a war. I am fairly militarily minded. It is a campaign; it is a two generation war at least" (in Byng-Hall, 1987, p. 24). Of course, he put up a good fight and entered topics pertaining to social and political issues (Bowlby, 1946a), but he was not a believer in Utopia.

Bowlby had a profound knowledge and understanding of the turmoil and violence that are present in the nature of humankind and mind. His hope was for an optimal, happier and more peaceful society in the future. That was more than evident in his writings and teaching. Eric Rayner (1991, p. 20) put it this way: "Bowlby has, I think, influenced social policy probably more directly than any other psychoanalyst ever".

A 'war' within British psychoanalysis

From January 1943 onwards, Bowlby energetically participated in the meetings of the British Psychoanalytical Society. That was a time where tensions between the followers of Melanie Klein and those of Anna Freud were running high, due to different positions regarding theoretical, training and organisational issues. It was decided in the Society to hold a series of monthly meetings to deal with these differences.

Over a year and a half, the quarrels at the meetings resembled something that was interpreted as "a great marital conflict between 'mamma', Melanie Klein, and 'papa', Sigmund Freud" (Kohon, 1986, p. 42). It would appear that, to quite a large extent, the difficulties centred on personalities rather than irresolvable theoretical disagreements.

Klein was a strong and ambitious character. Born in 1882 in Vienna, she first sought personal analysis with Sandor Ferenczi in Budapest – where she became a psychoanalyst and began analysing children in 1919. At the time, she did not have a proper concept of *professional boundaries*. She in fact analysed her own children; something that would be considered grossly inappropriate nowadays by any professional ethics committee.

In 1921, Klein moved to Berlin to further her studies on child development and complete her personal analysis with Karl Abraham. He strongly supported her pioneering work with children. Impressed by her innovative concepts and method, in 1926, Ernest Jones invited her to come to London, where she worked until her death in 1960. Her professional successes over the years were remarkable. However, she was wounded by traumatic events in her personal life.

Klein was the youngest of four children. Her much loved elder sister died at the age of eight, when Klein was four. Her marriage failed and her son died in a climbing accident, although some suggested that he might have killed himself. Her daughter, the well-known psychoanalyst Melitta Schmideberg, fought her openly in the British Psychoanalytical Society. Edward Glover, Schmideberg's analyst, also challenged Klein openly in the Society's scientific meetings. Mother and daughter were not reconciled before Klein's death. Schmideberg did not attend her mother's funeral.

Klein had a major influence on the theory and technique of psychoanalysis, particularly in Great Britain. As a divorced woman whose academic qualifications did not even include a bachelor's degree, she was seen as an iconoclast within a profession where male physicians had control. She had a great drive for power and, in many ways, was able to dominate the British psychoanalytic scene until the arrival of Freud and his daughter Anna, as refugees from Vienna, in 1938.

It is quite astonishing that, soon after this event, Melanie Klein accused Ernest Jones of having done "much harm to psychoanalysis" (quoted in Grosskurth, 1986, p. 255), as he had invited Freud and her daughter to come to London – which in her view compromised the status of her own authority. Klein was *right*: the new arrivals were shocked at realising her strong influence. They regarded her work as a drastic departure from Freudian psychoanalysis.

Through her analysis of children, Klein postulated novel formulations on the early development of the mind. She proposed an idea that *unconscious phantasies* played a major role in the mental life of the infant, particularly regarding the relationship with the mother's body (see Chapter 9). She emphasised the prominence of infantile aggression and destructiveness, as she took a radical view on Freud's concept of the *death instinct* – something that she maintained throughout her life.

In the other camp, Anna Freud had begun her own psychoanalytic practice with children in 1923. She drew on her own clinical experience and relied on her father's writings as the main source of her theoretical insights. During the war, she became concerned to observe the effect of deprivation of parental care on evacuated children, as we saw earlier. She set up a centre, the Hampstead War Nursery, where these children were received into foster care. Mothers were encouraged to visit as often as possible. The underlying idea was to give children the opportunity to form attachments by providing continuity of relationships.

Indeed, prior to Klein, Freud had used the concept of *phantasy* within the structure of the unconscious mind. For him, phantasy functions according to the pleasure principle, equating reality of thought with external actuality, and wishes for the fulfilment of libidinal drives. In his view, phantasies are likely to arise when instinctual wishes are frustrated.

Anna Freud respected her father's views but became more receptive to exploring the impact of traumatic experiences on the development of the ego. Unlike her father, she worked with traumatised children and considered that their experiences were more important in the genesis of psychopathology than the mere frustration of libidinal satisfaction. It is noteworthy that contemporary artists and psychoanalytical theorists like Ettinger have been moving in a similar direction: "In art today we are moving from phantasm to trauma" (quoted in Pollock, 2010, p. 829).

The conflict between the followers of these two powerful women was such that it transpired in social situations. Unfortunately, the issues sometimes acquired a personal as well as professional dimension. Bowlby was uncomfortable with this polarisation, and he was not the only one. Alexander Neill, a Scottish educator known for his philosophy of freedom from adult coercion, provided an enthralling account of a wedding that he had attended:

> Filled with followers of Melanie Klein … they can't laugh; Melanie has definitely showed them humour is a complex that no normal man should have. To my asking what Klein was doing to prevent complexes there was a silence. I said: you can't analyse humanity but you can attempt to get a humanity that won't need analysis. No answer. Gott, they were a dull crowd…. Rather like talking to communists with a blank curtain that you could not penetrate.
>
> *(quoted in Holmes, 1993, p. 22)*

James Strachey, best known as the general editor of the *Standard Edition of the Complete Psychological Works of Sigmund Freud*, provided further revealing insights: "I am very strongly in favour of a compromise at all costs. The trouble seems to me to be with extremism…. These attitudes, on both sides, are of course purely religious and the very antithesis of science" (in Grosskurth, 1986, p. 257).

Bowlby and others were concerned about the risk that the Society may break up, and tried their best to achieve a peaceful solution. He positioned himself in the Middle or Independent Group created within the Society, known later as the Independent Group, aiming to achieve a compromise and to hold the two conflictive groups of Kleinians and Freudians within the Society's umbrella.

The so-called Controversial Discussions did not resolve the scientific issues. The resolution achieved was more political rather than theoretical. A pragmatic agreement was reached according to which each side undertook never to attempt a take-over of the Society. This "gentleman's agreement" remained until 2005, with Freudian, Kleinian and Independent approaches co-existing alongside one another within the institution, and upheld in separate training divisions. The emphasis on the training of candidates was in itself an aspiration of future dominance.

Further psychoanalytic developments

Mario Marrone (1998, p. 20) gave a good account of the process through which the Independent Group was born: a wish to be loyal to a philosophy whereby a commitment to psychoanalysis is sustained together with an openness to greater flexibility in theoretical and clinical developments. It was an obvious choice for

Bowlby's independent mind. The group itself could be seen as an assemblage of independent psychoanalytic thinkers (like Bowlby, Balint, Fairbairn, Guntrip, Winnicott and others), rather than an independent psychoanalytic school: a 'group of independents' rather than an 'independent group'.

Rayner (1990) offered a balanced historical perspective on the evolution of what he described as *The Independent Mind in British Psychoanalysis*. He included Bowlby's concept of attachment and its evolutionary significance to survival – particularly so in view of the long period of immaturity in early human development. In a later work, Rayner further underlined that, although attachment does not replace other drives, like feeding or sexuality, it "cannot be subsumed to any of them, for it has its own releasers and terminators, what is more, proximity often takes precedence over feeding even in states of hunger" (Rayner, 1991, p. 21).

Knowledge derived from modern attachment research has been increasingly taken into account not only by members of the Independent Group but also by the Freudians and the Kleinians. Nowadays, the patient's attachment history is no longer ignored or dismissed. However, particularly among the Kleinians, there is still an emphasis on internal conflicts such as the clash postulated by Freud and Klein between life and death instincts, between love and hate.

Bowlby never really accepted that we are born with a death instinct. He in fact conceptualised hatred as a response to threats or perceived threats to our survival, rather than an original component of a basic human ambivalence. Only occasion- ally did he write about such an ambivalence between love and hate – about sometimes getting angry and wishing to hurt the very person who is most loved (Bowlby, 1959, 1979a). However, he remained consistent in his explanations of anxiety, anger and aggression as a reaction to loss or threatened loss of love; in the more severe cases, as a response to abuse, neglect and other major disruptions in the formation of secure attachments (Bowlby, 1988a).

Among the post-Kleinian theorists, Bion is by and large considered the most influential. His interest in the analysis of psychotic patients in the 1950s led to his formulation of startling assumptions about the thinking process: how it develops in healthy individuals and how it can go wrong. His observations in the consulting room directed him to the construction of his *theory of thinking* (Bion, 1967b).

This was chiefly built upon Bion's notion of the mother as a *container* of the distress experienced by the infant that is projected onto her: an acknowledgment of the significance of the early attachment between the child and the mother. In psychosis, like in severe personality problems, the influence of adverse environ- mental factors can be traced even more clearly than in what has been described as neurotic problems. Although Bion appeared not to have taken notice of Bowlby, he may have been influenced by him more than he had realised.

Among contemporary post-Kleinians, John Steiner (1993) is well worth reading. On my arrival at the Tavistock Clinic, in 1984, he had a god-like status (similar to that of Bion until he emigrated to California in 1968). He was indeed the most influential theorist and clinician in the Adult Department, for staff and trainees alike. His workshop on borderline psychotic pathology became one of the jewels of the Tavistock's training programme. He thoroughly explored the interaction between the patient's internal world and unbearable reality.

Steiner specifically focused on those who he and other colleagues described as *difficult to treat* patients: people who defensively create bizarre states of mind in an ineffective attempt to be protected from anxiety and pain. He conceptualised this as a *psychic retreat* which, in his view, patients perceive as places where they could hide to be out of contact with the therapist and other people. The attachment difficulties of these patients often prevent them from recognising the therapist as a potential 'secure base'. The treatment becomes more challenging.

Looking back to the war years, Pearl King (1989, 1991) provided a thorough recognition of Bowlby's further contributions to the British Psychoanalytical Society. In July 1943, an elected Medical Committee of seven members was formed, with Adrian Stephen as Chairman and Bowlby as Secretary. This group undertook the task of thinking about negotiations regarding the role of the Society in the future National Health Service. Bowlby drafted three important documents. In 1944, the Constitution of the Society was changed. Sylvia Payne was elected as the new President and Bowlby as the new Training Secretary, with a seat on the Board and Council.

Klein and Riviere wrote letters of complaint to Payne for allowing a non-training analyst to hold such an important position. However, Payne replied that the Society needed someone who was a good organiser and willing to share her outlook on the need for unity. Bowlby produced the first Training Prospectus with courses programmed to cover a four-year period, and organised a shared course of lectures on psychoanalysis for all students. Despite the theoretical and political differences within the Society, he was able to arrange greater coordination between the various courses.

Bowlby's achievements to make the psychoanalytic training more professional were duly recognised by Payne and others. He gave a lot of credit to her and stated that her fair dealing and deep concern for the future of psychoanalysis earned the respect and trust of all parties (Bowlby, 1991a). Besides his training role, he set up and chaired the Society's Research Committee and initiated several other committees like the Public Relations Committee and the Curriculum Committee. Between 1956 and 1961, Bowlby was Deputy President of the Society to Donald Winnicott, as well as chair of the Board and Council.

In addition, Bowlby instigated a committee to look at indemnity insurance for non-medical members, in order to guarantee that everyone would be well protected, not only from the potential hazards of clinical practice but also from unforeseen personal or family misfortune. During all those years he was "not only good at implementing other people's ideas, but active in thinking out what needed to be done to deal with problems or disquiets that arose in the Society" (King, 1991, p. 27).

A breakthrough and a conflict with the Prime Minister

During his time at the London Child Guidance Clinic prior to the war, Bowlby had observed that a large number of the children referred were affectionless and prone to stealing. Through detailed examinations and case notes, he was able to connect their symptoms and behaviour with histories of separation and maternal deprivation. In the research, Bowlby compared a group of 44 juvenile thieves with a control group of 44 adolescents who, though emotionally disturbed, did not steal. Both groups were taken from the Child Guidance Clinic's caseload.

The findings were significant. Fourteen of the thieves were classified as affectionless, compared with none in the control group. Seventeen of the thieves had been separated from their mother for more than six months before they were aged five, compared with only two who had experienced such separation in the control group. These results indicated a correlation between maternal deprivation in infancy and subsequent criminal behaviour in adolescence.

Digging further into the children's family life, Bowlby also noted that the traumatic early separations leading to psychopathology had almost always occurred after the first half year of life. This finding suggested that separation is most damaging after the child has developed a personal relationship or attachment with the parents. A new field worthy of further research was opened.

In early 1943, a Research and Training Unit was established in Hampstead, London. Indeed, Bowlby was a member. He refined his study with the statistical advice received from people at the Research Unit. This enabled him to put together what turned out to be the first psychoanalytic publication to include statistical data as well as detailed case histories. He used psychoanalytic concepts and insights to describe the behaviour of the juvenile delinquents who had lost their mothers and were craving for libidinal satisfaction and for love, as well as for its material symbols:

"The food they stole was no doubt felt to be the equivalent of love from the mother whom they have lost, though probably none was conscious of the fact" (Bowlby, 1944, p. 121). Furthermore, "juvenile delinquency … is also a problem of sociology and economics" (ibid., p. 125). The publication attracted great interest, including that of the Medical Director of the Tavistock Clinic: "Dr John Bowlby's fascinating paper … is perhaps the best work that has yet been done in this country on the problem and demonstrates the importance of this sense of deprivation of love in leading to delinquent conduct" (Rees, 1947, p. 21).

While at the WOSB, Bowlby was at first involved in testing cadets. At the time, they were usually selected following a short interview, of some 15 minutes, with a small board of senior officers. The method proved to be quite unsuccessful: "Evidence of the inadequate selection was found in the high rejection rates at the Officer Cadet Training Units which resulted in a serious wastage in training, and this large proportion of failures naturally had an adverse effect on the morale" (Fitzpatrick, 1945, p. 75).

The need to raise a large land army after the fall of France had increased the need for officers. The colonels had to select candidates for officer training but most were inexperienced about making judgements outside their own social bound. So, "they were overlooking good candidates and sending forward too many poor ones" (Trist, 1985, p. 6). In this context, in the summer of 1941, Bowlby carried out research on the rate of failure. In contrast to the poor outcomes that followed the 15-minute interview by senior officers, he found a high correlation between a proper psychiatric interview assessment and success of officer cadets during their training (King, 1989). These results helped diminish some of the military prejudices against psychiatrists.

Subsequently, in one of the Boards, a programme was designed in which potential officers came in groups of 32 and stayed for two and a half days. Their activities included taking part in leaderless group exercises, where each man was observed on how he coped with the normal tension of undertaking a group task, such as: "needing to co-operate for the achievement of the group purpose or goal, yet competing with others to demonstrate both a distinct personal identity and a competence for leadership" (Bridger, 1985, p. 91). The men were also given a battery of tests dealing with emotions and cognitions.

Initially, all the candidates were assessed by a psychiatrist. Only the doubtful cases were referred for psychiatric follow-up. One of the principles upon which WOSB's psychiatrists seemed to have worked was that: "It is the harmoniously organised man who is most capable of showing aggressive or cautious, tactful, deferential, firm or sympathetic characteristics whenever these may be needed, and he is less likely to give way under stress" (Vernon & Parry, 1949, p. 59). Or, as Bion (1946, p. 77) put it: the selection officers could "observe a man's capacity for maintaining personal relationships in a situation of strain that tempted him to disregard the interest of his fellows for the sake of his own".

Bowlby worked with Bion, Trist and Sutherland at the WOSB. He gradually became a role model for newly recruited psychiatrists and for senior Army officers. From the outset, he made his mark:

> John wanted plans to be adopted with little delay and gave a sense to the existing staff group of the new boy pressurising things, so that he was not at first warmly welcomed. Within a few weeks, however, it was recognised by all that his impatience was not the product of a forceful, insensitive character; it seemed to be a superficial manner which in fact concealed a person, who was deeply concerned to be with the group in all its work.
>
> *(Sutherland, 1990, p. 13)*

Throughout the war years, Bowlby's energy and determination were such that one of his contemporaries reflected it in a rhyme, as reported by Parkes (1995, p. 252):

> "Major Bowlby
> Goes flat out
> Whatever his goal be"

In 1944, Bowlby was given the task of planning a large-scale follow-up of candidates selected by number two WOSB in order to validate the group selection procedures. Bowlby's research showed that assessments made by psychiatrists who used group methods greatly improved retention of officers, reducing the failure rate from 45 per cent to 15 per cent (Dicks, 1970, p. 108). The results indicated that the most effective leaders were those who best understood the workings of the group and the preoccupations of its members (rather than those who were more athletic or charismatic, cleverer or better educated). Real leadership must include an attentiveness to the needs of others (Kraemer, 2011, p. 91).

In contrast to the stereotype of *masculine* heroism, the new conception of leadership included more feminine or maternal qualities. Harrison (2000, p. 91) suggested that

> an officer had to pay attention to such trivial matters as the men's pay problems, showing concern for their welfare and that of their families, and reinforcing the belief that if they were wounded or killed they would be properly cared for.

However, not everyone recognised the added value provided by psychiatrists – who were regarded with displeasure by many in the old guard because they were thought to have too much influence in the selection procedure. The Prime Minister, Winston Churchill, was sharply critical of psychiatrists in his statement of December 1942:

> I am sure it would be sensible to restrict as much as possible the work of these gentlemen, who are capable of doing an immense amount of harm with what may very easily degenerate into charlatanry. The tightest hand should be kept over them, and they should not be allowed to quarter themselves in large numbers upon the Fighting Services at the public expense. There are, no doubt, easily recognisable cases which may benefit from treatment of this kind, but it is very wrong to disturb large numbers of healthy normal men and women by asking the kind of odd questions in which psychiatrists specialised.
>
> *(in Ahrenfeldt, 1958, p. 26)*

Some years later, in 1945, Rees reacted publicly to this attitude:

> Earlier in this present war, we were often told that psychiatrists were the fifth columnists of the army, and this because they were advising the discharge of men who were obviously too dull or too unstable to soldier ... and much opprobrium has come to army psychiatrists because there has necessarily been a high discharge rate from psychiatric causes.
>
> *(in Van Dijken, 1998, p. 115)*

Bowlby's work in the selection and training Boards gave him a good level of methodological expertise in research, something unusual for a psychoanalyst at the time. He retrospectively pointed out: "My three years there were invaluable in giving me a postgraduate education in psychology and research method" (Bowlby, 1981, p. 3). His mentor was Eric Trist, a clinical and social psychologist. Bowlby's commitment, hard work and camaraderie at the WOSB were duly recognised. He formed long-lasting friendships that were to stand him in good stead after the war.

At the beginning of 1946, Bowlby was appointed as Director of the Children's Department at the Tavistock Clinic. His relationship with the institution was complex but immensely creative and fruitful. During the war, Bowlby seemed to have been preparing his mind for peace. But new battles were waiting for him!

4

JOHN BOWLBY AND THE TAVISTOCK CLINIC

Bowlby became attached to members of the Tavistock group during the war. My colleague Felicity de Zulueta, Head of the Trauma Unit at the Maudsley Hospital, met him in 1990 to discuss her book *From Pain to Violence: The Traumatic Roots of Destructiveness*, in which she challenges those who believe that mankind is innately violent. On the contrary, she expressed the view that violence is the outcome of man's traumatic experiences: *attachment gone wrong* (Bowlby, 1984; Zulueta, 1993).

Bowlby was pleased to learn about Zulueta's work and encouraged her to pursue it. He also told her that, in spite of its brutal destructiveness, the Second World War had given him the gift of a close friendship, an attachment with the group of men with whom he fought. This group, the *invisible college* (see Chapter 3), played a major part in the reorganisation of the Tavistock after the war. In an interview at 70, Bowlby recalled:

> We were a group for which the Tavistock acted as a kind of anchor so the notion was that some of the pre-war Tavistock people, together with some of the rest of us who were not Tavistock but who were in the party, should develop something or other as a post-war enterprise around the Tavistock.
>
> *(quoted in Van Dijken, 1998, p. 130)*

Was this anchor a secure enough base for him?

Besides Bowlby, the group included John Rees, Ronald Hargreaves, Wilfred Bion, John Rickman, Jock Sutherland, Harold Bridger, Eric Trist, Henry Dicks and others. They all advocated the democratic principles of social justice, equal opportunities and support for the more vulnerable. These principles made an important contribution towards the new *dynamic social psychiatry* (Dicks, 1970, p. 115). The reorganisation of the Tavistock as a whole was to some extent the result of military experience. There probably is more than a mere joke in the military name *Operation Phoenix* given to it by the participants (ibid., p. 138).

Historical and political context to Bowlby's professional growth

In the post-war world, it had become obvious that the Tavistock would need to change its image in order to continue the role that it had endeavoured to fill since it opened in 1920. In the early years, it had sometimes been called the *parsons' clinic* (Newcombe & Lerner, 1982), as a number of the staff had a Christian-based altruism rather than a scientific orientation. It was now necessary for survival to open new fields and raise professional standards to a very high level.

In 1944, Bowlby and Rickman had anticipated that the Tavistock Clinic would have to make adjustments after the war. They instigated a meeting with the Tavistock's management to build stronger links between the Clinic and the British Psychoanalytical Society. They both wanted the change in the relationship between official psychoanalysis and the Tavistock group, started through the war service, to be carried a long step further.

For Bowlby and Rickman the priority was joining forces and employing psychoanalysts to serve on the staff of the Clinic, lifting the hitherto official interdict of Ernest Jones against the Tavistock as a place where a true psychoanalyst may not work. They also discussed the possibility of fostering closer peace-time links with stakeholders from other psychiatric hospital services and university departments.

Dicks (1970) explained in detail the process of change, in his book *Fifty Years of the Tavistock Clinic*. An Interim Planning Committee (IPC) was established in the autumn of 1945. It was chaired by Bion, who was already considered an expert in group dynamics; he helped this planning group to get on with the task. At the top of the IPC's agenda was an impending political event: the Labour Government's project that would create a National Health Service (NHS) in 1948 had been intimated to senior members of the Tavistock.

The IPC recommended building up a modernised institutional structure to meet the NHS requirements. This involved the selection of the kind of staff who could be entrusted with the development of out-patient psychiatry, based on a dynamic approach and oriented towards the social sciences. The Committee also recommended creating a Human Relations Institute for the study of wider social problems.

The Tavistock's Board endorsed these recommendations; the timing was right. The contributions of the *invisible college* to the management of social problems in the war years had attracted interest in other countries, especially the USA. Prominent American professionals came to London, including Alan Gregg, medical director of the Rockefeller Foundation, to visit a number of the medical and psychiatric services that had operated during the war. They wanted to identify institutions interested in developing, under conditions of peace, the type of social approaches that had been used by Army psychiatrists under conditions of war.

Gregg supported a grant of £22,000 that was given by the Rockefeller Foundation to the Tavistock in 1946. It was agreed that the money would be used to expand work in social and preventive psychiatry, with the proviso that the development of such medico-social science should be closely linked to analytic and psychodynamic insights (Dicks, 1970, p. 141).

With these funds it was possible to implement the recommendations of the IPC and the Tavistock Institute of Human Relations (TIHR) was created, initially as a division of the Tavistock Clinic. TIHR attracted a core group of experts who would have otherwise been scattered in universities and institutes throughout the UK and abroad. From its inception, the Institute received many requests from industrial firms to help with various mental health and industrial projects.

Bowlby and Rickman's forward thinking of previous years, and their emphasis on group work and collaborative relationships, had contributed to pave the path of change. It would also be fair to add that, before the war, a significant number of members of the Tavistock staff had achieved eminence for their contributions to the growing mental health field. The volume of publications of papers and books flowing from the Clinic was quite considerable. By the mid-1930s, the institution had secured two research fellowships endowed by the generosity and belief in its work of the Rockefeller Foundation and of the Sir Halley Stewart Trust, respectively (Dicks, 1970, p. 4).

In February 1946, a professional committee, chaired by Rees, and a small Technical Executive, with Bion as its leader, were constituted. One of the objectives of this committee was the conversion of a large part-time staff team, appropriate for the pre-war Clinic as a voluntary out-patient service, into a selective group of full timers – supported by others giving substantial chunks of their time and a commitment to the redefined mission of the post-war organisation.

Important decisions had to be made as to who should leave, who should stay and who should be appointed. Criteria included willingness to employ a social approach and the requirement of personal analysis for those who had not completed it. Bowlby, Sutherland, Trist and other outsiders, who had played major roles in the war-time effort, were recruited as part of *Operation Phoenix*.

Sutherland and Bowlby were democratically elected by the staff as medical director and deputy medical director, respectively, in July 1947. Both represented the *new era*. Together with other members of the professional committee, they emphasised valuable links with potential client agencies and spent most of the following year building up the service's structure required for entering the NHS. Full timers would be able to do more research and training than part timers, in addition to the clinical work. In September 1947, TIHR became a separate entity from the Clinic. Trist played an important part in this process. *Phoenix* rose from the ashes and the NHS age began on 5 July 1948 (Dicks, 1970, p. 177).

There were, however, some important casualties. At the height of his power in his mid-fifties, Rees was pushed by the pace of events to resign as medical director of the Clinic. Under the pressure of the younger generation, he had realised that the institution needed to be modernised. He was generous and co-operative with the transition.

However, Dicks (1970, p. 174) had the impression that Rees

> was deeply hurt by the way the new group were taking power.... It was
> probably inevitable that the young men whom he had recruited and brought
> together, and given the opportunity of developing their ideas in the Army and
> in the first months after the war, must in the end supplant him. This seems
> to be one of those relentless historical processes by which the succeeding
> generations displace each other.

Bowlby's Department for Children and Parents

Prior to the developments outlined above, Bowlby had experienced a dilemma
with regard to his career choice. He had received a suggestion that he may start a
private full-time psychoanalytic practice, with a view to becoming a training
analyst for the Independent Group. However, he decided to give priority to the
more disadvantaged and so to devote most of his working time to patients who
could not afford private treatment.

The Children's Department, which had always been "a strongly 'separatist' or
autonomous body, despite Rees's efforts to integrate the whole Clinic" (Dicks,
1970, p. 150), needed drastic restructuring. There was fierce competition for the
full-time post of new Director of the Department. A strong field of candidates
included Evelyn Lucas, one of the earliest child guidance fellows in the USA, and
Donald Winnicott, one of the most charismatic figures in the world of child
mental health in the UK – and Bowlby's senior by 10 years.

Of course, there was intense deliberation through which the Tavistock's Council
realised the strong need for a "much more inclusive family clinic with a multi-faceted
approach to parents, children, adolescents, young mothers...." And

> John Bowlby emerged as the right person to head such a 'new' family service.
> Besides being a qualified psychoanalyst, Bowlby had a degree in natural science
> and psychology, had trained at the Maudsley and the Child Guidance Centre,
> and had been on the staff of the latter.
>
> *(ibid., p. 150)*

I gather that Bowlby's organisational skills and his capacity to get things done, as
well as his war connection with the Tavistock group, gave him an extra edge for
his appointment. His leadership qualities were present from the outset. In order
to highlight the importance of the parentchild relationship, he promptly renamed his
new service as the Department for Children and Parents in the year of his appointment. As recognised by his colleagues, Bowlby showed the "characteristic energy"
(ibid., p. 164) that had made him stand out during the war as *Major Bowlby* (see
Chapter 3) and stayed in the Director's role for more than 22 years.

By the end of 1946, the Tavistock's Child Department had seen 313 new
patients referred mostly from local health authorities. The 1944 Education Act had

put an obligation on the local authorities to provide child guidance services. The great increase in need for qualified workers made training a top priority, which added to the existing teaching status of the Clinic. In order to maximise resources, the Child Department took the decision to limit its intake of patients to the northwest London. This helped make room for the training of child psychiatrists, educational psychologists and psychiatric social workers (ibid., p. 165).

Bowlby was especially rigorous in adhering to the policy of restricting new patients to the number that could be handled and treated promptly by his Department, so as to eliminate a waiting list for treatment altogether. His idea was that once a child and his parents had been seen for an assessment, therapy should follow. This generated a waiting list for the initial consultations. However, he would give precedence to children under five – who were seen without delay.

Bowlby held the view that far more could be done for a young child and his parents than could be done for older children. The diagnostic procedure was rather more elaborate than hitherto used at the Tavistock. Bowlby also believed that the greatly improved cooperation obtained from parents and referring agencies, such as schools, children's homes, etc., added greater efficiency to the process of assessment and treatment (ibid., pp. 189–190).

The Tavistock Clinic had to develop therapeutic methods that would allow for the maintenance of a patient load sufficiently large as to satisfy the new NHS authorities that out-patient psychotherapy could be cost effective. War-time experience suggested that the best prospect would lie with group psychotherapy and Bion was asked to set this up. In order to attract patients for the groups, he offered two options: to wait one year for individual treatment or to start group treatment immediately. In fact, by the time the Clinic entered the NHS, many of the senior staff were already running patient groups under Bion's headship. He also conducted groups for industrial managers and professionals from the educational world.

In the early days, Bion was very enthusiastic about injecting his group ideas into the Tavistock's post-war culture. From his work at the *First Northfield Experiment* (see Chapter 3), he had advanced a notion that man is a social animal whose fulfilment can only approach completeness in a group. Neurosis started to be perceived as a problem of personal relationships and, therefore, it had to be treated as a group phenomenon rather than as a purely individual one (Bion & Rickman, 1943).

Group therapy was a most timely development at a key moment when war survivors needed to learn to help one another, and themselves. Bion's work had wider implications, as it laid the basis of a model focusing on the study of the group itself and the tensions within it. His corpus of intellectual axioms describing mainly unconscious group dynamics has been a major influence in the field until the present day (Bion, 1961). His ideas have contributed to the understanding of institutions and to the practice of organisational consultancy across the world.

Bion's model influenced Bowlby (1949), who found his own way of applying group methods. He laid the foundations of family therapy by seeing all the members of a family group together. He also started a weekly support group for mothers and their babies or young children, which he called the 'well-baby clinic'. He spent one afternoon every week on this project and ran it during three decades. Group membership, of course, changed when some mothers improved and were replaced by others. He created a therapeutic dynamic in which he was "trying to help the less experienced learn from those who knew more" (Bowlby, 1991a, p. 29).

As the decisions stemming from *Operation Phoenix* were being implemented, a great deal of guilt developed over the departure of those of the pre-war staff who did not meet the criteria for inclusion in the post-war team. An abdication crisis ensued. Tension and confusion invaded the whole institution. Bion did not wish to serve in the NHS any longer. He resigned as chairman of the technical executive committee and restricted himself to the roles of social therapist and consultant to staff groups within the organisation – in order to work through these conflicting feelings and issues.

In addition to the institutional crisis, Bion delegated his leading responsibility in the Tavistock's group psychotherapy programme for NHS patients to Henry Ezriel. Furthermore, some academics became critical of the Tavistock Institute and the Medical Research Council (MRC) dismissed some of the Institute's group work publications. As a result, obtaining research funds became more difficult.

Research takes off

Bowlby, who later joined MRC, had to start his own negotiations to identify suitable research funds and obtained a grant from the Sir Halley Stewart Trust (Dicks, 1970, p. 180). This enabled him to appoint James Robertson, a distinguished researcher who had made his mark working at Anna Freud's residential nursery for homeless children in Hampstead (see Chapter 3).

The Department for Children and Parents was the biggest of all the Tavistock units and operated rather autonomously. Bowlby was the only full-time consultant in his department but was well assisted by a large number of psychiatric registrars and senior registrars, including Molly Main. She was the wife of Tom Main, another prominent war psychiatrist and one of the founders of the therapeutic community movement (Main, 1946). Although Tavistock's management had wanted to recruit him, Tom Main had decided to accept the post of medical director at the Cassel Hospital. Nevertheless, he remained a friend and supporter of the Tavistock.

James Robertson was an experienced social worker training in psychoanalysis and a conscientious objector. He, his pregnant wife and their first child were living in a hostel for homeless people, where they remained for two and a half years. He later said: "surely very few psychoanalysts had done the major part of their training in such strange domestic conditions" (quoted in Karen, 1998, p. 73).

Robertson and Bowlby were poles apart in social background, outward manner and life experience. One of seven children from a poor Scottish family, Robertson grew up in appalling housing conditions. The family lived in a cold-water flat and shared an outhouse with two other families. Understandably, he became deeply sensitive to social injustice – something that he and Bowlby held in common, despite their differing origins.

During his war time with Anna Freud, Robertson had studied methodically the consequences of separating children from their parents. Bretherton (1991, p. 14) pointed out that Anna Freud required that all members of the staff write in full detail their observations about the children's behaviour on cards. These notes were used for clinical discussions. Soon after his arrival at the Tavistock, Robertson started to write up his observations of children who had been sent off to the short-stay ward at the Central Middlesex Hospital in London. This was part of a new research project led by Bowlby, who was hugely impressed by Robertson's work.

Right from the outset, Robertson picked up the children's distress – something that staff did not seem able or willing to recognise. He saw desolate children silently sitting on the cots. He saw a kind-hearted nurse rebuked for showing concern about a silent toddler. When parents came for a Sunday visit, the silent ward was inundated with anguished cries. But he was told by the hospital staff that the children's distress was inevitable and that they would all settle down soon (Karen, 1998, p. 74).

However, Robertson found that the children's *settled* state in the ward gave way to difficult behaviour at home, such as aggression against the mother, anxious clinging to her and temper tantrums. The hospital staff had an explanation for this: "the mothers were simply less competent than the nurses in caring for the children" (Robertson & Robertson, 1989, p. 13).

In the next two years, Robertson observed children in a long-term ward. He ascertained three stages in their emotional reaction, after their separation from the parents: protest, despair and detachment. He emphasised that, after a prolonged separation, some of these children no longer seemed to know their parents. Robertson became very frustrated and worried by the unwillingness of professionals, outside of Bowlby's team, to take his concerns seriously.

At the Tavistock, there was an aspiration that a research component should be built in to all current and future therapeutic work. That was with the aim of refining knowledge and feeding the conceptual refinement back into the sub-sequent clinical activities of the institution: "no research without therapy; and no therapy without research" (Dicks, 1970, p. 142).

Despite this motto, Robertson's talks to psychoanalytic colleagues at the Tavistock about his observations of children in hospitals were met with resistance. Talks to other audiences elsewhere, including psychiatrists and paediatricians triggered disbelief too. He was exasperated that he had been lecturing for three years and writing for three years to little effect – and decided to make a film on a little girl who would soon be admitted to hospital.

Bowlby supported Robertson's idea about film-making, and refined it with a suggestion that its main purpose should be to obtain neutral data on the child's response to her mother and father and to the staff. The plan was to pay specific attention in the film to the child's responses when her mother and father were present or absent, to how she treated the nurses and to how she behaved when alone. But there was no instant money to buy a camera.

Tom Main, probably under the influence of his wife Molly (psychiatric registrar to Bowlby at the Tavistock), identified funds from his budget at the Cassel Hospital. Institutional and personal boundaries enjoyed greater flexibility in those days. The donation permitted Bowlby to buy a Bell and Howell spring-wound 16 mm camera. With this Robertson was able to perform a hand-held shoot, relying on window light – which resulted in a vital and now classic film: *A Two-Year-Old Goes to Hospital*.

The film showed Laura, a beautiful, well behaved and self-controlled two-and-a-half-year-old child. She was much loved by her parents. Following separation, at the point of the hospital admission, she was apparently self-contained. But her feelings started soon to break through her composure. Karen (1998, pp. 76–77) provided a detailed account of what followed.

On the first day, after her bath, Laura ran naked and tried to escape. Her expression became dull and she periodically sobbed quietly to herself, grabbing her teddy. Several times she asked: "Where is my Mummy?" She later looked more tense and miserable. Although visiting was normally restricted to once a week, Robertson requested special permission for the parents to visit her every other day.

On seeing her parents at their first visit, Laura immediately burst into tears and pleaded with them to take her home. In a poignant moment, she looked into her father's face and clutched his tie while pleading: "Don't go Daddy". In each successive visit the parents were greeted by a colder response, until she seemed frozen. On the fifth day, she looked resentful when her mother appeared and wiped away her kiss.

When mother waved good-bye on the seventh day, Laura stood motionless with her head bent. The following day was her last day at the hospital. Mother came to fetch her but was greeted with shaking sobs. Laura initially resisted leaving but eventually scoured the ward for all her belongings. As she was walking out of the hospital, she refused to take her mother's hand. Two days after returning home, she was a bright-eyed child again, "as though a lamp had lit up inside her" (Robertson & Robertson, 1989, p. 41).

The film had been carefully planned to ensure that no one could later be able to claim that it was biased. Bowlby and Robertson decided to use time sampling, documented by the clock that was always in the picture, to prove that the film segments were not specially selected. According to Bowlby, "the film was dynamite" (quoted in Bretherton, 1991, p. 15). It certainly stimulated a great deal of interest and became known to child development experts throughout the world.

Despite the controversies, Anna Freud and her team were great enthusiasts. She commented positively on the film stating that for her it was a convincing and brilliant demonstration *ad oculos* of the outward manifestations of the inner processes that occur in infants who find themselves unexpectedly and traumatically without their families (Karen, 1998). In spite of the fact that she and Bowlby differed on theory, they "always saw eye to eye" (Bowlby, 1991a, p. 29).

The only criticism Bowlby could recall came from the Kleinians. They were sceptical about the connection between the child's distress and the separation from the parents, and put a greater emphasis on the fact the mother was pregnant. Bion, probably the strongest Kleinian voice at the Tavistock during this time, also criticised Bowlby for "missing the point" (Karen, 1998, p. 79).

It is not clear whether Laura was aware of her mother's pregnancy at the time the film was made. But, in any case, this additional element was not explored further or integrated in the wider picture. Bowlby (1969, p. 33) would later say that whatever part is played by other variables, "by far the most weighty is the loss by a child of his mother".

The reviews of the film in the medical journals were quite unanimously encouraging. The idea that hospitals would need to do things differently was taking shape. The medical superintendent at the Central Middlesex Hospital honestly said: "Well, I am sorry it is my hospital. But I accept that it is an objective record which should be shown widely" (Robertson & Robertson, 1989, p. 45).

In November 1952, Robertson and Bowlby presented the film at the Royal Society of Medicine in London to some three hundred professionals who were outside the field of mental health. This audience included general practitioners, paediatricians, nurses, managers and administrators. The general public and, very importantly, health economy policy-makers soon became aware of the film's simple, factual, but highly emotional, findings (Bowlby & Robertson, 1952a, 1952b).

The dissemination of the film marked the beginning of a major shift in professional and public opinion – leading to policy changes in hospitals and other child care institutions. Parents were now being allowed to make routine visits and to stay the night with their hospitalised children. Indeed, the film *exploded* previous denials of the needs of children. It was a landmark in improving the care of young people and in raising greater awareness on the effects of separation. The film also played a role in the development of attachment theory – as I shall spell out in the next chapter.

Robertson went on to make similar harrowing films that revealed the true nature and extent of the distress shown by separated young children in hospital. Additional films also explored another common situation, when a mother was hospitalised and the children in that way separated from her. In four of the cases Robertson and his wife Joyce became temporary foster parents. They wanted to see the impact of separations, without the previous potentially confounding variables of the child's illness and a hospital setting without adequate substitute care. In all these cases there was no previous history of separations or attachment problems.

The children were allowed to become familiar with the Robertson's home before moving in. Joyce Robertson tried to find out all she could about their likes, dislikes, routines and diets. The length of separation ranged from 10 to 27 days. The children showed different degrees of anxiety and distress, but this was far more manageable than in the case of Laura. Although separation from the mother remained a hazard for the young child, it was possible to demonstrate that planning for the situation and arranging proper care could make a difference (Karen, 1998, pp. 82–83).

Robertson became a bit distant from Bowlby. However, Bowlby continued giving credit to Robertson for his research and theoretical accomplishments, and specifically referred to the foster study films in the second volume of his *attachment trilogy* – acknowledging that, prior to this study, insufficient weight had been given to the influence of skilled care from a familiar substitute (Bowlby, 1973). He also wrote an endorsing paragraph for the back of Robertson's last book, which was published in 1989 – the year after Robertson had died. Bowlby's paragraph became a touching epitaph for his colleague and, for a long time, friend:

> James Robertson was a remarkable person who achieved great things. His sensitive observations and brilliant filming made history, and the courage with which he disseminated – often in the face of ignorant and prejudiced criticism – what were then very unpopular findings, was legendary. He will always be remembered as the man who revolutionized children's hospitals, though he accomplished much else besides. I am personally deeply grateful for all that he did.
>
> *(quoted in Karen, 1998, p. 86)*

Besides Robertson's contributions, the standing of Bowlby's separation research unit was boosted by the appointment of Mary Ainsworth (née Salter), in 1950. A few months earlier, she had married Leonard Ainsworth, a Second World War veteran and psychology graduate at the University of Toronto, where she herself was on the Faculty.

The Ainsworths decided that Leonard would continue his PhD studies in London, where they moved together. Upon arriving, a friend from the Army days drew her attention to an advertisement in *The London Times Educational Supplement* for a research position at the Tavistock Clinic, under the direction of Bowlby. The research was into the effects on personality development of separation from the mother in early childhood. This appointment reset the whole direction of her professional career (Ainsworth, 1983).

Mary Ainsworth was born in 1913 in Ohio, but her family moved to Toronto when she was a child. As a psychology student she became conversant with 'security theory' as formulated by Blatz (1940). In fact, the theme of the dissertation for her doctoral studies was *An Evaluation of Adjustment based on the Concept of Security*. Interestingly, one of the major tenets of security theory is that infants and young children need to develop a secure reliance on parents before launching out into unfamiliar situations where they must cope on their own.

According to Ainsworth, 'secure dependence' provides a basis for learning the skills and developing the knowledge that make it possible to confidently rely on oneself and confidently gain emancipation from the parents. Indeed, secure dependence on parents should gradually be supplanted by mature dependence on peers and partners. Ainsworth and Blatz, her mentor, believed that 'secure independence' is an impossibility (Bretherton, 1991, p. 13)

On her arrival at the Tavistock, Bowlby introduced the work of James Robertson to Ainsworth, particularly his method of observing children and keeping a
record of such observations. A similar method for the observation of infants at
home was running in parallel at the time, as developed by Esther Bick (see below).
Ainsworth was impressed by Robertson and emulated his technique of naturalistic
observation.

Bick and Bowlby worked together at the Tavistock for the next three years at a
crucial time when his ideas on attachment were beginning to take shape (see
Chapter 5). After her departure, they continued to communicate and collaborate
on the development of attachment theory. In fact, they gradually established a solid
and secure professional attachment with one another that lasted 40 years, until
his death.

Bowlby was immensely grateful for this loyal partnership and dedicated to
Ainsworth his seminal work, *A Secure Base: Clinical Applications of Attachment Theory*:
"To Mary D. S. Ainsworth who introduced the concept of a secure base"
(Bowlby, 1988a). This she had indeed done:

> Familial security in the early stages is of a dependent type and forms a basis
> from which the individual can work out gradually, forming new skills and
> interests in other fields. Where familial security is lacking, the individual is
> handicapped by lack of what might be called a secure base from which
> to work.
>
> *(quoted in Bretherton, 1991, p. 13)*

They both were most appreciative of each other's contributions. Ainsworth used to
say: "Bowlby does the theory", as if he were the commander in chief and she the
field marshal (in Karen, 1998, p. 434). Despite her own prominence, he remained
the senior partner. They were not driven by the rivalry and jealousies that had
destroyed so many other scientific enterprises but enjoyed their collaboration and
mutual respect for each other.

As well as Robertson and Ainsworth, Bowlby's separation research unit gathered
over the years an impressive group of professionals, including Anthony Ambrose,
Mary Boston, Dorothy Heard, Christoph Heinicke, Colin Murray Parkes, Dina
Rosenbluth, Rudolph Schaffer, Ilse Wertheimer and others. In recognition of
their loyalty, commitment and creativity, Bowlby (1979a) dedicated to them his
book *The Making and Breaking of Affectional Bonds*. The research and clinical activities of the Department for Children and Parents enhanced both Bowlby's and the
Tavistock's reputation.

In Chapter 5, I shall provide details of Bowlby's appointment by the World
Health Organization to produce a report on homeless children who had been
orphaned during the war. This gave him world-wide renown. He, of course, was
also active in the development of training programmes for child psychiatrists, educational psychologists, social workers and non-medical child psychotherapists. The
latter, however, became a different story in its own right.

The child psychotherapy training

From the beginning of his headship, Bowlby wanted to create a separate child psychotherapy training at the Tavistock to emphasise the importance of this treatment modality – something that he had appreciated during his years of education in Kleinian child analysis and his work at the London Child Guidance Clinic. He became conversant with the Hampstead child psychotherapy training course started by Anna Freud in 1947.

Bowlby's idea was to design a distinct course incorporating a combination of Kleinian and Independent orientations – thus complementing the training that Anna Freud had organised. Ultimately, he wanted to create a new profession. In 1948, he appointed Esther Bick to jointly organise the new child psychotherapy training. She had been in analysis with Michael Balint, so there was an expectation that on completion of her psychoanalytic training she would join the Independent Group.

Bick (née Esteza Wander) was born in Poland, in 1901. The first child in an orthodox Jewish family, she was six years older than Bowlby. At the age of seven her parents sent her to Prague to look after her aunt's baby. She then worked in a nursery while attending school. She moved to Vienna to read psychology and married the medical doctor Philip Bick. They escaped to Switzerland in 1938 after Austria was occupied by the Nazis.

Bick was determined to pursue a career as a clinical psychologist and came to England without her husband, as she could not obtain a Swiss work permit. During the war, she worked in various nurseries in Manchester and Salford. In 1945, she got a job at a Child Guidance Clinic in Leeds where she worked until her move to London.

Bowlby's relationship with Bick was reasonable during the first couple of years. He and the team had produced a document outlining the standpoint that the Children's Department was taking:

> We stress in particular the importance of the relationship of the child to his mother and the members of the family…. If these are happy relationships, we believe that there is every likelihood that the child will be able to develop similar satisfactory relationships in later life…; conversely, if this relationship develops adversely, we believe that he will probably become disturbed emotionally to a greater or lesser degree, and may be confronted throughout his life by difficulties in his personal relationships.
>
> *(Bowlby et al., 1948, pp. 1–2)*

That made sense to Bick. She had spent many years informally observing babies and young children – and suggested that observation of infants in ordinary families could be a component of the new training. Bowlby supported Bick's idea. In 1948, they jointly launched the Tavistock's child psychotherapy training programme. This has become the largest European training programme in the field – known as the *Tavistock Model*.

The training includes two years of infant observation and supervision seminars, based on hour-long weekly observations in a family home, soon after the birth of the baby and up to his or her second birthday. The aim is to gather as *objectively* as possible an observation – for which trainees should avoid any form of relationship with the family outside the strict observing task. One of the requirements is writing up, in as much detail as possible, everything observed and report it in a small supervision group.

Bowlby and Bick were the supervisors in the early years of the programme. They, in fact, had a number of points in common. For example, they were keen on naturalistic methods of observation, but also aware of the risks of intrusiveness and premature conclusions. Therefore, they conducted the infant observation seminars very much with an open mind. That is, looking for possible hypotheses about the observed interactions and communications – conscious or unconscious. They often reminded their supervisees that further observations over time would be the proper basis for confirming or refuting the line of interpretation being developed (Rustin, 2009, p. 31).

Bick gradually became closer to Melanie Klein and started training analysis with her in 1950. She turned to join the Kleinian Group at a time when Joan Riviere, Bowlby's analyst and one of the most devoted Kleinian disciples, was dissociating herself from the close circle that surrounded Klein. Coincidentally, the relationship between Bick and Bowlby deteriorated sharply. The conflict went over and beyond theoretical differences. It became a personal problem, as well as an ongoing professional argument.

Juliet Hopkins, Bowlby's niece, underwent training in child psychotherapy at the Tavistock, throughout the mid and late 1950s. She felt that Bowlby and Bick did not get on. Was this due to theoretical differences? Talia Welsh (2013, p. 98) gave her own view: "Perhaps accurate theorising is not the hallmark of human interaction. Something more primitive and less intellectual underlies the natural connections we form with others".

Bowlby himself felt that, as time went on,

> Bick's missionary zeal let the course become strongly Kleinian, a shift I was unable to stop owing to my many other responsibilities. Throughout the 1950s, the Kleinians were extending their grip on the Tavistock, which I regretted, since they were not interested in research.
>
> *(Bowlby, 1991a, p. 28)*

By 1959, the quarrel had become so notorious that it was a matter of 'either or'. Bowlby was the boss, which meant that Bick had to leave the Tavistock. Nevertheless, she had already made an outstanding contribution to the psychoanalytic understanding of child development through the naturalistic study of babies in the ordinary life of their family environment.

After Bick's departure, the Tavistock model of child psychotherapy training and its infant observation component continued growing. In 1960, Martha Harris, a

British child and adult analyst, also with a Kleinian orientation, was appointed new Head of Child Psychotherapy. She stayed in the role for more than twenty years and expanded the infant observation programme, which included the addition of one-year observation of a young child between the ages of two and five.

Harris appointed a new seminar leader, Gianna Williams, who would later supervise me on the infant observation course in the mid and late 1980s. As an observer, I came to appreciate the mutual influence of the developing relationship between mother and baby, and father and siblings. In supervision, I also had opportunities to reflect on the feelings aroused in me during the observation and how my presence may influence the family dynamic. Bowlby was on good terms with Harris; in spite of their theoretical differences, they worked well together.

From 1985 to 2007, the Head of Child Psychotherapy was Margaret Rustin, who had been a gifted student of Harris in the late 1960s and early 1970s. With Rustin and Williams, the infant observation course went from strength to strength to reach the pre-eminent role that it plays nowadays in training programmes across the world. The number of international trainees at the Tavistock grew exponentially.

From the distance of his late years, Bowlby was happy to see the increasing success of the child psychotherapy training, which he had jointly conceived with Bick in the late 1940s. This was duly recognised: "The international reputation of the Tavistock Clinic and of its child psychotherapy training owes him a great debt" (Rustin, 2007, p. 355).

Margaret Rustin's appreciation had a personal component too. In the 1960s she was interviewed by Bowlby following her application to train in child psychotherapy. She was anxious about how she would be able to cope with the demands of the training while starting a young family. Bowlby was very supportive, encouraging and understanding. He reassured her that being in analysis would be of help.

Clinical orientations

Bowlby was primarily an open-minded clinician eager to learn. His clinical observations guided his increasingly powerful research. He chose to live in both these two professional worlds and appreciated their differences. From his privileged position, he heard that some clinicians felt that researchers were remote from everyday life, whilst some researchers assumed that clinicians were fuzzy-headed, inclined to engage in leaps in the dark, hunches and guesswork. He gave his own perspective:

> The underlying cause for this difference in attitude is that clinicians have to take action, whereas researchers are able to reflect on a narrow area of study to unravel 'do-able' problems. Clinicians apply a theory, whereas researchers try to test it. Not many people find it congenial to work in both worlds, because doing so requires an often uncomfortable switch in frame of reference.
>
> *(quoted in Bretherton, 1991, p. 14)*

Though Bowlby was very successful in bringing together a team of outstanding researchers, it was more difficult for him to be accepted by a peer group of clinicians at the Tavistock. In his case, the disparities of these two worlds were sharp. He had to employ his own strategy to get on with this dual task:

> These are two distinct worlds ... when you are operating in the one world it is proper to have one frame of reference; and when you cross the road and are operating in the other world, it is proper to have quite a different frame of reference. Now, when I formulated that to myself ... soon after the war ... it helped me a great deal .... The point I want to make is that each point of view is appropriate within its own world, and that it is totally inappropriate in the other world. Unless you realize that, you can't operate in both.
>
> *(quoted in Van Dijken, 1998, p. 133)*

In the years he had worked at the London Child Guidance Clinic, before the war, Bowlby was introduced to the idea that unresolved conflicts stemming from the parents' own childhood may contribute to their children's problems. Upon his arrival at the Tavistock, he indeed introduced family interviews and therapeutic work for parents. As the norm, he included mother and father in the initial assessment of the child.

Bowlby also encouraged parents to participate in the treatment of their children one way or another, so they could at least realise what was involved and support the therapeutic process. Depending on the findings of the assessment, Bowlby sometimes carried on seeing the whole family together. He was very committed to the promotion of mental health and the prevention of the inter-generational transmission of problems.

However, Bowlby realised only too well that, at the time, fathers were often left out: "there are at present few facilities for fathers to improve their understanding of the emotional development of children" (Bowlby et al., 1948, p. 10). He was especially sensitive to the impact of paternal separation and loss during the war. He had in fact experienced his own father's war-time absence for nearly five of his childhood years.

Bowlby hoped that the need to involve fathers would be more widely recognised as time went on. He was pleased that formal family therapy, including fathers, developed healthily in the following decades. He also advocated a multidisciplinary approach, in which collaborative communication between professionals and agencies was highlighted to maximise the child's wellbeing.

Marcus Johns, the son-in-law of Molly and Tom Main, was Bowlby's psychiatric registrar in the late 1960s and early 1970s before becoming a consultant in what is now called the Child and Family Department. He was in training analysis with Hanna Segal during his Tavistock supervision with Bowlby, but this was not a problem for him. Bowlby was supportive of his Kleinian analysis. Hanna Segal, usually warm and sympathetic, in an uncharacteristic unguarded moment, said to Marcus Johns that 'John' [Bowlby] had never really got over being sent away to boarding school. Hanna Segal had in fact been supervised by Bowlby's analyst, Joan Riviere.

As part of his work as a child psychiatrist, Marcus Johns had to be involved in decisions about the placement of children who were received into care. He recalled Bowlby had been said to him in supervision that, before deciding on a new placement, it would be important to be as convinced as possible that such a new place would be better for the child than his or her current place – even when this one was considered suboptimal.

Bowlby also advised Johns that it would be in the child's best interest that his or her psychiatrist had been familiarised with the institutional setting where the child would live. Therefore, visiting it prior to the move would be highly recommendable. The child could perceive this, maybe for the first time, as grown-ups working together for his or her wellbeing.

In an influential book edited by Judith Trowell and Alicia Etchegoyen, *The Importance of Fathers: A Psychoanalytic Re-evaluation*, Johns (2002) values the relevance Bowlby gave to fathers. An example Johns remembers was a consultation with a young mother who attended alone and was eulogising her own mother and the support she had from her, therefore not requiring support from the clinic. It slipped out that her husband was sitting in their car in the car park waiting for her.

Johns went down, found the car and invited him into the consultation, which he was very pleased to accept. The young mother continued the idealisation of her own mother, at which her husband clearly became more and more uncomfortable. At last he burst out: "But your mother is an old witch!" The family dynamics could now be examined in a more realistic way, helpful to the young mother in her current pregnancy, her marriage and her family.

Bowlby's psychotherapeutic orientation in his work with children seemed to have taken a middle course between Melanie Klein's and Anna Freud's. Klein thoroughly used transference interpretations, in which she held the view that children project the internalised mother on to the therapist. This *transference* was then seen as an accurate reflection of the child's feelings towards the mother. On the other hand, Anna Freud held the view that the child's hostile behaviour towards the therapist could be compatible with a good relationship with the mother, or vice versa.

Bowlby used transference interpretations but was more interested than Klein in the child's real life experiences. He was also prepared to give advice to the child's parents – something that Anna Freud and her team did too. His clinical ideas were close to the psychoanalytic theorising of members of the Independent Group, particularly Michael Balint, Ronald Fairbairn, Donald Winnicott and Harry Guntrip. He often recommended their influential writings to me.

Bowlby placed an emphasis on early intervention. He practised and supported therapeutic work with infants and their parents. I can recall that, when I discussed this with him in supervision, he alerted me to the work of the psychoanalyst Selma Fraiberg, whom he had referred to in his own work (Bowlby, 1988a). In the 1970s Fraiberg had pioneered the analytic observation of infants with congenital blindness and described a number of additional developmental hurdles for them. These included difficulties in recognising parents from sound alone, in learning about the permanence of objects and in acquiring a healthy self-image.

Fraiberg also found that vision acts as a way of pulling other sensory modalities together and without sight babies are inevitably delayed in integration. Additionally, like Bowlby, she studied the intergenerational transmission of trauma. This she described in her landmark publication *Ghosts in the Nursery: A Psychoanalytic Approach to the Problems of the Infant-Mother Relationships* (Fraiberg et al., 1975). When there are congenital problems, early bonding is more difficult and sensitive early intervention is even more crucial.

Despite his openness and inclusiveness, Bowlby was very much criticised for not going along with the predominant Kleinian orientation of the child psychotherapists in his Department. Juliet Hopkins found herself in a difficult position at times when she witnessed the hostility that her Kleinian colleagues directed at her uncle: "These were not people you could disagree with. If you disagreed, you were wrong" (quoted in Karen, 1998, p. 108).

Hopkins' training was mainly Kleinian, but she tried to integrate Klein's and Bowlby's ideas. In fact, she found that attachment concepts added a valuable layer of meaning to her clinical work. According to Hopkins, the main criticism that Bowlby received at the Tavistock, namely that he did not pay attention to the *unconscious* and the internal world, was unfounded – as he in fact paid more consideration to intra-psychic processes than his detractors gave him credit for (see Chapter 9).

For example, "On Knowing what you are not Supposed to Know and Feeling what you are not Supposed to Feel", Bowlby (1979b) proposed the concept of 'defensive exclusion' – something that occurs largely at an unconscious level. He explained that there are situations where a child is put under pressure by his parents or carers not to talk about, or even to forget, some difficult events.

A child subjected to such a pressure is often pushed to conform to the parents' or carer's wishes, and may defensively exclude from further processing the events he knows they want him to forget – to the point that the child is no longer aware of these. Bowlby's insights on unconscious processes can help with the understanding of complex clinical phenomena, such as repression and dissociation (see Chapters 9 and 10).

Bowlby paid attention to fantasies but did not give to them the same prominence as the majority of his psychoanalytic colleagues. His thinking was straight-forward:

> Most of what goes on in the internal world is a more or less accurate reflection of what an individual has experienced recently or long ago in the external world. Of course, in addition to all that, we imagine things … but most of the time we are concerned with ordinary events. If the child sees his mother as a very loving person, the chances are that his mother is a loving person. If he sees her as a very rejecting person, the chances are she is a very rejecting person.
>
> *(Bowlby et al., 1986, p. 43)*

Right from the outset, well before formulating his attachment theory, Bowlby's clinical approach was primarily relational. Supporting children to develop a capacity for making satisfactory relationships was paramount: "children characterised by nervousness, tempers, delinquency, moodiness, reclusiveness and so on, are regarded as children whose capacity for forming personal relationships has become impaired and crippled in one or a number of ways" (Bowlby et al., 1948, p. 5).

In order to properly address this, Bowlby tried to provide a therapeutic environment where children could freely express their fears, wishes, anxieties, feelings, fantasies and conflicts. In turn, this would help them gain an age-appropriate understanding and develop a capacity to work through their difficulties. His main orientation remained psychoanalytic:

> The unconscious mechanisms in the child's mind are brought to the surface by allowing him to project them on to suitable chosen play or art material, the meaning of the phantasies represented being then interpreted to the child by the therapist.
>
> *(Bowlby & Caplan, 1948, p. 6)*

Wider institutional impact

The Tavistock Clinic organised a Conference in 2007 to celebrate the centenary of Bowlby's birth. The event generated a special issue of the journal *Attachment and Human Development*. This included a paper, "John Bowlby and the Tavistock Clinic", in which Margaret Rustin paid tribute to the less known but very significant contributions that he made as an *institution builder*. She wrote:

> His vision ... was pivotal. He had ... a picture of multi-disciplinary collaboration which was exemplary.... First, the wider context of the children's lives was to be taken account of, through attention to the child's school experience and the involvement of fathers in the clinical work. Second, he was part of a small group of psychoanalysts and analytically-minded child psychiatrists who believed that a new profession of child psychotherapy was needed.
>
> *(Rustin, 2007, p. 355)*

The early days of the new discipline, under the supervision of Bowlby and Bick, were not free from conflict. A certain degree of tension and uncertainty is needed for new ventures. Over the years, Bowlby time and again had to navigate through hostile opposing forces, which seemed to stimulate his creativity. As well as making the new training possible, he contributed to the creation of the Association of Child Psychotherapists – an umbrella under which a number of different standpoints came together. Rustin (2007, p. 356) concluded: "Bowlby's loyalty to the project remained solid and meant an enormous amount to this tiny profession as it emerged".

On his Tavistock appointment, Bowlby was aware that his professional status gave him new authority to propagate his knowledge on child guidance and preventive psychiatry. He became a prolific writer, who could be read by professionals and the general public alike. He spent much time and effort giving papers at scientific meetings and sitting on policy committees. This included membership on the Mental Health Standing Advisory Committee (MHSAC), which started in 1949. He was described as "a live member, with embarrassing enthusiasm for his own specialty" (Van Dijken, 1998, p. 143).

Bowlby pleaded in this committee for a separate governmental department of child welfare. Bowlby was also influencing the new children officers who were striving, after the Children Act 1948, to create child-centred services. He was still alive to learn with pleasure that the new Children Act 1989 had replaced the old terms 'parental custody' and 'place of safety' by more attachment-friendly concepts such as 'parental responsibility' and 'secure accommodation'.

The Ministry of Health had, in 1956, approved a plan for new premises in Belsize Lane, in Hampstead; which would be a more fitting home for both the Tavistock Clinic and Institute and the Child Guidance Training Clinic. Following a long administrative process, in October 1965 Rees was invited to lay the foundation stone of the new construction. Bowlby was in favour of this, in recognition of Rees' contributions as former medical director.

The present building was officially opened by the late Princess Marina, Duchess of Kent, on 4 May 1967. It is about three times larger in floor space than the previous edifice in Beaumont Street. This is a good indication of the huge success the Tavistock had in the 20 years that followed the war (Dicks, 1970, pp. 10–11).

Bowlby made a special contribution to the new edifice. Tirril Harris remembered him, after a research seminar, pausing on the staircase descending from the Tavistock Canteen and casually saying that he rather liked the view. One glance was enough to reveal the link between psychotherapy – this most indoor of pursuits– with an outside world of long gardens where cats and children could play. Bowlby explained that it had been fortunate that the architectural plans permitted the relocation of the staircase from the original design. Harris (1990, p. 309) added: "It was only after his death that I learnt that it was he himself who had played the crucial architectural role in amending the plans. Yet again by relocating the initial viewpoint he had incomparably broadened our perspective". Bowlby always tried to maintain a natural link with the total environment.

Soon after the move to the new building in 1968, Bowlby retired from his role as Director of the Department for Children and Parents, "which he had so creatively reorganised and shaped over 22 years, in order to devote more time to the research and training activities of the growing School, of which he had been chairman from the beginning" (Dicks, 1970, p. 278). The following year he published the first volume of his trilogy on *Attachment and Loss*. Prior to this, he produced an internal document on the working philosophy and scientific principles of the Department. These could be summarised as follows:

- First, to promote the health of families and children growing up within a community;
- Second, to gain a better understanding of the conditions making for healthy growth;
- Third, to devise more varied and better techniques for bringing those conditions into being;
- Fourth, to train professional personnel for those functions;
- Fifth, to encourage and support the cross-fertilisation between clinical work and research.

Bowlby made his theoretical position clear. He emphasised not only intrapersonal factors but also human environments and interactions, as playing their part in the creation of either good mental health or mental illness in the child. Therefore, the task was not to sit in a clinic and receive sick children but to work with families and the wider community – especially with schools and other children's institutions.

The document further stated that much clinical work could be done at earlier stages by the staff actually going out and dealing with incipient trouble in the places where children were living and socialising. The work should never be done with the child patient in isolation. Bowlby constructively recognised that the staff in his Department "had individual differences and sometimes a conflict of working theories, and that this conflict and controversy was a respected part of a growing subject rather than suppressed for the sake of uniformity" (Dicks, 1970, p. 278).

As chairman of the Children's Department, Bowlby was supportive of working mothers in most practical ways. He bypassed official maternity leave restrictions as much as he could. For example, he allowed his junior colleague Freda Martin (see Chapter 12) to work two half days a week for a couple of years and negotiated changes in time meetings to accommodate her and other working mothers. She wrote:

> I can think of no other institution in the 1970s, where because of the incoming Chair-person of a department (myself) had young children, the time of the Clinic Professional Committee Meeting, by long tradition held at 4.00 in the afternoon, was altered without a murmur to 11.00 in the morning.
>
> *(Martin, 1991, p. 65)*

Peter Bruggen and his Tavistock colleague Sandy Bourne (see Chapter 1) published over half a dozen papers on distinctions awards for consultants. They criticised the allocation by committees in secret and focussed on sexism in NHS management (Bruggen, 1997, p. 282). They examined all sorts of factors: age and specialty of recipients, specialty of members of committees, collection of data. Women were grossly under-represented both on the committees and as recipients of awards. At one point they had asked Bowlby, just before his retirement, about his experience as a recipient of awards at the Tavistock. Choosing his words carefully, he responded that whatever happened had already happened and that it was in the past!

It would appear that Bowlby might not have received the recognition that he deserved for his NHS work at the Tavistock. It is quite tempting to speculate that, maybe, his theoretical differences with the Kleinians could have influenced some of the committees' secret decision-making. But who knows? Van Dijken (1998, pp. 175–176) gave a summary of his main twenty major awards. He received only one of these prior to 1971, the year before his retirement from the NHS. Sixteen out of the twenty awards arrived after his retirement (see Appendix).

Despite the history of tension and conflict, the institution did give him a permanent honour, as reported by Harris (1990, p. 305):

> It is difficult to work in the new reading room at the Tavistock Centre library without being struck by the photograph on the wall. The man in whose honour the room was built, John Bowlby, looks down with that gentle intensity of attention, common alike to good therapists and great scientists. The photographer has captured a quintessentially expression, questioning enough to inspire us to tell our story without distortion, but tranquil enough to convey that we may tell it in our own good time and still be heard with acceptance.

5

GENESIS OF ATTACHMENT THEORY

Nicolaus Copernicus postulated that our planet was not the centre of the Universe and that it was the Sun at the centre around which the Earth rotated: a blow to man's egocentricity. His masterpiece *De Revolutionibus Orbium Coelestium* (On the Revolutions of the Celestial Spheres) is considered a major breakthrough in the history of science. It was published in 1543 just before his death. The work had been completed by 1532 but he delayed publication as he did to wish to risk the scorn to which he would expose himself on account of the novelty of his discovery and the extended religious beliefs of his time. He carefully expressed his fears in the dedication of the book to Pope Paul III.

Isaac Newton initiated another scientific revolution. He published *The Principia* (Mathematical Principles of Natural Philosophy) in 1687. He used a simple Latin word *gravitas* (weight) to define the complex law of universal gravitation. Isn't it ironic that the same *apple* that, in the Christian tradition, had caused the original sin and eternal human suffering on Earth would finally illuminate Newton to discover Earth's gravity?

Charles Darwin published his revolutionary theory of evolution with undeniable evidence in his 1859 book *On the Origin of Species*. The idea that we descend from the *beasts* met, of course, much criticism and hostility from religious groups. A further blow to our egocentric view of ourselves. Despite this opposition, by the late 1870s the scientific community and much of the general public had accepted evolution as a fact, rather than a theory. Nevertheless, a tiny minority of fundamentalist creationists are still reading the *Book of Genesis* literally and continue rejecting evolution.

Sigmund Freud delivered the ultimate blow to our narcissism with the publication of *The Interpretation of Dreams* in 1899. The conscious mind could no longer be seen as the centre of our existence. We had to give up the illusion that we might be able to be completely aware of what is going on in our everyday life, let alone our internal world. Non-conscious forces had been known to humankind for centuries, but no one before Freud had investigated the *Unconscious* systematically. This led to the development of psychoanalysis as a new theory of the mind and a treatment method for human torment.

John Bowlby did not attempt to deal with the Universe. But his formidable intellect and historical circumstances interplayed creatively: he formulated a 're-evolutionary' dimension of human survival and wellbeing. The individual cannot exist in isolation: attachment to other human beings is as vital an instinct as the hunger for food and sex. We rotate about our larger attachment figures. Similar to the gravitational force that keeps our feet on the floor, we are born with a powerful energy that seeks meaningful human connection. This stays with us across the life cycle: from cradle to grave. The first volume of his trilogy on *Attachment and Loss* was published in 1969. He dedicated it to Ursula, his secure base and life companion of 52 years – with whom he was able to survive the blows of the world.

The word 'theory' comes from the Greek *theoria*, meaning to contemplate, to look at. I find it helpful to think that theories are aids or spectacles: ways of looking at reality or unreality. As such, they should be seen as neither right nor wrong, but as being more useful or less useful. Indeed, there is nothing as useful as a good theory. Expectations, plans and meaning can be based upon it. In this chapter, I invite the reader to use the *attachment spectacles*.

Conceptions of attachment

As I understand it, attachment is both an 'instinct' and a 'relationship'. As an instinct it is deeply rooted in evolutionary biology. However, it would be plausible to say there is no such thing as an instinct but a continually evolving interaction between an instinctual substrate and the environment. As a human relationship, the concept of attachment visibly evolved from psychoanalytic thinking. However, it is possible to trace a deep understanding of the nature of human attachment in existentialist writers. The Danish philosopher and poet Søren Kierkegaard is widely considered to be the 'father' of *Existentialism*.

Despite his premature death at 42, in November 1855, a few months before Freud was born, Kierkegaard had a profound influence on psychology and existential psychotherapy – a school of thought that had guided my training as a junior psychiatrist in Spain. He tried to understand what today we call *separation anxiety*, in the face of threats to an attachment bond. In 1846, he wrote a moving account of what secure attachment might be about:

> The loving mother teaches her child to walk alone. She is far enough from him ..., but she holds out her arms to him. She imitates his movements ..., so that the child might believe that he is not walking alone.... And yet, she does more. Her face beckons like a reward, an encouragement. Thus, the child walks alone with his eyes fixed on his mother's face, not on the difficulties in

his way. He supports himself by the arms that do not hold him and constantly strives towards the refuge in his mother's embrace, little supposing that in the very same moment that he is emphasising his need for her ... he is walking alone.

(quoted in Sroufe, 1979, p. 462)

Bowlby was born at a time when the existential work of Søren Kierkegaard and the phenomenological work of Edmund Husserl, ontology and epistemology, were coming together to create an existential phenomenology tradition that permeated European thinking, particularly during the first half of the twentieth century. Human life was looked at from the observation and analysis of *dasein* or being-there, in the context of *lebenswelt* or life-world.

Within this tradition, the Baltic-German doctor and philosopher Nikolai Hartmann, in his *Philosophische Grundfragen der Biologie* (Philosophical Questions of Biology), wrote about two ways of being: *verankertsein* (attached being) and *orienkertsein* (oriented being). The first could today be described as a clinging and anxiously attached individual; the second as a securely attached and trusting person, able to explore the world with confidence (Hartmann, 1912).

Etymologically, the most likely origin of the term attachment appears to the Germanic word *stakon* (stake). It evolved through the French *estachier* and *attacher* meaning to tack on, fasten or join to. A less likely origin might be the Greek *tassein* and the Latin *taxa* meaning to order, dispose or put in place. Is the spelling proximity between attack and attach significant or a mere contamination?

In his *Three Essays on the Theory of Sexuality*, Freud (1905) had mentioned the presence of a 'grasping instinct' an extension of the grasp reflex, linked to catching hold of some part of another person. He noted that an infant of 18 months disliked being left alone. He tried to accommodate his observations into his new theorising. Originally, he postulated that this tie was a secondary consequence of the mother providing satisfaction of physiological or erotic needs and that fear of losing her was a growing tension of non-satisfaction – that needed to be discharged. However, his position on this was not at all unequivocal, as his thinking was open to the influence of new observations.

Freud often appeared to try to conciliate his observations of attachment with his belief that, in the earliest stages of our development, we go through an autoerotic or narcissistic phase. He wrote in 1922:

In the first instance the oral component instinct finds satisfaction by attaching itself to the sating of the desire for nourishment; and its object is the mother's breast. It then detaches itself, becomes independent and at the same time auto-erotic, that is, it finds an object in the child's own body.

(quoted in Klein, 1952, p. 435)

Melanie Klein later pointed out that, here, Freud is talking of a *libidinal attachment* to an object, the mother's breast, which precedes auto-eroticism and narcissism.

She elaborated on this and stated that, while Freud was referring to the object of an instinctual aim, she meant, in addition to that, "an object-relation involving the infant's emotions, phantasies, anxieties and defences" (Klein, 1952, p. 435).

Nevertheless, Freud gradually realised that his own theorising alone was insufficient to explain the whole of our instinctual life. He wrote in 1925: "There is no more urgent need in psychology than for a securely founded theory of the instincts on which it might then be possible to build further. Nothing of the sort exists" (quoted in Bowlby, 1969, p. 37). Towards the end of his life, Freud became more able to recognise that understanding the true nature of this powerful, early bond was beyond his grasp. He wrote in 1931: "Everything in the sphere of this first attachment to the mother seemed to me so difficult to grasp in analysis" (quoted in Bowlby, 1969, p. 177).

The first psychoanalyst who used observations of anthropoid apes in an attempt to understand the intricacies of the early mother–child relationship was the Hungarian Imre Hermann. Initially a neurologist, he trained as a Freudian analyst and developed an interest in experimental psychology. After becoming a member of the Hungarian and International Psychoanalytical Societies, in 1921 his interest turned towards the behaviour of primates. He noted a distinctly instinctive behaviour in the offspring of chimpanzees. He was particularly struck by the fact that they spend the first months of their lives clinging onto the fur of their mothers. He set forth a tentative theory of the 'clinging instinct' (Hermann, 1923). In some way, this made him one of the forerunners of what we now call attachment theory.

In *L'Instinct Filial*, a strangely fascinating book, almost *Planet of the Apes*-like read, Hermann (1972) synthesised his thinking on this primeval clinging instinct. The book lacks scientific rigour but explores filio–maternal attachment with a touch of nostalgia and poetry. He suggested that, at the earliest developmental episode, there is a primordial *paido-mater* unity. That was not an infant within the mother (or introjected into her) but an infant clinging to the mother.

According to Hermann, for several hundred-thousand years the infant gripped the mother's fur until the *universal catastrophe* of the loss of long body hair – that is, the loss of the grip on the mother. He postulated a filial instinct (manifested by a searching and clinging drive) to recover the *paradise lost*. This implicitly suggests that babies yearn for a return to the womb and that this craving draws them to seek the mother's embrace.

This, of course, would later be challenged by Bowlby (1958a, p. 369): "It is difficult to imagine what survival value such a desire might have, and I am not aware that any has been suggested". In this respect, I can recall a true anecdote about one of my supervisors who had a reputation for recruiting beautiful secretaries and trainees, with whom he usually ended in bed, in a clear exploitation of his status. When he was confronted with his professional misconduct, he justified it as a need to return to his mother's womb – which, according to him, was fundamental for his emotional survival.

Hermann's contention that the self is always a fragmentary vestige of a dual unity was not completely discarded. He was able to elaborate on it and put forward a thought that, ultimately, the filial instinct replaces *Eros* as the life drive: to seek out and grasp, to form attachments to figurative substitutions for the mother – including sexual partners, by a maturing capacity to introject. Hermann's ideas were later described by Geyskens (2003) as a *Freudian theory of attachment*, where consideration is given to the attachment instinct as an interesting alternative to Freud's death instinct. Hermann's thinking contained ideas about attachment, separation and loss – something that acquired a more mature and accurate shape with Bowlby who *introjected* updated scientific knowledge. Eventually, the dual unity became a social or *group unity*.

Bowlby was significantly influenced by the work of Scottish psychoanalyst Ian Suttie (1889–1935) who was working within the Freudian tradition but developed his own independent thinking. In his book *The Origins of Love and Hate*, which was published a few days after his death at the age of 46, Suttie (1935) postulated that the infant is born with a mind and instincts adapted to infancy of which 'attachment' to the mother would be predominant. In line with Bowlby's later theorising, Suttie highlighted the survival value of this attachment, not only in terms of feeding but also protection, and started to challenge the idea that the strength of this early bond was primarily related to the satisfaction of bodily needs.

Suttie in fact considered that the need for company and emotional relationship with the mother was what really mattered for the infant. His influence on Bowlby's future thinking is clear in the following passage:

> Love of the mother is primal in so far as it is the first formed and directed relationship. Hate, I regard not as a primal independent instinct, but as a development or intensification of separation anxiety which in turn is roused by a threat against love.
>
> *(Suttie, 1935, p. 25)*

Suttie had been influenced by the Hungarian school of psychoanalysis, particularly Imre Hermann and Sandor Ferenczi. Like them, Suttie saw sociability, the craving for companionship, the need to love and to be loved, to exchange and to participate, to be as primary as sexuality itself. He understood anxiety, insecurity and hate as a reaction to the failure in having a response for this sociability of which mother was the primal base. For him, when separation anxiety is in full force the infant devotes all efforts to restore the relationship with the mother. When this restoration is successful, anxiety, anger and hate will be put behind and the infant will feel emotionally secure. In a harmonious relationship, anxiety is kept to a minimum and resentments are only transient.

In spite of his untimely death, Suttie's fundamental insights left a mark on the pre-war Tavistock group (Dicks, 1970) and in the young Bowlby's mind as he was going through his psychoanalytic training. Suttie's concepts and terminology (such as innate need for companionship, attachment to mother, separation anxiety, anger, insecurity, etc.) were similar to the ideas and formulations that Bowlby would later develop with the support of systematic research. But that was still a long way off.

In the next few years after Suttie's death, other psychoanalytic authors reported observations of the interaction between mother and child, which increasingly challenged Freudian views on child development. Most of these authors had their ideological roots in the school of 'object relations', although they gradually separated from mainstream Kleinian thought as well. Similarly, Anna Freud evolved from her father's emphasis on libidinal drives to a more direct provision of maternal care. Bowlby was always respectful and appreciative of her work.

However, Bowlby was theoretically closer to the work of Michael Balint (1937, 1952) – a Hungarian physician who spent most of his professional life in England and developed reflective groups for General Practitioners, now called *Balint groups*. Like Hermann, Balint talked about the infant's sturdy needs to cling – something that was not linked to any of the erotogenic zones. He coined the concept of 'primary love': an immature form of affection present in the demanding infant, who is expecting to be at the receiving end. As the child grows healthily, he or she develops a capacity for secondary or mature love, which is based on reciprocity – that is, giving as well as receiving.

During the Second World War, there was an increasing interest in the understanding of the nature of human attachment. Another object relations analyst from the British Independent Group, Scottish-born Ronald Fairbairn (1943), gave an account of the vigour with which an infant relates to the mother. The following year, Anna Freud and Dorothy Burlingham described the child's needs for attachment in terms of an important instinctual need. From their direct observations, working with children and families, they suggested that it was not until the second year of life that the child's attachment to the mother comes to its full potential (Freud & Burlingham, 1944). Donald Winnicott (1945), a leading member of the Independent Group, considered that for the baby's survival it is vitally important that the mother is available to be sensed in all possible ways.

On the other side of the Atlantic, the American psychoanalyst Margaret Ribble (1944) suggested that infants are born with a need or instinct for contact with the mother. She became a major voice against maternal deprivation. The Austrian-born analyst Rene Spitz emigrated to the safety offered by the USA, away from the European fronts. He coined the term *anaclitic depression*, seen as a result of partial emotional deprivation (the loss of a loved object). From his direct observations, he stated that when the love object is returned to the child within a period of three to five months, recovery is prompt.

However, if the child is deprived for longer than five months, he or she would show the symptoms of increasingly serious deterioration – that Spitz called *hospitalism*. He quoted a passage from the 1760 diary of a Spanish bishop: "In the foundling home the child becomes sad and many of them die from sadness" (in Spitz, 1945, p. 53). He later produced a film on grief in infancy and, finally, stressed the importance of skin contact in the relationship between mother and baby (Spitz, 1947, 1957).

The American neo-Freudian analyst and son of Irish emigrants, Harry Stack Sullivan (1953, 1955) claimed that infants have a primary need for closeness with mother and for human relationships. He held the view that human development happens as a result of complex interpersonal relations. Similar ideas were put forward by Therese Benedeck, a Hungarian psychoanalyst who had trained in Budapest and worked in Berlin. Like Spitz, she also needed to flee Europe for the USA, in 1936.

Benedeck played a central role in the development of American psychoanalysis. She wrote about the early mother–infant attachment, depicting in plain English the child's basic needs to be smiled at, picked up and talked to. She added that a crying fit could be seen as an attempt to communicate emotionally. But she used traditional psychoanalytic jargon, like 'emotional symbiosis' to conceptualise the early attachment relationship (Benedeck, 1956).

The kindness of strangers

It seems sufficiently clear that, during more than half a century, there had been a growing emphasis among psychoanalytic authors on the strength of the early mother–child relationship. In a compelling analysis, Newcombe and Lerner (1982) stressed, in particular, the importance of the period between the two world wars in the development of British psychoanalysis and its influence in the development of Bowlby's theory of attachment.

However, in the mid-1950s, there was no suitable theoretical framework that would convincingly explain the nature of such a strong early bond. How would it become possible for Bowlby to put together a new theoretical framework? In order to address this, I shall now look further into some of the circumstances that shaped his motivation and thinking.

An investigation into the origins of attachment theory (Grossmann, 1995) should indeed consider the historical context, including the massive losses and disruptions to family life caused by the two world wars. But we should not neglect the intellectual climate that had been progressively generated by existential, phenomenological and psychoanalytic writers, nor should we underestimate the value of Darwinian evolutionary thinking. Human survival was being gradually drawn into sharper focus, at all levels.

Bowlby's own attachment history and intellectual development are highly relevant to the development of attachment theory. He was seven when the First World War erupted and his father was absent for more than four years. Bowlby and his brother Tony were sent away to boarding school – a significantly difficult separation (Hunter, 1991). At the age of 14, Bowlby was sent to the Royal Naval College, Dartmouth but asked his father to buy him out of the Navy, after which he went to Cambridge University for his pre-medical studies in 'natural and moral sciences' (1925–28).

Freud had already made an important contribution to contemporary thought. Psychoanalytic literature was becoming increasingly popular. The number of related articles published in the British press in the early 1920s was such that the progressive magazine *New Statesman* declared:

We are all psychoanalysts now. That is to say that it is difficult for an educated person to neglect the theories of Freud and his rivals as it would have been for his father to ignore the equally disconcerting discoveries of Darwin.

(Hynes, 1990, p. 366)

Few Cambridge undergraduates having any pretentions to advanced thought in the 1920s, failed to have curiosity about Freudian ideas (Glover, 1966).

At Cambridge, indeed, Bowlby became aware of psychoanalysis and developed an interest in it. In a retrospective interview, he said: "And I decided to take it up – whatever that meant" (Smuts, 1977, p. 1). In his last undergraduate year, he enjoyed the tutorship of Frederic Bartlett. The climate that Bartlett fostered was one of understanding psychology as a biological science. Students were trained in the technique and methods of psychological experiments for the study of the conditions that regulate any type of animal and human response to stimuli. Bowlby was not only trained in external observation, but in introspection as well: "Very often the most valuable information can be given in terms possible only to the person himself who responds" (Bartlett, 1961, p. 42).

Bartlett was interested in real life problems and in memory research. He believed that past experiences are organised in schemata, forming a whole that influences decision-making in the present. Van Dijken (1998, p. 43) referred to the many similarities between Bartlett's work and Bowlby's later work. Both regarded observation as a sound method for gathering data: "the data drawn on are observations of the behaviour of young children in real-life situations" (Bowlby, 1969, p. 5). Both were interested in real life problems, in spite of the fact that psychoanalytic literature at the time was not paying much attention to these.

Like Bartlett, Bowlby used the concept of the schema: "members of all but the most primitive phyla are possessed of equipment that enables them to organise such information as they have about their world into schemata or maps" (Bowlby, 1969, p. 48). Additionally, both valued research on primitive cultures as giving insight into contemporary human culture. It would be reasonable to believe that Bartlett was a good intellectual role model for Bowlby at the crucial sensitive period of his university education.

Rather than going straight to Medical College, Bowlby wanted to have an experience observing and working with children. In September 1928, he started a job at Bedales Junior School (Dunhurst) that was serving boys and girls from six to twelve years. The Dunhurst curriculum was based on Montessori principles. He realised how much there was to be learned about education, but he was unhappy about the multitude and diversity of duties expected of him, as these prevented him from getting to know the children well: "one cannot be expected to deal with children properly before one knows them thoroughly" (Bowlby's letter to his mother, 1 December 1928, quoted in Van Dijken, 1998, p. 51).

At the end of 1928, Bowlby decided to move on. For the next six months he worked at Priory Gate School in Norfolk – a progressive mixed school, operating on psychoanalytic principles, for maladjusted children aged three to eighteen. This experience ignited his curiosity about human development:

> One boy of eight years followed me around all day every day, so I became familiar with him and developed an attachment to him. An opposite experience that occurred involved a boy of fifteen or sixteen who had been thrown out of a well-known school. He was very emotionally shut-up in character ... and had had a much disrupted early childhood ... and the opinion of the people running the school was that such an experience in his early childhood had caused his current condition. So that was the origin of all that I've followed ever since.
>
> *(Bowlby's interview, January 1990, quoted in Tondo, 2012, pp. 16–17)*

Bowlby's father died on 7 April 1929 when Bowlby still was at Priory Gate. He did not refer to his father's death in any of the letters to his mother. On the advice of John Alford, his mentor at the school for whom he had great respect, he decided to pursue a career as a child psychiatrist. For this, the first step was coming to London in the autumn of 1929 to study clinical medicine at University College Hospital.

At the end of that year, he started his personal analysis, also called training analysis. This lasted nearly 10 years, during which he successfully completed his medical studies and general psychiatric training. The latter, from 1933 to 1936, was under the mentorship of Aubrey Lewis at the Maudsley Hospital. Lewis was also a good role model who helped him develop an enquiring, sceptical mind that would protect him from dogmatic beliefs.

By the time of his appointment to train and work as a child psychiatrist at the London Child Guidance Clinic in 1936, Bowlby was a well-trained, open-minded and intellectually powerful professional. He had developed a sort of attachment to three strangers – Bartlett, Alford and Lewis. Each of them provided a positive role model for him. In some way, they became *paternal* figures in his life from whom he learned a great deal. Maybe they partly compensated for Bowlby's father who was largely absent and to some extent a stranger.

I can imagine that the lack of a warm, intimate and continuous relationship with his father might have made it more difficult for him to grieve his father's death. The quality of attachment with his father appeared to have been predominantly avoidant. However, with the passage of time, Bowlby increasingly used explicit surgical metaphors in his writings. Was this perhaps a late homage to his not so estranged father, whom he admired as a successful surgeon and hard-working man?

I wonder if his strict Kleinian analysis with Joan Riviere may have provided Bowlby with a facilitating-enough environment for him to emotionally work through his difficult bereavement. He would later say about his analyst:

> Mrs Riviere was a tall good looking woman, always well turned out.... Her voice and manner were often a little haughty and she sometimes seemed rather

patronising … I was in analysis with Mrs Riviere for ten years 1929–39 which was too long. After the war I used occasionally to have supper with her at her house before a Society meeting. She was supportive of my work, though I suspect she did not regard it as psychoanalysis, since she held strong views that psychoanalysis was in no way concerned with external events…. During the thirties and forties she was a close friend of Mrs Klein, but later, she told me, she felt she had no place in the circle of disciples that came to surround Mrs Klein.

(quoted in Kahr, 2012, p. 36)

Bowlby appeared to have formed an ambivalent attachment with his analyst. Was it secure enough?

Bowlby's education in evolutionary biology, developmental psychology, clinical medicine, eclectic psychiatry, Freudian ideas and Kleinian psychoanalysis proved to be a powerful combination. This he exploited conspicuously in the 60 or so years that followed his transforming experience at Priory Gate. Studying the early mother–child relationship, and the impact that deprivation of maternal care would have on the child's development, became his priority. His work at the London Child Guidance Clinic provided further evidence for him to suggest that children raised in institutions may develop significant emotional problems, since they had had no chance to form a close bond to a parent. As a number of the depressed patients whom he was seeing at the time had suffered recent bereavement, he also started to make links between depression and loss.

His initial ideas were presented in a ground-breaking paper: "The Influence of Early Environment in the Development of Neurosis and Neurotic Character" (Bowlby, 1940). Bowlby later called this paper the first statement of his position (Bowlby et al., 1986). He had been made aware before this of the difficulty of convincing his sceptical psychoanalytic colleagues of this causal relationship. Thus, he tried his best to deliver the dissertation in a non-controversial and palatable form. This, in fact, enabled him to become a full member of the British Psychoanalytical Society (see Chapter 2).

Bowlby's first formal research publication, *Forty-Four Juvenile Thieves: Their Characters and Home Life* (Bowlby, 1944, 1946b), was well received and gave him due recognition in the wider mental health community. Following his appointment as Director of the Children's Department at the Tavistock Clinic, in 1946, he soon created a *Separation Research Unit*. The timing was right, as Britain had been severely traumatised by massive war-time separations and losses.

Bowlby's work received international appreciation. Ronald Hargreaves, Chief of the Mental Health Section of the World Health Organization (WHO), contacted him at the end of 1949. He originally proposed an extended research on juvenile delinquency for the WHO, but Bowlby declined. Hargreaves then suggested a report on some of the many homeless children who had been orphaned during the war. Bowlby accepted this and wrote to his wife Ursula to let her know how pleased he was with the assignment and, also, with Hargreaves' compliment that his research on separation was one of the most important happenings in mental health at the time.

He also conveyed his enthusiasm with the new appointment: "the job looks very much to my liking" (Bowlby's letter to Ursula, January 1950, in Van Dijken, 1998, p. 145). This work put him in close contact with leading figures in child development research in the USA, such as William Goldfarb, Rene Spitz, Loretta Bender and Milton Senn. It was reassuring for him to learn that they had been independently coming to similar conclusions. However, he felt that the research findings needed the flesh of a good theory that would make them more meaningful.

With a disquiet mind, Bowlby made a synthesis of expert opinions, including his own, and delivered a ground-breaking document for the WHO in the summer of 1950 – while still attempting to figure out a coherent theoretical framework. The report was published the following year as a monograph, *Maternal Care and Mental Health* (Bowlby, 1951). He was determined to communicate his message to the general public and a popular edition of his work was soon published under the title *Child Care and the Growth of Love* (Bowlby, 1953a). This became an instant bestseller and was soon translated into ten other languages.

Bowlby had concluded that prolonged deprivation of maternal care for the young child may have grave and far-reaching effects on his character and emotional wellbeing: "mother-love in infancy and childhood is as important for mental health as are vitamins and proteins for physical health" (Bowlby, 1951, p. 158). He conceived maternal care in a broad sense – meaning that it can be provided by either parent or by relatives, or carers, acting as substitutes for the parents. For him, the quality and consistency of the *mothering* is what really matters and, although this role is usually played by the biological mother, "adoption can give a child nearly as good a chance of a happy home life as that of the child brought up in his own home" (ibid., p. 108).

Bowlby was especially sensitive to the needs of homeless children. In his view, the proper care of those children severely deprived of ordinary home life is essential for both the child's health and the social welfare of a community. He ultimately saw childhood deprivation as a social problem: "Deprived children, whether in their own homes or out of them, are a source of social infection as real and serious as are carriers of diphtheria and typhoid" (ibid., p. 157).

Being consistent with his clinical practice at the Tavistock (see Chapter 4), Bowlby did not study the child in isolation. For him, child welfare and family welfare are two sides of the same coin, which should be linked. He made calls for supportive social networks for the parents to maximise healthy relationships in the family: "If a community values its children it must cherish their parents" (ibid., p. 84).

The work for the WHO had a far-reaching effect on Bowlby's professional development. However, throughout his career he would always be guided by a principle that "evidence is never complete … knowledge of truth is always partial, and to await certainty is to await eternity" (ibid., p. 158). This attitude enabled him to be curious and open-minded in his search for further evidence.

Noticeably, the word attachment was not included in the index of his *Child Care* book. But he was actively working on it: "If disruption of a bond had such powerful emotional effects, what is the nature of the bond which is being disrupted?" (Bowlby's 1990 interview, quoted in Tondo, 2012, pp. 17–18). That is the question that was top of his mind in 1951. He thought that trying to answer this basic and fundamental question was worth a whole professional life.

And the trouble began ...

Norman Hotoph, a psychologist and acquaintance of Bowlby, drew his attention to Lorenz's work with new-born goslings. Hotoph asked Bowlby: "Do you know the work of Konrad Lorenz on imprinting? I think it would interest you" (Bowlby's 1990 interview, quoted in Tondo, 2012, p. 18). That was a stray remark made at the end of a committee meeting in July 1951. And well-timed. Bowlby soon obtained an English translation of Lorenz's article *Der Kumpan in der Umvelt des Vogels* (The Companion in the Bird's World), which was originally published in 1935, and found it thought-provoking. Was this serendipity?

Bowlby had been interested in natural history since his childhood. During his upbringing, a positivist idea of science (something that had developed during the Victorian era) was becoming increasingly prominent in Britain. Things had to be proved rather than speculated upon. In his youth, he regularly observed and identified plants and animals under the guidance of his mother and grandfather. They read natural history books aloud to him, which stimulated his love for nature. Marcus Johns, consultant child psychiatrist at the Tavistock Clinic in the 1980s, told me that he was struck by Bowlby's knowledge and descriptions of the trees and plants that surrounded the Clinic, as emerged during some of their informal chats at break times.

As an adolescent, Bowlby had been a fervent beetle collector, as well as an enthusiastic bird watcher and bird photographer. (Incidentally, his eldest son, Sir Richard Bowlby, became a professional medical and scientific photographer.) In their summer holiday in Scotland in July 1951, the Bowlbys received a visit from Julian Huxley who was a friend of Ursula's family and the brother of Aldous Huxley (see Chapter 8). Julian Huxley later became a well-known British evolutionary biologist – being considered one of the early ecologists. Bowlby was intrigued by Lorenz's work but uncertain about its value for humans; he asked Julian Huxley if he knew anything about Lorenz and ethology. That led to an enthusiastic commendation from the biologist who knew Lorenz well and who had done work of his own in the field.

In fact, Julian Huxley had written the foreword to the English translation of *King Solomon's Ring*, Lorenz's (1952) new book which was due to be published the following winter. He promised to get an advance copy for Bowlby (Karen, 1998, p. 453). At a later stage in his career, Julian Huxley studied how cultural traits may stay in a society and persist over generations. Conversely, Bowlby was to develop an interest in the transmission of attachment patterns through generations. (I cannot help thinking that some of the idiosyncratic cultural and character traits described by Miguel de Cervantes in *Don Quixote*, 400 years ago, may still be relevant to contemporary Spanish society.)

Julian Huxley also encouraged Bowlby to read Nikolaas Tinbergen's (1951) work on the nature of instincts. Bowlby later remarked:

> I spent the whole winter of 1952–53 studying ethology, and that's how it all started. The more I studied it, the more impressed I was by the high scientific quality of their work and the extent to which they were studying in other species, problems similar to our own in the clinical field. So I became a great enthusiast for the ethological approach, which led to my attachment theory.
>
> *(Bowlby's interview, January 1990, quoted in Tondo, 2012, p. 18)*

The information obtained from ethological methods of observing animals in their natural environment inspired Bowlby and gave him a confidence boost – at a time when he and his 'separation' research unit were thriving. But he could not have imagined the hornet's nest he would later disturb.

Following Bowlby's death, Ainsworth (1990, p. 13) paid tribute to him and recalled his intellectual eagerness during the early 1950s, which coincided with the time she was working with him at the Tavistock: "It is my conviction that Bowlby's attachment theory began with a sudden flash of insight, sparked by ethology, that led to a scientific revolution". After years of searching for an explanation of the true nature of the mother–child attachment, he now had a hunch that the formation of early social bonds did not need to be tied to feeding or sex.

Indeed, as I discussed earlier, many authors had previously referred to attachment, but it is remarkable that no one before Bowlby had been able to formulate it so accurately and clearly. In order to put together a well-constructed and meaningful theory from something so basic and obvious, Bowlby had to work hard and fight quite a few battles. These extended over the next three decades: from his insights in the early 1950s to the publication of the last volume of his trilogy on *Attachment and Loss* in 1980 (see Chapter 6).

Bowlby made an initial attempt to introduce ethological concepts in an original paper, "The Contribution of Studies of Animal Behaviour" (Bowlby, 1953b). An elaborated version of this paper was published the same year, under the title "Critical Phases in the Development of Social Responses in Man and other Animals" (Bowlby, 1953c). His new ideas were received with some degree of suspicion, even by his Tavistock research colleagues – who were sceptical about the value that ethology might have for the understanding of the mother–child relationship.

Mary Ainsworth, his much trusted research partner, at one point commented that, though much enamoured of ethology, she was somewhat wary of the direction Bowlby's theorising was beginning to take. It was obvious to Ainsworth at the time that "a baby loves his mother because she satisfies his needs" (quoted in Bretherton, 1992, p. 767). Bowlby and Ainsworth had quite prolonged debates on ethology before she left for Uganda in 1954, which might have influenced her to develop her own ethological orientation (Smuts, 1977).

As a good scientist, Bowlby did not want to draw premature conclusions. Although enthusiastic and determined, he was unprejudiced and cautious in his explorations into the emerging field of ethology. He continued learning from his direct clinical work and from his child development research. He found it useful to study Piaget's (1951, 1953, 1954) new empirical work on cognitive and psychosocial child development.

Additionally, Bowlby took an active part in a WHO's study group on the *Psychobiology of the Child.* This was a forum of world experts who met monthly in Geneva, between 1953 and 1956. The meetings were attended by Ludwig von Bertalanffy, Julian Huxley, Erick Erikson, Jean Piaget, Margaret Mead, Konrad Lorenz, James Tanner, Barbel Inhelder and others. It was in this forum where, at the end of 1953, Lorenz told Bowlby about a young Cambridge ethologist by the name of Robert Hinde.

Bowlby and Hinde met for the first time in London in February 1954 during a scientific meeting on ethology and psychiatry – which was organised by the Royal Medico-Psychological Association. Each of them read a paper and afterwards had lunch together. Bowlby was vastly impressed by Hinde's expertise and invited him to join a weekly research seminar at the Tavistock – where professionals with wildly diverging views discussed clinical cases (Smuts, 1977). That was a mutually enriching experience.

Bowlby (1991a) reported that he was trying to master the principles of ethology and that, as a *student* of a new discipline, he very much appreciated Hinde's tutorship. On the other hand, Hinde said that it was difficult to describe the excitement of the seminars, which for him were "a very important scientific experience" (quoted in Van der Horst et al., 2007). Over the years, he widely used Bowlby's insights for his experimental and naturalistic studies of social separation in non-human primates.

In the next few years, Bowlby continued working towards an integration of concepts from psychoanalysis and ethology, as well as from cognitive and learning theories. Eventually, he became confident enough to produce a landmark paper, "The Nature of the Child's Tie to His Mother" (Bowlby, 1958a), in which he outlined the initial scheme of his attachment theory. Bowlby showed the draft to Hinde for his comments before the official presentation at the British Psycho-analytical Society on 19 June 1957. Prior to introducing ethological concepts, the paper reviewed current knowledge of child development and challenged the main four contemporary explanations of the child's tie to the mother. These were as follows:

- First, a 'cupboard-love' theory. This referred to affection that is given to gain a reward. The physiological and libidinal needs of the infant are met by the mother, through which he gradually learns to love the mother as the source of such gratifications.

- Second, a primary 'object-sucking' theory. This stated that the infant has a built-in need to orally attach to a 'breast'. Subsequently, he learns the breast is attached to the mother and then relates to her as well.

- Third, a primary 'object-clinging' theory. This described a built-in need the infant has to touch and cling to the mother or to another human being, which is as important as the need for food.

- Fourth, a primary desire for 'returning to the womb' theory. This postulated that attachment is basically a craving for regaining the unity that mother and baby had before birth.

Bowlby considered that, in some way, his own formulations related to the theories of primary object sucking and clinging; but he went far beyond these theories. To support his views, he reviewed empirical studies and research on child development, as well as his own research and direct clinical work and observations. In the previous 12 or so years, he had been running an ongoing, weekly support group at a well-baby clinic. In this group he made regular longitudinal observations of a random sample of babies and young children interacting with their mothers. He also learned about these mothers' day-to-day experiences with their children.

In the second part of the paper, Bowlby introduced the idea of a set of 'instinctual social releasers', including (among others): sucking, clinging, following, and the signalling behaviours of smiling and crying, directed at eliciting social responses from the mother and forming a bond with her. He explained that, through clinging and following, the child actively seeks to keep proximity to the mother. On the other hand, he observed that crying and smiling are also powerful social releasers of maternal behaviour.

Bowlby incorporated animal studies that showed the mother responding immediately to a cry of the offspring. He remarked that although the human infant's cry is frequently terminated by being fed, babies very often cry when they are not hungry, but frightened, distressed or in any other need. They will habitually stop crying after being picked up, rocked, or talked to – that is, through an attachment relationship. He also noted that the smile has an effect that is comparable to crying but more agreeable.

McCluskey (2002, p. 138) elaborated on this: "eye contact is the greatest source of information and emotional connection between the nonverbal infant and his or her caregiver". In healthy babies, social smiling is clearly present by the sixth week, often much earlier. Human faces are equipped with the most sophisticated system of muscles of all living beings. The mutually dependent muscular movements that need coordinating to produce a smile are extremely complex.

Bowlby (1958a, pp. 366–367) emphasised that a baby's smile powerfully attracts the mother unless she is impaired – for instance, by severe trauma or depression. Healthy smiling promotes attachment: "Can we doubt that the more and better an infant smiles the better is he loved and cared for?" Bowlby often smiled in our supervision sessions, which was deeply engaging. He at one point told me that it is important for patients to be able to find themselves reflected in the face of the therapist. And this comment came from someone who had been in personal analysis for 10 years, five times a week, lying on the couch!

Other psychoanalytic and group-analytic thinkers have used the *mirror* metaphor to describe the face of the mother in relation to the face of the child (Pines, 1998). Interestingly, in the second half of the nineteenth century, Charles Darwin had studied the expression of emotions in humans and other species and paid attention to a child's reaction to his mirror image. And, in the first half of the sixteenth century, the Spaniard Bartolomé de las Casas (1474–1566) had observed the Native American Indians' fascination at seeing their own images reflected in the mirrors that the *conquistadores* brought from Spain to the New World.

Human beings have developed the most expressive faces on Earth, which are fundamental for attachment. Something similar could be said of the musculature of the human hand, which is crucial in order for the infant to reach out when seeking proximity to an attachment figure. In "The Child's Tie" paper, Bowlby was beginning to advance the idea that *attachment* is a two-way system of stimuli and responses that mutually influence one another. For him, these stimuli and responses can be both external and intra-psychic. In contrast to his psychoanalytic predecessors and contemporaries, he proposed a scientifically updated understanding of the concept of *attachment*.

While acknowledging that the term had been used before in psychoanalytic and psychological theorising (by Freud and a number of other authors) Bowlby challenged the view that attachment was a 'secondary drive' to satisfy primary libidinal and physiological needs:

> Psychological attachment and detachment are to be regarded as functions in their own right apart altogether from the extent to which the child happens at any moment to be dependent on the object for his physiological needs being met. These [attachment functions] were independent of the need to be fed and the satisfaction of sensuous need.
>
> *(Bowlby, 1958a, p. 371)*

Unequivocally, he considered this hunger for attachment at least as basic as the desires for food and sex.

Bowlby (1991a, p. 29) would later recall in his autobiographical paper:

> The crunch came when I presented The Child's Tie paper. I had shown a copy to a friend beforehand and, without my knowing, it had been passed to members of the Kleinian group. A number of them spoke in the discussion, criticising first one aspect then another.

Other colleagues received Bowlby's ideas with respect but without any enthusiasm.

Anna Freud did not go into an outright attack – that had never been her style. In fact, as a reaction to witnessing the Kleinian hostility towards Bowlby, she commented: "Dr Bowlby is too valuable a person to get lost to psychoanalysis" (quoted in Grosskurth, 1986, p. 404). But to say that he was cold-shouldered by her response to the paper would be an understatement. Bowlby commented: "She banned it" (quoted in Karen, 1998, p. 113). She was probably anxious to protect her father's legacy. Nevertheless, the relationship between Bowlby and Anna Freud stayed on cordial terms; they shared concerns about the wellbeing of children as well as approaches to treatment.

In some psychoanalytic circles, as in other fields, an allegiance to a particular theory can represent a complex set of emotional commitments – to one's own analyst, supervisor or mentor. It may also represent a loyalty to oneself and to the way one has worked with patients. So, to challenge an existing theory may sometimes be tantamount to threatening the meaning of one's own previous work. Anna Freud and, especially, Melanie Klein expected strong loyalty from their followers.

Bowlby challenged drive theory and the death instinct. And underplayed the role of the *Oedipus complex*! The emotional reaction that many colleagues had to his *re-evolutionary* theory prevented them from realising that attachment was of huge consequence. In 1997, the Australian journalist Peter Ellingsen came to London to interview British psychoanalysts. He was struck by the fact that a large number of them made dismissive comments about Bowlby's work while admitting that they had not read it (Marrone, 1998, p. 26). Sadly enough, 30 years after the initial blueprint of attachment theory, leading Kleinian analysts like Hanna Segal believed that Bowlby "was attacking psychoanalysis and that his goal was to destroy it" (Karen, 1998, p. 112).

In his book *The Structure of Scientific Revolutions*, Thomas Kuhn (1962) provides an explanation of resistance to conceptual change. His analysis is that, in the development of science, the first accepted paradigm is frequently considered to be the essential explanatory truth. In his view, however, the evolution of scientific knowledge requires the periodic renewal of paradigms; any subsequent attempt to change the original paradigm meets considerable resistance in scientific communities. Additionally, "scientists are political beings and resistance to theoretical and methodological change often takes the form of political action" (Marrone, 1998, p. 113).

In her remembrances following Bowlby's death, Ainsworth recalled that attachment theory was initially met with a hostile reception by psychoanalysts, despite the fact that he tried to frame his arguments in a non-contentious way. She admired the manner in which Bowlby reacted to these antagonistic criticisms:

> He persisted in expositions of his new approach without feeling it necessary to be defensive and with no sign of reactive hostility. Although undoubtedly feeling quite confident that he was on the right track and recognising the difficulty encountered by those thoroughly dedicated to one theoretical paradigm, in accommodating themselves to a new one.
>
> *(Ainsworth, 1990, p. 13)*

The concept of attachment, like the concepts of gravity, evolution and the unconscious mind, is now well established. Attachment is no longer a theory. It is understood to be a vital component of our social existence, present from cradle to grave. But reaching this conclusion took time – and there were further obstacles getting in the way, as we shall see in the next chapter.

6

CROSS-FERTILIZATION IN THE DEVELOPMENT OF ATTACHMENT THEORY

Bowlby had turned 50 a few months before presenting his initial sketch of attachment theory at the British Psychoanalytical Society. He was in his prime and a force to be reckoned with. He was prominent at home and abroad, in child psychiatry, hospital paediatric units, social work, adoption agencies and ordinary homes. Additionally, his publications were powerful, persuasive, clearly grounded on a thorough knowledge of psychoanalytic and other developmental theories, as well as on updated scientific studies (Karen, 1998, p. 115).

Bowlby's eldest son, Sir Richard Bowlby, intimated to me that his father was deeply hurt by the hostile response received from his psychoanalytic colleagues at the presentation of "The Nature of the Child's Tie to his Mother" paper on 19 June 1957. Richard was 16 at the time. He can still recall that his father expected intellectual debate and opposition but not personal hostility. In September that year, Bowlby, accompanied by Ursula and their eldest daughter Mary, went to Palo Alto in California for nine and a half months: an academic year sabbatical at the Center for Advanced Study in the Behavioral Sciences (CASBS). Richard, with his younger sister Pia and younger brother Robert visited the family for the Christmas and New Year holidays.

CASBS was founded in 1954 and has hosted generations of scholars and scientists who usually come for a year as Fellows, as Bowlby did. Former Fellows include 22 Nobel Laureates, 14 Pulitzer Prize winners, 44 winners of MacArthur Genius Awards and hundreds of members of the National Academies. Fellows have played key roles in starting new fields, ranging from cognitive science to behavioural economics to the sociology of urban poverty, and have developed new policies and practices in fields as diverse as medicine, education and electoral politics.

During his sabbatical, Bowlby had breathing space from the conflict generated by "The Child's Tie" paper at home. He felt reasonably confident that he was on the right track and hoped that by his return to London he would have gathered additional evidence to persuade his psychoanalytic colleagues that his attachment hypothesis made sense. He worked intensely in reviewing experimental and developmental research, as well as psychoanalytic literature.

During his time at CASBS, Bowlby wrote two further papers that were intended to be chapters in the single volume monograph on attachment that he was planning to write. Things, of course, would turn out differently. The first paper was "Separation Anxiety", of which two versions were published (Bowlby, 1960a, 1961a). The second paper was "Grief and Mourning in Infancy and Early Childhood" of which three versions were published (Bowlby, 1960b, 1961b, 1961c). Both articles were to consolidate the hypothesis he had advanced in "The Child's Tie" paper (Bowlby, 1958a). Interestingly, each of the three papers would constitute an embryo of each of the three volumes of his future trilogy – Volume 1: *Attachment*; Volume 2: *Separation: Anxiety and Anger*; and Volume 3: *Loss: Sadness and Depression* (Bowlby, 1969, 1973, 1980).

Bowlby was particularly mindful after the rebuff to which he had been subjected at home and actively sought to make meaningful contacts with his American colleagues. Among them, he made friends with David Eaton, an open-minded political scientist, and with Frank Newman, a lawyer with an interest in the resolution of conflict – something that Bowlby was experiencing first-hand with his psychoanalytic colleagues. He also made an important connection with the psychologist and ethologist Harry Harlow, who became a significant influence and provided a bridge to the scientific observation and study of attachment that Bowlby had long sought.

Harlow was born in 1905 and married Clara Mears in 1932. She had been one of his most talented students. They had two children together but divorced in 1946. That same year, Harlow married child psychologist Margaret Kuenne. They were very close and Harlow became deeply depressed when cancer killed her in September 1971. He was treated with electro-convulsive therapy but was only able to overcome his depression after he remarried Clara Mears in March 1972. They lived together until his death in 1981.

A detailed description of the scientific and personal relationship between Bowlby and Harlow, upon which the following passages are based, can be found in Frank Van der Horst (2011) and Van der Horst et al. (2008). Just a couple of months prior to Bowlby's controversial presentation of "The Child's Tie" paper at the British Psychoanalytical Society, Harlow had given a talk on *Experimental Analysis of Behaviour* at a conference in Washington DC on 20 April 1957. He emphasised the importance of developing longitudinal studies – a departure from the traditional cross-sectional approach employed by most psychologists at the time. Harlow was on the threshold of his rhesus monkey affectional studies, something that grabbed Bowlby's attention. Their mutual interest in socio-emotional behaviour and development directed Bowlby and Harlow to a fruitful period of intellectual collaboration.

Bowlby introduced himself to Harlow by letter:

Robert Hinde tells me that you were interested in my recent paper... and at his suggestion I am now sending you a copy.... I would be most grateful for any comments and criticism you care to make. I shall be at the centre at Palo Alto from mid-September.... Hinde told me of your experimental work on maternal responses in monkeys. If you have any papers or typescripts, I would be very grateful for them.... I would try to visit you next Spring when I hope to be moving around USA.

(Bowlby's letter to Harlow, 8 August 1957, quoted in Van der Horst et al., 2008)

Harlow replied by return of post, thanking Bowlby for the paper, which he would later describe as a 'reference bible'. They exchanged eight additional letters before Bowlby attended one of Harlow's lectures on 26 April 1958. After this first encounter, Bowlby wrote to Ursula with great enthusiasm:

You may remember I went to hear ... Harry Harlow of Wisconsin on mother infant interaction in monkeys. His stuff is a tremendous confirmation of the Child's Tie paper, which he quoted. Afterwards Chris [Heinicke] heard him remark, in very good humour, to a friend: 'You know, I thought I had got hold of a really original idea ... to find that bastard Bowlby had beaten me to it'! This is not really true. I think we can say it's a dead heat – the work of each supports the other. We had a very amiable chat [and] arranged to meet in June.

(Bowlby's letter to Ursula, 28 April 1958, quoted in Van der Horst et al., 2008)

As promised, Bowlby visited Harlow at his Madison laboratory in June that year for a couple of days and on 26 June wrote to thank him for his hospitality: "I shall look forward to keeping in touch ... I hope too you will put me on your list to send mimeograph versions as and when your stuff goes further forward. We will reciprocate". The earlier formal salutations and closings 'Dear Professor Harlow' and 'Yours sincerely' or 'Dear Dr Bowlby' and 'Cordially' had changed to a much more informal tone, becoming 'Dear Harry' and 'Yours ever, John', or 'Dear John' and 'Best personal wishes, Harry' (in Van der Horst et al., 2008).

Bowlby's (1958a) first reference to Harlow's work appeared in the expanded version of "The Child's Tie" paper that was published by the *International Journal of Psychoanalysis*. In this version, Bowlby stated:

The longer I contemplated the diverse clinical evidence the more dissatisfied I became with the views current in psychoanalytical and psychological literature and the more I found myself turning to the ethnologists for help. The extent to which I have drawn on concepts of ethology will be apparent.

(Bowlby, 1958a, p. 351)

He particularly used Harlow's observations of non-human primates, published in "The Nature of Love" later that year (Harlow, 1958), to challenge the idea that attachment develops through oral gratification.

Bowlby considered his hypothesis on attachment was "rooted firmly in biological theory and requires no dynamic which is not plainly explicable in terms of the survival of the species" (Bowlby, 1958a, p. 369). His insights received further backing in a piece of ethological research that would become widely known (Harlow & Zimmermann, 1959). In this study, infant rhesus monkeys were raised with two surrogate-mothers; one made of bale-wire mesh, the other covered with terry cloth. Even when the 'bale-wire mother' was the only one providing food, the infant monkeys became more attached to the 'terry-cloth mother', cuddling it, running to it when frightened, and using it as a base for explorations. These findings stimulated rethinking about the nature of human attachment.

In order to frame his hypotheses, Bowlby paid more attention to direct observation of infants and young children in their relationship with their mothers than to retrospective inferences from the psychoanalysis of adult patients – upon which Freud based his early theorising. Bowlby also reframed some of the concepts of traditional psychoanalysis and social learning theory such as 'dependency' and 'regression'. He explained these phenomena as a reactivation of attachment behaviour, in the face of threats or difficulties, and viewed such response as natural and healthy in all stages of human development:

> In much theorizing … all manifestations of attachment behaviour after infancy are conceived as 'regressive'. Since this term inevitably carries with it the connotation pathological or, at least, undesirable, I regard it as misleading and failing to do justice to the facts.
>
> *(Bowlby, 1958a, p. 371)*

After his sabbatical in California, Bowlby attended the 21st Congress of the International Psychoanalytical Association in Copenhagen in July 1959. He read a paper on "Ethology and the Development of Object Relations" in which he amalgamated ethological and psychoanalytic insights. That was eight years after his interest in ethology had been aroused, initially by Lorenz's work on imprinting. During this time, Bowlby had been cautious about the value of ethological research. However, he published three papers in which he started to tentatively explore possible links between psychoanalysis and ethology (Bowlby, 1953b, 1953c, 1957).

At the Copenhagen conference, Bowlby showed that his inclination toward ethology was on the increase:

> The further I read and the more ethologists I met the more I felt a kinship with them. Here were first-rate scientists studying the family life of lower species who were not only making observations that were at least analogous to those made of human family life but whose interests, like those of analysts, lay in the field of instinctive behaviour, conflict, and the many surprising and sometimes pathological outcomes of conflict…. A main reason I value ethology is that it gives us a wide range of new concepts to try out in our theorizing.
>
> *(Bowlby, 1960c, p. 313)*

Bowlby was careful about extrapolating or generalising from one species to another. However, he justified the importance of animal research in providing a better understanding of human social behaviour:

> Man is a species in his own right with certain unusual characteristics. It may be therefore that none of the ideas stemming from studies of lower species is relevant. Yet this seems improbable.... We share anatomical and physiological features with lower species, and it would be odd were we to share none of the behavioural features which go with them.
>
> *(ibid., p. 314)*

In his attempt to further understand the instinctual response systems present in the infant, which facilitate the attachment to a mother figure, even when she is not participating actively, Bowlby referred to Harlow and Zimmermann's surrogate mother research:

> A new born monkey will cling to a dummy provided it is soft and comfortable. The provision of food and warmth are quite unnecessary. These young creatures follow for the sake of following and cling for the sake of clinging.
>
> *(ibid., p. 314)*

Thus, he was determined to emphasise that, although related to them, attachment occurs independently from feeding and sexual gratification.

In discussing some of the consequences of disrupting the early mother–infant bond, Bowlby also mentioned the substitution of one type of behaviour by another; for example, thumb sucking or overeating when denied maternal access. He drew a parallel with non-nutritive sucking in chimpanzees and rhesus monkeys:

> In Harlow's laboratory I have seen a full-grown rhesus female who habitually sucked her own breast and a male who sucked his penis. Both had been reared in isolation. In these cases what we should all describe as oral symptoms had developed as a result of depriving the infant of a relationship with a mother-figure.... May it not be the same for oral symptoms in human infants?
>
> *(ibid., p. 316)*

Further controversies

In the autumn of 1959, Bowlby presented at the British Psychoanalytical Society the paper on "Separation Anxiety" (Bowlby, 1960a, 1961a) that he had written during his California sabbatical. He structured the presentation in a rigorous way (Bretherton, 1991), similar to "The Child's Tie" paper. He started with a critical review of traditional psychoanalytic theories of anxiety related to the child's attachment to the mother conceived as a secondary drive. He suggested that none of these theories alone was sufficient to explain the intensity of young children's attachment to a mother figure and their extreme responses to separation. He postulated that separation anxiety is primarily experienced when attachment behaviour is activated but there is no adequate response to it, so it cannot be shut off or terminated.

Bowlby referred to the work of his Tavistock research unit and added new insights from ethology. He recalled Laura, the two-year-old child filmed by Robertson in 1952 (see Chapter 4), and compared her response with a strange man entering her room to the behaviour of the infant rhesus monkeys who froze in a bent posture when facing a strange situation in the absence of mother. He discussed the experiments of Harlow and Zimmermann (1958) from whom he took the concept of 'haven of safety': "One function of the real mother, human or sub-human, and presumably of a mother surrogate, is to provide a haven of safety for the infant in times of fear or danger" (Bowlby, 1960a, p. 97). He later replaced this with the notion of a 'secure base' (Bowlby, 1973) from which to explore – for which he gave full credit to Mary Ainsworth (1967) who formulated this concept following her research studies in Uganda.

The difference between safety and security became important in Bowlby's thinking (see Chapter 9). He would conceive safety mainly in relation to external circumstances; if there is external danger, the child would be frightened or fearful in the absence of a haven of safety. On the other hand, Bowlby would relate security more to the internal experience; the child can be anxious, without there being an external frightening stimulus, if the mother is not available. The child may also experience 'expectant anxiety' in situations where he anticipates that mother is not likely to be available. However, a child held in his mother's arms may feel secure even when the external situation is unsafe – as in the case of a storm or military bombing.

Internal experience and external circumstances intertwine. Bowlby described situations in which extreme separation anxiety was due to repeated threats of abandonment or to serious illnesses in the family – especially when the child is blamed for these. Liza Glenn, a fellow supervisee of Bowlby, told me that he once referred to having heard in a playground, on more than one occasion, mothers threatening to abandon their child or saying: "You'll be the death of me!"

Bowlby also described situations where separation anxiety might be paradoxically low or absent, due to defensive processes, which can give a misleading impression of maturity or self-reliance. Additionally, he suggested that 'overprotection' is a mis-nomer, often an expression of parental anxiety projected onto the child – sometimes a type of overcompensation for unresolved unconscious hostility in the parent towards the child.

In a further scientific meeting at the British Psychoanalytical Society at the end of 1959, Bowlby presented the other controversial paper that he had drafted during his sabbatical: "Grief and Mourning in Infancy and Early Childhood" (Bowlby, 1960b, 1961b, 1961c). He confronted the prevailing psychoanalytic views that very young children cannot mourn because they are immature and their ego has not developed sufficiently, and that infantile narcissism is an obstacle to the experience of grief upon loss of a loved object. He also challenged Melanie Klein's assertion that weaning is the greatest loss in infancy. For him mourning in infancy is triggered by the loss or unavailability of the primary attachment figure, rather than the loss of the feeding breast.

Bowlby emphasised the importance of evidence from direct observations and described similarities between children and adults with regard to processes of mourning. These included: longing for the lost person, hostility, appeals for help, despair, disorganisation and reorganisation. In addition to longing, bereaved young children frequently become aggressive and reject the care offered by other people before they are able to accept a new primary attachment figure. He also looked at childhood mourning from an evolutionary perspective: "In the light of phylogeny it is likely that the instinctual bonds that tie human young to a mother figure are built on the same general pattern as in other mammalian species" (Bowlby, 1961c, p. 482).

The papers on "Separation Anxiety" and on "Childhood Mourning" were received with as much hostility as "The Nature of the Child's Tie" paper. Some considered that the response was even more heated (Karen, 1998). Negative comments came not only from the Kleinians and the Freudians, but also from the Independent Group. Guntrip wrote:

> I think it is very good for an eminent psychoanalyst to have gone thoroughly into the relationship between ethology and psychoanalysis, but my impression is that he succeeds in using it to explain everything in human behaviour except what is of vital importance for psychoanalysis.
>
> *(quoted in Holmes, 1993, p. 28)*

Donald Winnicott, President of the British Psychoanalytical Society at the time, wrote to Anna Freud, as quoted by Holmes (1993, p. 28): "I can't quite make out why it is that Bowlby's papers are building up in me a kind of revulsion although in fact he has been scrupulously fair to me in his writings". Adding to the highly emotional nature of the controversy, an unnamed psychoanalyst apparently exclaimed: "Bowlby? Give me Barabbas" (Grosskurth, 1986).

Even Joan Riviere, Bowlby's former analyst, was amongst those who protested. Only newcomers seemed to have been free enough from prejudice to openly defend him. David Malan, then a young analyst, became very upset by the strength of the hostile reactions against Bowlby and rose to his defence. Malan later recalled: "I went away somewhat terrified about the consequences of being so passionate a supporter of John's position – would I be excommunicated at once?" (quoted in Karen, 1998, p. 115). Anton Obholzer (former Chairman and Chief Executive of the Tavistock Clinic) recently told me that Malan's work, like Bowlby's, has been better appreciated outside the Tavistock than within the institution.

Bowlby, who had been Deputy President of the British Psychoanalytical Society in 1956 and 1957, was now intensely hurt. But, it seems, he managed to be phlegmatic enough about it. He would say in an interview with Smuts, in

1977: "Although in the natural course of things I might well have been elected the next president, it had become clear that there would be too much opposition and, with my agreement, those supporting me did not propose me" (quoted in Karen, 1998, p. 115).

Robert Karen further reported:

> Indeed, after the hellish response to his attachment papers, Bowlby decided to stop attending scientific meetings at the British Psychoanalytical Society. Unread, uncited, and unseen, he became the nonperson of British psychoanalysis, and was lost to his peers and to new psychoanalytic trainees for the better part of the next three decades.
>
> *(ibid., p. 115)*

It was exactly 30 years after the presentation of the blueprint of his attachment theory when, on behalf of the British Psychoanalytical Society, Pearl King publicly stated her regret that many members had been unable to appreciate Bowlby's important scientific contributions. She also regretted that he no longer felt at home after the vicious criticisms that he received from certain sections of the Society (King, 1991). She delivered the speech at Bowlby's 80th Birthday Conference, organised by the Tavistock in June 1987. Although he never discontinued his membership of the Society, a large number of colleagues assumed that he had abandoned psychoanalysis. Bowlby, however, saw himself as a psychoanalyst and defended his position by arguing the following:

> You can define psychoanalysis in one or two ways: one way is to refer to Freud's theories, which is very commonly done. An alternative is to refer to the phenomena to which he called attention, which, of course, is what I'm concerned with. My own position, regarding Freud's work, is that the phenomena to which he called attention are immensely important; but the theories he came up with are very dated and inadequate.
>
> *(Bowlby et al., 1986, p. 45)*

For the avoidance of doubt, Bowlby would further state that, historically, attachment theory was developed as a variant of object relations theory (Bowlby, 1988a).

Additionally, Bowlby was criticised by groups of feminists who interpreted his message that 'good mothering' was essential for a child's healthy development as being a threat to the independence of women. Advocates of feminism and women's rights were insisting on a mother's right to a career equal to that of her partner. Besides, two incomes were more often needed to meet household expenses. However, the crucial question is not whether a mother should stay at home or go out to work, but about other realities around the new-born, including father, extended family, wider kin group and community. Adequate support around the mother, whether at home or out at work would maximise the chance for her children to feel securely attached.

Many feminists gradually changed their views when they realised that they had misunderstood Bowlby's message and that there was no incompatibility between women's rights and good quality child care. In fact, an emotionally secure mother–child attachment enhances the wellbeing of the child, mother, father, family and, ultimately, society. Strongly committed feminists, like Anna Brave and Heidi Ferid, reconsidered the hostile views of the past and eventually came to feel comfortable enough with attachment theory:

> It is to Bowlby's credit that attachment theory in itself is not fundamentally sexist, but rather sees both genders as having equally deep attachment needs. He has taught us that, as the child is born innocent, he or she is also born with a need and an ability to form attachments. These we need to respect, rather than criticise.
>
> *(Brave & Ferid, 1990, p. 32)*

These authors also advocated greater levels of co-parenting as beneficial for the child, mother and father. 'Maternal' qualities are indeed present in fathers, in male therapists and to some degree in all men.

Peter Marris (1996) formulated larger questions about how resources and roles are allocated in society, about how flexibly work can be organised and about how people manage uncertainty – particularly those with the fewest social and economic resources. According to Marris, there is an increasing need for strategies of group co-operation and reciprocity rather than greed and financial profit, and these strategies should be deployed at both personal and political levels to maximise the chance of survival for all.

The skill, the will and the group

Bowlby was immensely talented – too valuable to be lost to psychoanalysis, as Anna Freud put it – and his will appeared to have been built to withstand bombs. Richard Bowlby told me that his father was a very loyal person – always wanting to be connected with his group of psychoanalytic colleagues and to offer them scientific food in order to make psychoanalysis stronger. So, how was he able to cope with the aggressive responses he received at the British Psychoanalytical Society?

According to Inge Bretherton (1991, 1992), Bowlby showed through his professional life a distinct ability to draw to himself outstanding individuals who were willing and able to help him acquire expertise in new fields of inquiry that he needed to master in the service of theory building. Individual enterprises are in fact group enterprises (Caparrós, 2004). At the Tavistock Clinic, Bowlby made important connections and collaborated with Robert Hinde, James Robertson, Colin Murray Parkes and quite a few others among whom Mary Ainsworth was particularly prominent: "a mutual admiration society", as Ursula put it (quoted in Karen, 1998, p. 434). Ainsworth especially admired Bowlby for not showing signs of reactive hostility (see Chapter 5).

In the early days of his career (see Chapter 3), Bowlby had written two papers on aggressiveness in children: "The Abnormally Aggressive Child" (Bowlby, 1938) and "Jealous and Spiteful Children" (Bowlby, 1939). I cannot help wondering if he might have been trying, in some way, to understand the complex relationship with his brother Tony. Their brotherly friendship contained episodes of sibling rivalry, jealousy and physical fights during their childhood, as portrayed in Holmes (1993) and Van Dijken (1998). There is also much evidence to suggest that Bowlby learned to manage his own aggressiveness and became an assertive person – a crucial distinction, as there might be a fine line between the two (Parkes & Stevenson-Hinde, 1982; Ainsworth, 1990, 1991; Sutherland, 1990; Parkes et al., 1991; Byng-Hall, 1991a, 1991b; King, 1991; Holmes, 1993; Marrone, 1998; Karen, 1994, 1998; Van Dijken, 1998; Coates, 2004).

Assertiveness has been described as

> feelings and actions directed towards achieving some desired goal, which continue in the direction of that goal in spite of obstacles in the environment or the opposition of others. The attitude of assertive people towards others is generally held to be positive and action taken to secure goals is not aimed at attacking obstructing individuals.
>
> *(Randall, 2001, p. 78)*

No doubt Bowlby's assertiveness was another factor that helped him survive against the odds. The more barriers he found on his way the more determined he became. But he was never alone: he was a group person.

In his autobiography *Long Walk to Freedom*, Nelson Mandela (1994) confessed that for him it would not have been possible to survive 27 years in prison if he had not been part of a group of comrades fighting together against *apartheid*. The group made him stronger and more determined in his fight for freedom. For one person alone it would have been extremely difficult, if not impossible, to resist suppression. Despite being in jail, group members supported and comforted one another. They shared every piece of news, worry or discovery. Not everyone was equally resilient. Human beings have different capabilities and respond differently to extreme situations. In Mandela's group, the stronger looked after the weaker.

Group attachments can be key to survival, particularly at times when people are pressed into a collaborative and egalitarian struggle against a common enemy. In Chapter 5, I referred to Bowlby's experience of cross-fertilisation during the meetings of the WHO's interdisciplinary study group on the *Psychobiology of the Child*, held in Geneva between 1953 and 1956. I believe this was a valuable group experience that, once internalised, helped him develop confidence and resilience – despite the rejection of many of his psychoanalytic colleagues. So, I shall now explore further the import of this experience of creative group interdependence and networking for Bowlby's professional growth.

James Tanner and Barbel Inhelder (1971) provide an excellent account of the workings of the WHO's study group, in which they were active members.

Initially, Bowlby was the only advocate of psychoanalysis among this group of psychiatrists, psychologists, research fellows, biologists, cultural anthropologists, ethologists and electro-physiologists. Two other eminent theoreticians, Erik Erikson and Ludwig von Bertalanffy, were to join the group at a later stage.

Erikson, German-born to Danish parents, was a leading American developmental psychologist and psychoanalyst. He became widely respected and quoted across a wide range of disciplines. His theory on psychosocial development as an open-ended task and his concept of 'identity crisis' (Erikson, 1950, 1971) made sense to professionals, patients and public. He and Bowlby seemed to be on a similar wavelength, proving that psychoanalytic notions and attachment ideas did not need to be at war. In the first meeting that Erikson attended, he connected meaningfully with Bowlby:

> The terms basic trust and basic mistrust [both most relevant to attachment theory] summarize much that has been emphasised recently in psychiatry and in public health, especially by Doctor Bowlby....
>
> *(quoted in Tanner & Inhelder, 1971, vol. 3, p. 170)*

Erikson tried to integrate attachment ideas with his own thinking:

> The baby will certainly feel secure only with one or two persons, especially at critical times. Each of the stages which I outlined coincides with an extension of the social radius of interaction: from the family to the known 'world'. Therefore, with each crisis, security has to be re-established within a wider radius, from a mother or maternal person to that of parental persons in general ... to the basic family, to the neighbourhood, to the peer group, to the apprenticeship organization and so on. Each of the early securities is basic for the later one, but it has first to find its own establishment in its own social radius.
>
> *(ibid., p. 212)*

Bertalanffy was an Austrian-born biologist known as one of the founders of general systems theory, in which self-regulating-systems are a central object of study. These are systems that self-correct through feedback. They can be found in ecosystems and physiological systems within the body, as well as in human learning processes and relationships, within the family, social groups and organisations. Bertalanffy (1956) challenged traditional models as they did not explain adequately the behaviour of complex living organisms. His view of living systems as sets of elements interrelating with one another provided a theoretical base for the development of systemic family therapy and organisational consultancy.

Attachment and cybernetics

General systems theory is related to cybernetics: a corpus of ideas that developed through an attempt to integrate basic principles across a number of disciplines, such as evolutionary biology, neuroscience, logic modelling, mechanical engineering, electrical network theory, anthropology, sociology and psychology. The term *cybernetics* derives from the Greek word *kybernetike*, meaning 'governance'.

Cybernetics aims to navigate through different regulatory systems, their structures, constraints and possibilities. It was originally defined by Norbert Wiener (1948) as the scientific study of control and communication in the animal and the machine. Simon (1996, p. 172) viewed cybernetics as a combination of feedback control systems, information theory and computer programming. He emphasised: "Feedback control systems show how a system can work towards goals and adapt to a changing environment".

There are many other definitions of cybernetics; most would agree that its domain includes the study of multiple signalling, communication and regulation; many consider that systems theory and cybernetics should be viewed as two facets of a single approach, basically studying the same problem. Systems thinking and cybernetics constitute a meta-disciplinary language through which we may better understand and modify complex systems. Initially, the emphasis was on observed systems (first-order cybernetics). That was followed by the study of observing systems (second-order cybernetics). The trend now is to consider that each system is observing and being observed at the same time, and that they cannot be understood separately (third-order cybernetics).

The WHO study group was committed to the development of a 'common' rather than a 'single' language – a sense of inclusive commonality rather than exclusive dogma. The search for a trans-disciplinary common language that navigates across and transcends several disciplines is a basic tenet of general systemic theory and cybernetics. Interestingly, some members of the group were not explicitly familiar with systemic concepts but conveyed ideas that were consistent with systemic thinking, prior to the arrival of Bertalanffy. For example, in one of the discussions, Lorenz stated: "All organisms are open systems and all of them live only by achieving a regulative equilibration between their inner processes and the requirements of the outer environment" (quoted in Tanner & Inhelder, 1971, vol. 4, p. 29).

Bowlby incorporated ideas from cybernetics and systems theory in the development of his own thinking. In one of his presentations in the WHO group, he stated:

> It is plain that the structure and activity of the organism as a whole cannot be understood simply in terms of structure and activities of its parts and that the process of organization of the separate activities into a whole must have laws of its own and that, in so far as the organism persists and develops, there must be an equilibrium of forces.
>
> *(ibid., p. 45)*

Piaget interacted constructively with Bowlby in the ensuing debate:

> I had understood that Bowlby does not consider, as did Freud in certain passages, that we are fixed in the past and that there is necessarily regression…, but

rather that the past is continually reorganised according to the present needs and present structures.... Bowlby's reply contains an idea which seems to me very clear and fertile. He says that an affective reaction in the child – for example, the relations between the child and his mother – is the product of a group of reactions which are at first isolated or uncoordinated between themselves, such as suckling or smiling or imitating, but later becomes more and more closely coordinated until they finally constitute a whole.

(ibid., p. 91)

Piaget (1951, 1953, 1954) often discussed the interaction of the individual with the environment – essential for learning and psychosocial development. He proposed an interesting distinction between the processes of 'assimilation' and 'accommodation'. The first consists of the incorporation of new experiences into existing structures or schemata; the latter refers to the modification of existing schemata as a result of new experiences. Adaptation can be seen as a dynamic balance between assimilation and accommodation. Neither the environment nor the organism are static; there is a constant co-evolving interaction; equilibrium can only be dynamic.

In some later explanations of attachment, Bowlby (1988b, p. 3) would postulate the existence of a control system within the central nervous system analogous to the physiological control systems that maintain physiological measures, such as blood pressure and body temperature, within certain limits. He proposed that "in a way analogous to physiological homeostasis, the attachment control system maintains a person's relationship to his or her attachment figure between certain limits of distance and accessibility".

Bowlby termed this 'environmental homeostasis' and added:

Control systems, by nature, can operate effectively only within a specified environment. For example, the system regulating body temperature cannot maintain an appropriate temperature when environmental conditions become either too hot or too cold, which means that whenever conditions go beyond certain limits the whole organism becomes stressed or dies.

(ibid., p. 3)

Further group work

Following his positive experience of the WHO study group and his productive sabbatical year, Bowlby was keen to set up a similar interdisciplinary forum. From 1959 to 1965, he convened and chaired a new study group on mother–infant interaction. Membership of this group included colleagues involved in studies of the behaviour of infants and young children, scientists engaged in similar behavioural studies of animals and clinicians who contributed from the perspective of their observations in the consulting room.

This Forum was known as the Ciba Foundation Symposia and also as the Tavistock study group. Bowlby was joined by Mary Ainsworth, Anthony

Ambrose, Jack Gewirtz, Harry Harlow, Robert Hinde, Thelma Rowell, Harriet Rheingold, Rudolf Schaffer, Theodore Schneirla, Peter Wolff, Heinz Prechtl and others. The meetings were held at the Ciba Foundation premises in London, at two-year intervals. Bowlby took a leading role and was very pleased with the meetings, as conveyed in his correspondence with Ursula:

> There is widespread enthusiasm at the way the study group is going … communication is quick, spontaneous, effective … plenty of time to digest the first meeting … [and] much private visiting between the members since … it is the atmosphere of a house-party. Harry H[arlow] … is on the platform … we should probably have some fireworks. I confess I feel rather proud of this party, both as a convenor [and] chairman, I can take much credit for the party atmosphere … much of the work reported owes its origin to my stimulation. We have had excellent presentations (Mary Ainsworth, Peter Wolff [and] Heinz Prechtl).… In addition, Robert [Hinde] has shone [and] Rudolf Schaffer did very well in a brief contribution.…
>
> *(Bowlby's letter to Ursula, 7 September 1961, quoted in*
> *Van der Horst et al., 2008)*

The contrast between the atmosphere in these scientific meetings and those of the British Psychoanalytical Society was sharp. At the Ciba Symposia, Bowlby felt at home emotionally and intellectually:

> The study group is over [and] has been a tremendous success. Everyone has enjoyed it [and] feel they have profited from it. It has been extremely friendly [and] intense, together with cautious and effective discussion. We managed to cover a lot of ground without hurry. It is striking how far [and] fast people have developed.… In a sense it has become a kind of club [and] seems likely to have far reaching effects.
>
> *(Bowlby's letter to Ursula, 9 September 1961, quoted in*
> *Van der Horst et al., 2008)*

Van der Horst et al. (2008) further reported that after the last meeting of the Symposia, Bowlby wrote to Harlow to express his gratitude: "I was very glad indeed that you were able to be with us last week and to give us such a stimulating account of your work" (Bowlby's letter to Harlow, 21 September 1965). Bowlby's sentiments concerning the ultimate success of the four-part series were reciprocated by Harlow: "I personally believe that the Tavistock series … achieved a great deal" (Harlow's letter to Bowlby, 18 October 1965).

Harlow and Bowlby kept each other informed about their work and cited each other's work extensively. They continued their scientific collaboration and warm personal contact until Harlow's retirement in 1974. One of Harlow's students, Suomi (1995) highlighted Bowlby's influence in animal research, including the development of attachment and other social relationships in non-human primates.

Bowlby successfully navigated through his *identity crisis* and extended his professional *radiuses*. Entering and sustaining a dialogue with leading researchers, clinicians and theorists from diverse disciplines and schools of thought, over several decades, gave him an exceptionally large and creative lineage. He sought legitimacy through science and group work, which helped him survive fierce opposition – and he produce a monumental piece of work, a masterpiece.

The trilogy on *Attachment and Loss*

The rejection at the British Psychoanalytical Society of the three papers ("The Nature of the Child's Tie to his Mother", "Separation Anxiety" and "Grief and Mourning in Infancy and Early Childhood") that Bowlby presented between 1957 and 1959 was a painful experience for him. Richard Bowlby believes that, while remaining assertive, his father was cautious and tried to walk a fine line to prove that his formulations worked without further antagonising his psychoanalytic colleagues.

Bowlby in fact spent some six years gathering evidence to build a solid theory that could withstand the close scrutiny of both the psychoanalytic and scientific communities. He started writing his trilogy on *Attachment and Loss* after the Ciba Symposia had ended in 1965. He told his son Richard that he had originally planned to write only one volume on attachment but, as the book unfolded, relevant material kept coming up and he ended up producing a Magnum Opus of three volumes written over 15 years – one volume for each of the three papers rejected? Was this a cathartic experience?

Attachment, the first volume, was published in 1969. Bowlby dedicated it to Ursula, his secure base. In this volume he makes ample use of control theory and evolutionary biology, drawing substantially on the results of Harlow, Hinde and other ethologists' experiments as empirical confirmation of his ideas. Bowlby drew most heavily on Ainsworth's extensive research on the nature and quality of infants and young children with their mothers or mother-substitutes. She was primarily a researcher who helped Bowlby to grow as a formidable theoretician.

The British–Chilean psychoanalyst Ignacio Matte-Blanco, while anticipating that the book would be met with strong opposition by fellow British psychoanalytic colleagues, gave due recognition to Bowlby from the outset as exemplified in a thorough book review:

> Attachment renders a great service to psychoanalytic thinking.... Bowlby's topics of study ... represent the base upon which psychoanalysis stands. By presenting a map of the region in which psychoanalysis moves, by discovering the gross facts of instinctive behaviour, as well as the great number of subtleties connected with it, this book provides psychoanalysis with a fertile ground for entirely new developments ... to proceed upon firm ground.
>
> *(Matte-Blanco, 1971, p. 198)*

Some 23 years after Matte-Blanco's book review, my wife María received a letter and a present from Skye:

Dear María,

It is such good news that you have your baby son. Please thank Arturo for letting me know that he arrived safely on August 2nd. I knew he was due about then but hadn't heard this – Pia and Carlos and Co. being away in Vigo (they returned to London a week ago).

By now the baby must be about a month old, which is a lovely age – still very new but starting to feel 'established'. I'm hoping that the gap between the two boys is big enough (I'm for good long gaps, so was John) that his elder brother finds him more interesting than jealousy evoking!

I love the baby's name. He is the second Ignacio in our lives. The first one, Ignacio Matté Blanco (from Chile) was one of the few friends John and I already had in common when we met, in 1936/7. He and John were the two 'babies', the two youngest members to be elected to the Psycho-Analytic Society, at that time, around, 1936/7 (John was aged 30, Ignacio about the same).

He was a close friend and one of our ushers at our wedding in April 1938, and godfather to our firstborn who arrived in October '39. So one of Mary's names is Ignatia, after her godfather.

I am well and happy and have the family with me now (some of them – we are 7, and will be 9 a week hence). In London again Sept 20th.

Love, Ursula

P.S. I realise the enclosed won't fit for a while yet! It's the Black Watch Tartan, a famous regiment.

[Ursula Bowlby's letter to María Cañete, 29 August 1994. The Tartan referred to the gift of a child's romper suit.]

Although María and I received many letters from Ursula, since Bowlby's death in 1990 to her own death in 2000, this was the only letter she addressed solely to María. A loving way of highlighting the shared privilege and specialness of motherhood.

Like our son Ignacio, the *Attachment* volume had been born healthy. Firmly grounded on refined Darwinian principles, Bowlby noted that each species is endowed with its own repertoire of behaviour patterns in the same way as it is endowed with its own peculiarities of anatomical structure. He referred to Darwin's emphasis that instincts are as important as corporeal structure for the welfare of each species, and that all instincts have originated through the process of natural selection having preserved and continually accumulated variations which are biologically advantageous. Thus, Bowlby conceptualised attachment as the main basis for our sociality – and essential for survival:

Attachment behaviour is regarded as a class of social behaviour of an importance equivalent to that of mating behaviour.... It is held to have a biological function specific to itself.... In this formulation, it will be noticed, there is no reference to 'needs' or 'drives'. Instead attachment behaviour is regarded as what occurs when certain behavioural systems are activated. The behavioural systems themselves are believed to develop within the infant as a result of his interaction with his environment of evolutionary adaptedness, and especially of his interaction with the principal figure in that environment, namely his mother. Food and eating are held to play no more than a minor part in their development.

(Bowlby, 1969, pp. 179–180)

While bearing in mind that this volume was primarily focussing on the nature of the child's attachment to the mother within the family environment, the compass of the book takes us to manifestations of attachment across the life cycle. Bowlby (1969, p. 207) specifically refers to the fact that during adolescence and adult life an increasing measure of attachment behaviour is "commonly directed not only towards persons outside the family but also towards groups and institutions other than the family".

Most of the literature concentrated initially on primary attachments. However, there has been a growing interest in secondary attachments. Some authors have looked at attachment theory from a systemic perspective, spelling out the reciprocal and hierarchical qualities of attachment relationships. Antonucci (1986) described an interesting *convoy* model with three circles of socially supportive networks – that in part echoes Erikson's ideas on *radiuses*, as outlined earlier.

The inner circle represents the closest and most important relationships; usually (but not always) these are relationships with parents, spouse and siblings. The middle circle represents relationships that are less close but still significantly close. These are likely to be other relatives and friends with whom one has multi-level relationships. The third circle is conceptualised as including those with whom one has special social or professional relationships, but relationships that are role-specific and punctual; examples of such people include co-workers and managers. Such relationships are important and potentially influential but are dependent on a specific role connection and are likely to end if that connection is not sustained.

The convoy model acknowledges the supremacy of primary attachments, and aims to integrate these with other significant interpersonal experiences that we have over time, including relationships with friends and colleagues. These are important for the development of abilities to seek and meet the challenges that a person faces during the course of life – certainly they were important in Bowlby's life. The systemic concept of 'asymmetrical reciprocity' (Robinson, 1980) is consistent with the power differential in parent–child relationships, which has a counterpart in therapist–patient relationships and in organisations where there are also power differentials between managers and other staff.

Indeed, Bowlby's formulation is that of a hierarchical dimension of attachment figures. He also taught me that systemic thinking is a useful framework for observing, mapping and understanding the world, breaking it into smaller parts interconnected with each other. It is not necessarily an explanatory theory, but it provides a body of concepts and techniques for hypotheses-making. Bowlby had a rare ability to construct, deconstruct and reconstruct ideas, which he did as he composed his *Attachment and Loss* first volume. And he finished with a touching message:

> In conclusion let me outline the picture of personality development proposed. A young child's experience of an encouraging, supportive and co-operative mother, and ... father, gives him a sense of worth, a belief in the helpfulness of others, and a favourable model on which to build future relationships. Furthermore, by enabling him to explore his environment with confidence and to deal with it effectively, such experience also promotes his sense of competence ... personality becomes increasingly structured to operate in moderately controlled and resilient ways, and increasingly capable of continuing so despite adverse circumstances.
>
> *(Bowlby, 1969, p. 378)*

The completion of the second volume, *Separation: Anxiety and Anger* (Bowlby, 1973), took him a further four years during which he also wrote a number of papers on the consequences of disruptions to affectional bonds too. He dedicated this volume to three friends: Evan Durbin, Eric Trist and Robert Hinde. The year before *Separation* was published he had at 65 retired from both his NHS and Medical Research Council consultant posts, but he remained an honorary consultant of the Tavistock Clinic and continued running his research unit. He enjoyed writing until the end of his life. As with the first volume, he thought that *Separation* would be the last – but while working on it he realised that a third volume would be required.

In *Separation*, Bowlby draws considerably on the empirical studies of his colleagues, but includes significantly more studies of his own research than in the previous volume. He keeps an evolutionary perspective to explore the survival value, or otherwise, of certain reactions to separation or threatened separation – and digs further into the potential danger of being alone. He also proposes, for the growth of the personality, a revised model of developmental pathways inspired in Waddington's (1957) formulations of an ever evolving and mutually influential relationship between organism and environment.

In order to explain his perspective on personality development, Bowlby elaborates upon ideas from the previous volume about his dynamic conception of 'innate' genetic structures and instincts. He made an important distinction between features that are relatively insensitive to changes in the environment, terming them 'environmentally stable', and features that are relatively sensitive, terming them 'environmentally labile'. A low degree of sensitivity to environmental change may ensure adaptive development within a greater variety of environments but at the price of an inability to adapt should the environment change beyond certain limits (Bowlby, 1973, p. 414).

In an interview, Robert Hinde considered that the introduction of the concepts of environmentally stable and labile human behaviour led to fresh thinking. In his view, there is a quite stable and species-specific genetic bias to become attached which goes together with individual differences in attachment security – emanating from environmentally labile strategies for adaptation to a specific childrearing niche (Van der Horst et al., 2007).

When applying these concepts to the development of human personality, Bowlby (1973, pp. 415–416) postulates that psychological processes resulting in personality structure are endowed with a fair degree of sensitivity to the environment during early childhood. This sensitivity usually diminishes during late childhood and becomes even more limited during adolescence.

From Bowlby's perspective, the developmental process is perceived as more able to adaptively vary its course during the early years, according to the environment in which development is occurring. Subsequently, with the reduction of environmental sensitivity, development becomes increasingly constrained to the particular pathway already taken.

It is accepted that people who did not enjoy secure attachments in childhood tend to have greater difficulties in achieving secure adult attachments. However, many people are able to recognise the limitations and failures of early attachment relationships and recover from them. An advantage of a developmental model based on an array of possible pathways allows for a process of recovery from disrupted or damaging early attachments.

It is also understandable that people who have been abused, neglected or emotionally damaged become more vulnerable to future adverse events or further environmental failures – but this does not necessarily result in permanent severe psychopathology. People can continue to develop throughout their lives, moving on up from one pathway to another under the influence of other significantly close persons and new environmental circumstances.

Bowlby was 73 when the third volume, *Loss: Sadness and Depression*, was published in 1980. This volume resulted from eight years of work following his retirement from the NHS. He was now able to confirm many of the hypotheses he formulated in the 1950s and 1960s on childhood mourning, particularly regarding his belief in the child's germinal capacity to grieve at least from 16 months onwards (Bowlby, 1980, p. 437). He further validated his original findings that very young children's responses to loss are influenced by the conditions prevalent in the family after the loss. He pointed out a change in his position:

> I now give much more weight than formerly to the influence on a child's responses of the conditions in which he is cared for whilst he is away from his mother, whether the separation be temporary or permanent. With regard to this the work of the Robertsons with children in their second and third years has been especially valuable by calling attention to the mitigating effects of good foster-care.
>
> *(Bowlby, 1980, p. 438)*

The third volume is the most clinical of the three. Bowlby in fact dedicated it to his patients – "who have worked hard to educate me". He, of course, followed the

Darwinian principle that variation and natural selection have resulted in each organism's structural and physiological systems being so constructed that they operate effectively in the environment to which the species has become adapted, and that they will become stressed or fail in others. But he went beyond that: "We have at all times to think in terms of the interactions and transactions that are constantly occurring between an ever developing personality and the environment, especially the people in it" (Bowlby, 1988b, p. 6). So, he firmly believed in the positive developmental influence of sensitive psychotherapists, helpful teachers, loyal friends or inspiring supervisors – as well as in the healing potential of groups and our own capacity for self-healing.

Bowlby continued searching, exploring, growing until the end of his life. Following his retirement, he had numerous demands for lectures, seminars and workshops at home and abroad, especially in the USA. A good number of his lectures were published in two books: *The Making and Breaking of Affectional Bonds* (Bowlby, 1979a) and *A Secure Base: Clinical Applications of Attachment Theory* (Bowlby, 1988a). He formulated attachment not only in terms of physiological homeostasis but also in the context of an emotional and social environment – encompassing relationships across the life span. And this in fact was Bowlby's (1980, p. 442) final message in his trilogy:

> Intimate attachments to other human beings are the hub around which a person's life revolves, not only when he is an infant or a toddler or a schoolchild but throughout his adolescence and his years of maturity as well, and on into old age. From these intimate attachments a person draws his strength and enjoyment of life and, through what he contributes, he gives strength and enjoyment to others.

7

THE GROUP AS AN ADAPTIVE ATTACHMENT

Sibling and peer relationships constitute a profound part of growing up. They influence the character traits that people develop, as well as the capacity for social and emotional understanding, for adjustment and wellbeing. Until recently, sibling relationships have been a relatively neglected area in the psychoanalytic literature. The main emphasis has been on rivalry, envy and jealousy. However, the equation has to include other important aspects such as friendliness, loyalty to each other and ability to form a united front in response to an external threat or discomfort. Sibling and peer experiences provide frequent and ongoing opportunities for children to develop a capacity for empathy (Sanders, 2004, p. 59).

Freud mainly wrote about the sibling as a displacement in the relationship with the mother. In 1917, he stated: "A child who has been put into second place by the birth of a brother or a sister, and who is now for the first time almost isolated from his mother, does not easily forgive her this loss of place" (quoted in Sanders, 2004, p. 56). Bowlby (1969, p. 260) put together a more detailed observation of a young child's reaction to the presence of a new sibling and linked it to attachment:

> In most young children the mere sight of mother holding another baby in her arms is enough to elicit strong attachment behaviour. The older child insists on remaining close to his mother, or on climbing on to her lap. Often he behaves as though he were a baby.... The fact that an older child often reacts in this way even when the mother makes a point of being attentive and responsive suggests that more is involved....

Sibling relationships are indeed likely to be the longest standing that any of us has: longer than the relationships with our parents, or with our children or with our partners. Dunn (2014) describes the sibling relationship as distinctive in its emotional power and intimacy, as well as its qualities of competitiveness, ambivalence and mutual understanding. The child learns who he is – and who he is not – through ongoing comparisons with siblings and peers, selectively imitating, contradicting, or avoiding the other, depending on circumstances.

Siblings and peers might represent a potential self that the child can reflect on in relation to himself and future relationships. The sibling is a unique figure in the child's early life and can be considered the first 'peer group', as it were. Sibling relationships in early life are commonly seen as preparations for the kind of relationships children will establish with peers and friends outside the family. Initially, the sibling is not really an attachment figure. However, "as parents are absent either emotionally or physically, the siblings may be forced to reach out for one another" (Bank & Kahn, 1997, p. 123).

There is an ongoing debate about this 'compensatory' model of sibling relationships and parent–child relationships. The idea that if one is bad or absent, the other is good does not always apply. There are situations where it is possible to observe a 'congruent' model, in which relationships with parents and siblings are both either bad or good. Whether the link between the two is compensatory or congruent may depend on other variables such as the developmental stage of the child, environmental factors and individual differences between children (Sanders, 2004).

The traditional psychoanalytic view of the sibling as mainly a rival attachment system has been under increasing review and a wider picture, where collaboration plays an important part, has been provided in the last 30 or so years (for example, Dunn & Kendrick, 1982; Dunn & McGuire, 1992; Fonagy & Target, 1996, 2007; Akhtar & Kramer, 1999; Coles, 2003; Sanders, 2004; Dunn, 2014; Kriss et al., 2014; Music, 2014).

Competitive interactions are undeniable and frequent among siblings, but they represent only one aspect of the wide range of capabilities that children possess. Despite the undeniable stress involved with the arrival of a younger sibling, it can also be a stimulus for cognitive and emotional growth on the part of the older child as well as on the part of the baby. The mutual efforts to understand each other can form the basis for a loving and enduring attachment bond. Siblings and peers can adopt various relational roles with one another, including acting as comforters and teachers, as devious and manipulative bullies or as sensitive companions who can enter the play world of the other (Dunn & Kendrick, 1982).

Bowlby made a distinction between attachment figures and playmates. According to him, a child seeks his attachment figure when he is tired, ill, or alarmed, and also when he is uncertain of that figure's whereabouts. By contrast, a child seeks a playmate when he is in good spirits and confident, and wants to engage in playful interaction with him or her. Bowlby further elaborated on this:

> The roles of attachment-figure and playmate are distinct. Since, however, the two roles are not incompatible, it is possible for any one figure at different times to fill both roles: … an older child who acts mainly as playmate may on occasion act also as a subsidiary attachment figure.
>
> (Bowlby, 1969, p. 307)

Peer relationships as a desperate survival strategy

Bowlby supported me, from 1987 onwards, through the setting up and development of a group psychotherapy programme for very disturbed children living in a residential unit that was described as a 'traumatised institution'. He told me that, in his view, children's subsidiary attachments with siblings and peers may ameliorate or compensate for the negative consequences of traumatic experiences. He considered that these attachments could become essential for survival, particularly under extreme circumstances. Bowlby had always kept in good terms with Anna Freud and advised me to read a dramatic report of peer relationships in a group of children survivors of the Jewish holocaust: *An Experiment in Group Upbringing* (Freud & Dann, 1951).

This experiment was not artificially designed but occurred as a result of tragic and fateful circumstances. Six children (three boys and three girls), born between December 1941 and October 1942, were orphaned during the first year of their lives as their parents were murdered by the Nazis in the gas chambers. The six children spent more than two years together at the transit concentration camp of Tereszin, where they had arrived individually after months of being handed on from one refuge to another. They were liberated by the Russians in the spring of 1945 and were taken to a Czech castle where they received special care until their arrival in England with other rescued children in August 1945.

The children were originally destined to be fostered in the USA, but the plan changed and the Americans provided one-year funding for a rehabilitation programme in England instead. In October 1945, accommodation was loaned to the project in a country house with peaceful and quiet surroundings, including a field and adjoining woodland at *Bulldogs Bank*, in West Hoathly, West Sussex. Staff were drawn from the Hampstead Nursery run by Anna Freud, and from the English original reception camp in Windermere where the children had spent a couple of months.

Initially, the children were hypersensitive, restless, aggressive and difficult to handle. All reacted badly to the move. They destroyed toys and responded with cold indifference or active hostility to the adults in a way that made it impossible to treat them individually. They behaved as a very compact peer group that stuck together, each of them showing a strong need for clinging to the group:

> The children's positive feelings were cemented exclusively in their own group. It was evident that they cared for each other and not at all for anybody or anything else. They had no other wish than to be together and became upset when they were separated from each other, even for short moments. No child would consent to remain upstairs while the others were downstairs, or vice versa, and no child would be taken for a walk or on an errand without the others. If anything of that kind happened, the single child would constantly ask for the other children while the group would fret for the missing child.
>
> *(Freud & Dann, 1951, p. 131)*

As a further example on the nature of relationships within the group, the following was reported:

> The children's unusual dependence on each other was borne out further by the almost complete absence of jealousy, rivalry and competition, such as normally developed between brothers and sisters or in a group of contemporaries who come from normal families. There was no occasion to urge the children to 'take turns'; they did it spontaneously....
>
> *(ibid., pp. 133–134)*

However, some discrimination against one of the girls, whose arrival had been delayed by an infection, occurred on the part of the other two girls. At some point in the first half of 1946, another girl (one who had been known to have a short attachment to a mother figure previously) began to express feelings of envy and jealousy; but this was an exception.

At meal times, handing food to another child was usually of greater importance than eating one's own food. They would always insist on everyone getting the same. In the early months (October to December 1945), the children did not physically hurt or attack each other with the exception of one boy. There were at times verbal quarrels, insults and shouting among themselves and they would turn on any adult who tried to interfere. They also hit or smacked adults when restricted; for example, while walking in traffic. From January to July 1946, the battles of words gave way to some physical fights, which are not unusual at this age. After this phase, they expressed less aggression towards one another and towards the staff.

The children had originally regarded the caring adults as outsiders and did not exhibit demanding or possessive behaviour towards them. That was in sharp contrast to the usual conduct that tends to be displayed by children of their age. In the autumn 1946, there was a significant change: the orphans started to treat staff in ways that were similar to how they, the children themselves, were treating one another. They would often insist that the adults should take turns and have their fair share at all times.

This change indicated that, to some extent, the staff were included in their group and were expected to respect its rules. Certainly, the adults were no longer seen as enemies or outsiders and some form of individual attachments between children and adults began to emerge. However, during the remaining time of the therapeutic project, "these ties of the children to the adults in no way reached the strength of their ties to each other" (Freud & Dann, 1951, p. 144).

These orphans had been severely deprived of the usual early social development that has its origins in the attachments to mother and father. They presented themselves with a very patchy picture. On the one hand, they were emotionally and behaviourally immature and disturbed. On the other hand, they showed qualities, such as empathy, fairness and concern for others, which would normally appear at an older age. The developmental path of peer relationships was overdeveloped as a desperate survival strategy.

The start of the therapeutic experiment was very difficult. In the early stages, the children were unable to use any play material; instead, they damaged the furniture, destroyed toys and showed great hostility towards the adults. Staff members were patient, understanding and consistently caring. That was helpful and, together with the children's peer group support and the beautiful surroundings, contributed to the development of a facilitating and healing environment. Gradually, the children were able to use soft toys and the sandpit. As they became more interested in the adult world, they also acquired an appetite for reading and writing.

Towards the end of the project, the children's behaviour and emotions were closer to what is normally considered age-appropriate at nursery schools. This meant that a combination of new favourable situations and the staff quality of care enabled these orphans to form new, less anxious, attachments – which, in turn, help them find a healthier developmental path. The pace of progress quickened. Making up for their missed learning and balancing their uneven psychosocial development became possible to a significant extent.

Although peer group attachments on their own are not sufficient for optimal human development, they are an essential component to it. The above study demonstrates that strong and meaningful attachments to a group of peers can be made at a very early stage, in the absence of secure attachments to parents or other caring adults, under extreme conditions. The process of establishing a compensatory primary attachment to a group of peers at such an early age was fundamental for the children's survival in the absence of individual attachments.

This validates the conceptions outlined in previous chapters that attachment is a primary and powerful instinctual force serving survival – at a level that is as important as the need for food and sex. The orphans at Bulldogs Bank nursery vividly showed that, when survival is at stake, the peer group itself can be perceived as stronger, wiser and more able to cope with the world than the individual self – in order to provide a much needed feeling of emotional connectedness to a secure base, which can protect them from psychic death.

The peer group certainly contained a powerful quality of mutual care and psychological protection. In contrast to other cases of more common deprivation, these orphaned children did not become deficient, delinquent or psychotic. This remarkable upbringing could be seen as an adaptive attachment on the edge – in the face of a most deficient or non-existent early care-giving environment. The bonds between the children were made and sustained in a highly united peer group experience, since no other attachment figures were available to them. And, so, Anna Freud's experiment in group upbringing gives an unusual backing to the therapeutic potential of group work with children.

Ordinary peer development

Bowlby's advice and openness about Anna Freud's remarkable project presented a new dimension to my thinking on childhood peer development. At the beginning of this chapter, I provided some recent references on the subject. In order to keep a historical perspective, I shall refer in this section to the literature I used at the time of supervision with Bowlby. Michael Rutter (1980) and Daniel Stern (1985) had reported systematic studies showing that infants are socially responsive from birth onwards. For a baby, people constitute the first source of interest and attraction. Babies can recognise the mother's smell within hours after birth and her voice within days. They can take and keep a firm grasp with their hands within a few weeks. By the age of two or three months, healthy infants show preferential responses to mother and father (Bowlby, 1969).

At about five or six months there is a clear sense of social reciprocity and mutual enjoyment in the interactions between parent and infant, as well as an incipient awareness of other babies. However, this interest in 'peers' does not appear to be a source of enjoyment until the end of the first year (Dunn & Kendrick, 1982). Wariness of strangers begins to manifest itself after six months, in parallel with an increase of the intensity of attachment behaviour towards the mother or the main caregiver. The timing of this distinctive proximity-seeking towards main attachment figures makes sense: the infant is rapidly becoming more aware of its separateness and in need of protection from potential dangers.

In supervision, I was learning from Bowlby that the early relationships with parents and caregivers form the basis for future psychosocial development, for which sibling and peer relations are also a crucial part. He did not consider himself an expert in the field of peer development and recommended that I should look further into the literature, prior to starting a children's group psychotherapy programme. As he had not conducted therapy groups for children, he encouraged me by making comments such as: "we can learn together" and "with our [his and mine] existing clinical knowledge some degree of experimenting should be safe". He was clearly providing me with a safety net.

I read Grunebaum and Solomon (1980, 1982) who gave a comprehensive description of the developmental stages of peer relations from infancy to pre-adolescence. They postulated a controversial idea that, although influenced by the early mother–infant relationship, sibling and peer relations can develop quite autonomously following a different pathway of social development. This would be consistent with the experiences that the orphans described above went through. In their review of the research literature on friendship formation, these authors identified a set of developmental phases, including toddlerhood (ages one to three years), the pre-school child (ages three to six), middle childhood (ages six to nine) and pre-adolescence (ages nine to twelve years).

Under normal circumstances, the capacity for meaningful contact with peers grows steadily throughout childhood. Grunebaum and Solomon (1982, pp. 284–285) supplied a coherent description of this process. At the age of one year, toddlers are egocentric and play in parallel with other toddlers, rather than cooperatively. Around 18 months, they begin to take complementary roles with one another (e.g. one child throws the ball and the other receives it). By the age of two years, they start to form significant secondary attachments with specific peers and show delight on meeting them. From the age of three onwards, there is a dramatic decrease in solitary play and a corresponding increase in co-operative play.

Playing pretend games begins to emerge during the pre-school phase and the child also shows awareness of similarity of feelings in other children. This achievement had been described elsewhere as "resonant empathy" (Slavson & Schiffer, 1975, p. 374). It is towards the end of the pre-school period that children become aware that their peers may have feelings and expectations different from their own (Garvey, 1977). This primitive reflective function of exploring the meaning of actions of others has been more recently linked to the child's ability to recognise and find his or her own experience meaningful (Fonagy & Target, 1996, 2007).

Emotional ambivalence can be an important feature in the child's relationship with his peers and siblings: "Yesterday's best friend will be today's worst enemy and tomorrow will become best friend again" (Stringer, 1971, p. 11). Friendships appear after social interaction and play, and can be viewed as a culmination of toddler social skills (Vandell & Mueller, 1980). The quality of early peer friendship is a good index to predict future social competence. At about the age of three or four, and usually up to the age of six, some children have an imaginary companion usually to compensate for absences in their lives. These children are often creative, of average intelligence, with good verbal skills, co-operate with adults and generally do not have siblings. Imaginary friends can have a positive effect on the child's social and cognitive development (Bettelheim, 1976).

As the child gets older, relationships with peers become increasingly more important: "Friendship among peers is imperative to the normal development of a latency child" (Kaplan, 1976, p. 65). This is crucial in order to become emotionally more autonomous from the parents, during this so-called *latency period*. In the traditional psychoanalytic literature this stage goes from the *resolution* of the 'Oedipus complex' to puberty. Although a substantial majority of psychoanalytic authors tend to place such resolution after the age of six, it varies according to the individual child (see a different perspective of this in Chapter 11).

Bowlby warned me about the danger of being dogmatic in respect of the Oedipus complex. He preferred to look at this theme from the perspective of triangular situations. A likely dynamic is that one of the individuals in the *triad*, particularly if he or she is a child, can easily feel left out when the other two are close – even when they do not mean to exclude him or her. Feelings of jealousy may run high. Inevitably, everyone needs to deal with triangular situations in all periods of the life cycle. *Triangles* might be handled better or worse, but it would be unwise to state that they can be completely resolved once and for all.

On the other hand, *quartets* are considered a basic group constellation and have an advantage that they can be divided up in two *pairs*. There is less direct exposure to potential jealousy for which three people are needed, while for envy and rivalry two people are enough. However, in a group configuration, there might be a greater risk of becoming a 'scapegoat', especially for those individuals who had previously experienced problems in their psychosocial development. Being the *single one out* in a group may also generate a devastating feeling of isolation. Being left alone and unaided by the other group members can be particularly difficult to handle.

In *latency*, sexual impulses are not absent but dormant; they are less evident or actively manifested. It is a time when the child gathers resources in preparation for the dramatic psychosexual changes of adolescence – which I shall spell out in Chapter 9. Until the age of five, friends had been mainly selected on the basis of availability. From this age onwards, children look for friends with whom they can share common interests and exclude other children who do not enjoy the same activities. Around the age of eight the foundation of friendships shifts from playing together to an increasing interest in the character traits of one's peers. This is also a time when an important motive for going to school is to be with one's friends.

By the age of nine or ten, children have developed their own ideas of what constitutes "matching of give and take, fairness in exchange for fairness, dependability in exchange for dependability, and so on" (Stringer, 1971, p. 32). This enables pre-adolescent children to establish some kind of social contracts and resolve some of their earlier ambivalent feelings. For a number of people latency friendships are erratic but for others they continue through high school. With age, friendships tend to be more constant.

During the pre-adolescent period, from the ages of nine to twelve, there is a strong predisposition to make close friends with a particular member of the same sex. At this time, there is a significant shift in the quality of these friendships:

> the child begins to develop a real sensitivity to what matters to another person and this is not in the sense of 'what should I do to get what I want' but instead 'what should I do to contribute to the happiness or support, the prestige and feeling of worthwhile-ness of my chum.' ... Nothing remotely like that appears before the age of say eight and a half, sometimes it appears decidedly later.
>
> *(Sullivan, 1953, p. 245)*

In this pre-adolescent phase, there is also a need to be part of gangs and cliques. Gangs tend to be of the same sex, with sexual secrets becoming a source of intergroup curiosity and giggling: "The gang character has the quality of being subversive to adult (parental) standards. The courage to stick to his pal against the parent (no matter how much he loves the parent) is a step forward in the youngster's growth" (Redl, 1966, p. 404).

Children with insecure patterns of attachment may find it more difficult having to share friends: "being exposed to the constant dangers of rivalry and loss makes it hard for some children to dare to make any deep relationships at all" (Redl, 1966, p. 448). Additionally, pre-adolescents need their own space and time for privacy and freedom from group exposure. This has to be negotiated against the back-ground of a powerful drive for intimate association. The experience of *chumship* in pre-adolescence is usually a positive one. The developing sense of intimacy, and the capacity of seeing one's self through the other's eyes, may often foster the validation of one's personal worth and the growth of self-esteem. On the other hand, youngsters who did not experience childhood friendship would be more vulnerable to enter adolescence with a greater risk of isolation.

Child group psychotherapy

Psychotherapy groups for children can have a number of advantages. They operate as a peer group and have a developmental as well as a therapeutic value. They are also a cost-effective form of treatment. Children can overcome feelings of loneliness while in a therapy group. Belonging to such group can help members to develop self-esteem and to become more confident to make friends. Children can also see the impact of their own behaviour on other people, and the impact of others' behaviour on them, without being as exposed to the consequences as they might be in their own daily lives. Strengths and weaknesses are exposed in the group in a safe and confidential way. This provides good opportunities to learn about oneself in relation to other children, as well as in relation to the therapists who represent the adult world.

Some parents can perceive the group as less threatening than individual therapy, where the child could be seen as being singled out. Denial of real life experiences is more difficult in a group, as these are shared by members. In turn, the positive experiences in the group can be applied to other situations outside the group's life, such as home or school. Apart from clinics and hospitals, groups can be provided in many settings like children's homes, schools and remand homes. For school-age children, the group situation fits well, developmentally, into their ordinary lives.

In parallel with the stages of social development described earlier, children may form occasional groups at the age of four or five. These groups can be short-lived and may serve the purpose of some opposition to adults or exclusion of other children. By the ages of six and seven, it is possible to see more stable groups in which more mature forms of sharing and social learning can take place; like give and take and a sense of fairness. Conflicts may become more apparent between the authority of parents and teachers, on the one hand, and the new principles set by friends, on the other.

During the *latency* years, the need to belong to a peer group is increasingly stronger. For this reason, group work is a particularly effective therapeutic approach as it recreates important social, emotional and learning aspects of the child's life. Slavson (1940) paid special attention to this age group. Aggressiveness in the *latency* years is not uncommon and can manifest itself in both boys and girls (Kaplan, 1976). Indeed, with the more severe cases of aggression, it is quite likely to find a link to past experiences where the children themselves had been the recipients of aggression, or exposed to witnessing it (Bowlby, 1938, 1939, 1979a, 1988a).

The psychiatrist Jacob Moreno (1946) is considered a pioneer of therapeutic group work with children. In 1911, he developed a technique of puppetry and drama, which he called 'psychodrama', in a Child Guidance Clinic in Vienna. However, the concept of the small therapy group in therapy, consisting of five to eight children between the ages of eight and twelve, was introduced in 1934 by Samuel Slavson (an engineer and school teacher interested in psychoanalysis). In his view, the therapist had to show a profile of being a warm, accepting, non-directive and relatively permissive adult. In this model, children were allowed to act spontaneously in order to facilitate the expression of feelings and conflicts.

The technique became known as 'activity group therapy' (Slavson & Schiffer, 1975). In group work with children there is a tendency towards action, anyway. Slavson (1940, p. 526) put it this way:

> The members of the group work together: they quarrel, fight – and sometimes strike one another; they argue and haggle, but finally come to some ... understanding with one another. Sometimes this process takes six months or more, but once it has been established becomes a permanent attitude on the part of the individuals involved.

I think this is a basis for new peer attachments.

A similar technique, called 'group play therapy', was developed by Virginia Axline (1947, 1950) in the 1940s. This was expanded by Haim Ginott (1961) in the 1950s and has continued growing until the present day. Incorporating some of the strategies of individual child analysis, play can be used as a developmentally natural tool to communicate thoughts, wishes, fears and other feelings to their peers and the therapists. This is particularly useful as verbal expression is not entirely developed yet.

Group play can provide a path to a deeper understanding of conflicts and emotional situations of which children are not consciously aware. In any case, playing is a normal activity through which younger children can have a more rapid access to group formation. Toys such as dolls, puppets, animals and a range of characters, as well as materials such as water, sand or plasticine, can be used. Through the play characters children can create symbolic dialogues. Such materials are particularly attractive to the younger children and help them to feel less anxious and to hold their interest in the group.

It is generally accepted that, in young children, play can be the therapeutic equivalent of 'free association' in adults:

> Gradually, children are able to move from egocentric, solitary, exploratory motor (playground type), oral (cooking, and so forth) and anal (messy) levels of play to more social, representational and constructive play.... Various characters, toys, dolls, animals and so forth become endowed with feelings, intentions and relationships representing those from the world of the child. Social play allows the children to experiment with new ways of relating, with improved ego strength, attitudes and insight gained during the work of the group.
>
> *(Dwivedi, 1998, p. 118)*

Group psychotherapy with children has proven to be as effective as individual psychotherapy (Hoag & Burlingame, 1997; McRoberts et al., 1998; Shechtman &

Ben-David, 1999). This type of group work can help children to overcome primitive narcissism and egocentricity, to postpone gratification, to manage difficult feelings, to develop symbolic thinking and to explore new values, as well as to develop creativity, empathy, altruism and pro-social behaviour. The areas of improvement more widely reported are social skills, self-esteem and reality testing (Kymissis, 1996; Rose, 1998; Schaefer, 1999). A meta-analysis of 111 research studies, published between 1970 and 2003, indicated that "the average recipient of group treatment is better off than 72% of untreated controls" (Burlingame et al., 2003, p. 3).

Institutional change

I can recall Bowlby saying to me with a sweet smile: "You have been thrown in at the deep end". That was on my appointment as the child psychiatrist to a maintained special school for five- to eleven-year-olds who had emotional, communication and behavioural problems affecting their learning. The school offered 20 weekly boarding places as well as additional day places, ad hoc. Initially a hospital for autistic and psychotic children, the institution had opened in 1954 and had a strong individually orientated therapeutic tradition; group psychotherapy had never been tried.

In his remarkable book, *A History of Autism*, Adam Feinstein presented some helpful descriptions of the early years at the hospital, when the children were particularly challenging and showed major difficulties in forming attachments. In Feinstein's (2010, p. 83) book, Golding (2006) provided one of these accounts:

> I well remember picking mushrooms in the early hours of the morning – anything rather than have to get up and face those strange children who did not seem to respond to all my lovely, carefully planned activities.... The general ethos was to keep the children calm and not disturbed them further so that hopefully with all the therapy (both for them and their parents) they would emerge from their 'psychotic' or 'schizophrenic' state.
>
> *(quoted in Feinstein, 2010, p. 83)*

When I joined the staff team, the institution was still struggling to come to terms with major bereavements, following the sudden death of its director – a founding member who had been a charismatic leader and parental-like figure to the team. The loss appeared to be so painful that hardly anybody talked about it. Additionally, the institution was going through important structural changes, from being centrally managed by the regional Health Authority to being locally managed by the Education Department. These changes were generating significantly high levels of anxiety among many members of the staff, particularly as there was a threat that the Unit may have to be closed altogether.

In the circumstances, I had been appointed with a view to help both the staff and the children. Since the institution opened, its therapeutic culture had been one in which individual sessions were considered best because of their traditional one-to-one nurturing. Therapy had been strongly linked to feeding, both meta-phorically and literally. In view of the gross developmental deficits, staff had tried "to return the children there to their infancy so that they could restart their development. One technique was to give them baby-feeding bottles to suck from ... the children used these to squirt milk at the ceiling" (Feinstein, 2010, p. 83).

Of course, Bowlby challenged this approach and encouraged me to give priority to helping children, parents and carers feel secure – rather than focussing on feeding. Additionally, in his view, using a diagnostic label of psychosis or schizophrenia was unhelpful – since children are still developing a personality structure, which is too tender for adult-like psychopathology. While recognising that some children are more vulnerable than others to the risk of psychosis, such an adverse course can be prevented with adequate environmental support.

On the other hand, Bowlby agreed with the diagnosis of autism as a complex neuro-developmental disorder. Autistic children have great difficulties in using language and abstract concepts, which makes it very difficult for them to communicate and form relationships with other people. This puts additional demands on the parents and carers, which may sometimes stretch the care-giving and attachment systems to breaking point.

Bowlby also suggested to me that, before introducing group psychotherapy for the children, it would be helpful to run support groups for the staff. This took the form of reflective practice meetings, which I ran weekly. Over a number of months, the task was twofold. First, to facilitate the process for the staff to grieve the loss of their leader: *mourn, then organise* (see Chapter 2). Second, to work through the anxieties experienced in connection with the uncertainty about the future of the institution, with a view to giving staff a greater sense of control.

Bowlby considered this work with the staff was crucial in order to protect the children, as much as it would be possible, from the unresolved institutional bereavement. Certainly, without his guidance at the time, it would not have been possible for me to do this job. He was an expert on bereavement and loss but chose to direct me towards the work of his colleagues. I very much appreciated that he gave me a copy of *Bereavement: Studies of Grief in Adult Life* (Parkes, 1978). The book, now in its fourth edition, helped me understand the mood and feelings of the staff. Talking about it helped us all to move on.

When the team seemed ready, Bowlby gave me *licence* to introduce the group psychotherapy programme. He thought that the school would be an especially suitable setting for this type of therapy: children were naturally organised in groups and could perceive group work as part of their daily routine. I was further reassured by Sue Reid who pioneered group therapy for children at the Tavistock Clinic (Reid & Kolvin, 1993), and by reading Irvin Yalom's book *The Theory and Practice of Group Psychotherapy*. The book helped me understand group principles and therapeutic factors (Yalom, 1985).

When I formally proposed group psychotherapy for the children, it was still met with concerns about economic rather than therapeutic criteria – no matter that I had spent several months preparing the team for the change. However, despite the initial reluctance, the school eventually accepted the group idea on a trial basis. I had previously provided elsewhere a reflective description of some these institutional processes, including the introduction and development of the child group therapy programme (Ezquerro, 1995, 1997a).

As an integral part of the programme, I also arranged regular review meetings with the parents and foster families responsible for the care of the children. This development was unanimously welcomed. The meetings, to which the teachers were also invited, became an effective tool to evaluate the therapeutic project and monitor the progress of the children. The local Education Department came to be receptive to and appreciative of the institutional changes and decided to keep the Unit open. This helped the organisation with long-term planning.

There were further meetings to discuss the composition of the group. Children were already allocated to classes on grounds of similarities in development and ability, and so it was natural for teachers to argue for homogeneity of disordered behaviour in the group. But I felt that including an excess of violent children could keep the therapists occupied most of the time in preventing disasters; on the other hand, a group of very timid children together would become flat.

Bowlby also advised me to run the group with a colleague and I followed his advice. Alice Byrnes, an art therapist, became the co-therapist. She and I agreed to set up a mixed group of children with heterogeneity of personalities and presenting problems. We hoped that this would enhance the therapeutic potential for both identification and differentiation among the children in the group.

During the selection process, we gave priority to those children who were not receiving individual psychotherapy. We also managed to persuade my colleagues that group therapy could make sense after a period of individual therapy, or vice-versa. We started with two boys and two girls in a slow-open group, which children joined and left when ready. Maximum membership was six, with an average stay of a year and a half to two years.

After three years, the co-therapist changed jobs and Bowlby died. The group continued running for a further two years until I left. Running it on my own was harder for me and appeared so for the children; but gave them further opportunities to explore their feelings about separation, loss and single parenting. Over the five years, more than 20 children were treated in the group.

> John, a seven-year-old, became very upset when his parents split up, around the time Alice, the co-therapist, had left. He had a number of aggressive reactions in the group but one day burst into tears, and said that he was very angry with his parents and with me; he added: "Nobody wants me". Peter, an eight-year-old, put his arm around him and said: "Don't worry John; I'll be your friend".

Friends are governed by different sets of rules at different stages of development. Qualities of friendship include trust, loyalty, reciprocity, emotional fulfilment and a validation of each other's identity. We had told the children that there would be a regular meeting for one hour, on the same day and time each week, in the same room, to talk about things that were important to them. The therapists' attitude was usually reflective – unless disrupted by violence. We encouraged contributions consisting of verbal communication and interpretation. The group was not formally structured but carefully planned and thought about.

> Clare was five when her single-parent mother, as a result of psychotic break-down, had a long stay in a psychiatric hospital, during which Clare was received into care. In the group she broke toys and threw the pieces at other children. Alice, the co-therapist, held her in a caring but firm way, saying: "I am doing this because I care for you, Clare, and want to keep you and the other children safe". Clare did not listen but shouted: "She is going to hurt me, she is going to hurt me!" Then, Jane, a nine-year-old, said: "Alice is not hurting you, Clare; she is only trying to keep you safe", following which Clare stopped shouting and calmed down.

The children were expected to stay in the room, not to damage the furniture, or hurt each other physically, and to keep confidences. The last was clearly important for the children. When a child did bring up group matters outside, the others usually reacted angrily in the next meeting, insisting that the group was private and different from the rest of the week. We, the therapists, did not primarily seek to alter surface behaviour, but to help the children towards a deeper understanding of their feelings and reactions.

All of them had a considerable need to *belong*, particularly those who were *not wanted* in their own lives outside the group. The relationship between group members, including the therapists, was emphasised. For many of the children, this was the first experience of becoming an important part in the life of a peer group. The setting was safe, which helped to create learning opportunities for them about how to make friends. Interpersonal learning was one of the main therapeutic factors.

> Paul, a seven-year-old, had serious difficulties in forming relationships of any kind. He was playing on his own with two dolls, which would kick and punch each other increasingly hard. Sue, a nine-year-old, was watching him when she picked up two other dolls, making them shake hands and kiss each other, which trapped Paul's attention. I said that it would be easier for Sue's dolls to make friends. Then, Paul uttered: "I also want to have a friend but I don't know how". I added that maybe the best way to have friends is to try to be friendly with them. John joined the conversation with a smile….

Fostering peer relationships is an important part of group therapy. The experience of making friends is not only a source of gratification and learning social skills, but an opportunity to experience a companion who is supportive at times of adversity. Friendship is a unique form of pair bonding and one of the most precious human experiences. It is reciprocal, established between equals and can be fragile or enduring. Friendships, unlike familial bonds but like group-analytic bonds, are voluntary.

Co-therapy enabled us to offer the best of both worlds. In children's groups, the level of activity is such that it becomes difficult to keep an eye on all the moves, while preserving an analytic mode. Flexibly sharing both roles (looking after the safety of the group and creating thinking space) enhanced the therapeutic potential. For some of the children this was the first time they experienced a kind of *parental couple* working together. When I became a sole therapist, I needed to be more proactive and leader-like at the expense of interpretation.

The majority of parents and carers were appreciative of the changes observed in the children, particularly an improvement in relationships with peers and grown-ups, and in school performance. Staff sensitivity groups continued running weekly. In the second year of the children's group, in addition to the periodical individual reviews (usually every half term), we set up a monthly psycho-educational group for the parents; which contributed to the overall success of the project.

When I left, the school employed a child psychotherapist to continue the group work. The institution changed its approach: despite the initial doubts about the value of such groups, they became an accepted form of treatment. I, too, changed through this experience. I learned from the school, from Alice and, above all, from the children – something that Bowlby helped me discover.

Moving on up

This positive group experience was encouraging and influenced my decision to train as a group analyst working with adult patients. Bowlby was pleased about this move. He considered that the Institute of Group Analysis was a more democratic institution than the British Psychoanalytical Society. However, at no point did he try to influence my decision-making. He was respectful of my choices. My career as a child psychiatrist shifted to that of a consultant psychiatrist in psychotherapy. It was done gradually, over five years, during which I held two part-time jobs.

This arrangement enabled me to continue co-running hour-long weekly therapy groups for children aged seven to eleven (junior school), at a child and family psychiatric clinic. The format was similar to the one described above. The groups were reasonably heterogeneous and included a range of emotional, behavioural and communication problems, attention difficulties, aggressiveness and inability to relate to others. I also co-conducted a weekly group for the children's parents (mostly mothers), where the themes oscillated from discussing preoccupations about their children to working on memories about the difficulties they had themselves experienced as children.

Therapeutic results for the children were satisfactory, particularly regarding the development of social skills, with greater confidence in making friends, as well as improved self-esteem, reality testing and situational awareness. Children also learned to delay the need for immediate gratification, to manage difficult feelings, to tolerate frustration and to contain anger and aggressive feelings. Some schools reported improved behaviour, concentration and academic performance.

The dynamics (and needs) in children's groups are different from those of adults, in pace, style and manner of communication. The state of children's emotional and cognitive development determines their ability to conceptualise, to cultivate insight, to grow out of *primitive narcissism* and egocentricity and to develop empathy. A capacity to tolerate and contain difficult and conflictive feelings also develops gradually.

Modes of communication and ability for concentration have important implications for the choice of group interventions. Group therapy with children also differs from that of adults in the quality and quantity of *dynamic administration*. In view of the strong tendency towards action, groups for children require an even more careful advanced planning than for adults, as well as special attention to boundary activities and incidents that impinge on the group processes (Anthony, 1965; Behr, 1988; Woods, 1993; Behr & Hearst, 2005).

Boundaries are heavily tested in children's groups by demands for self-disclosure, physical contact and, at times, discipline. Themes of conversation may change rapidly, jumping from topic to topic, often unconnected and in parallel. Moods can be very volatile with strong, non-verbal, emotional expressions. An inability to fully comprehend each other's language can lead to conflict between children and therapists. Spilling over of the group into the waiting room before or after the session and, in fact, anywhere inside or outside the building is not uncommon. There might also be discussions among the parents in the waiting room influencing the entire process.

For most school children, the small therapy group can be a highly attractive setting, because of the resemblance and kinship with the natural peer group. In individual therapy the huge disparity between the status of the child and the therapist is too obvious and can lead to an intense *transference*. Such transferences tend to become diluted and might be better managed in a therapy group. Certainly, such groups can openly stimulate the children's relational capacity and offer them many opportunities to make valuable contributions. Groups also offer good chances for identifications and counter-identifications: working on one child's problems can be beneficial for other children in the room.

Previous attachment patterns can be observed in the group, as well new interactions. These may trigger perceptions, attitudes and behaviours that have proved to be problematical in day-to-day life. Such materials being enacted in the group can generate helpful feedback, experimentation with and practice of alternative perspectives and options. In well-functioning groups, the *group as a whole* may represent a secure base for the individual child; something that he or she can use to explore and overcome fears and difficult feelings. However, therapists must be prepared to provide a more parental-like secure base by giving special attention to a particular child, when required.

Overall, however, group psychotherapy with children, in particular the group-analytic approach, has been a relatively neglected area. This seems especially so when compared with group therapy with adults or with individual child psychotherapy. I believe that the primacy of the parent–child relationship in early development has influenced the structure of children's services. Indeed, most of the therapeutic work with children continues to take place on a one-to-one basis by practitioners trained in individual child psychotherapy or child analysis – while family therapy remains the second treatment option, often combined with individual psychotherapy.

Child psychotherapists and other care professionals have shown indeed a growing interest in child group work in the last 25 years. However, in contrast to the Institute of Psychoanalysis, which provides specific training in child analysis, the Institute of Group Analysis (the main provider of group psychotherapy training in the UK) has not incorporated a distinct child group therapy training. This had been somehow predicted by the late Jim Bamber (1988, p. 102): "Unless future group analysts are trained to conduct such groups, they will be left to the less well trained and group analysis will be the more impoverished for neglecting such a potential area for group analytic application".

Bowlby taught me that relationships with siblings are precious and should not be discounted. In this chapter, I believe I have shown that siblings, peers and group attachments play an increasingly important role in a child's development, healthy functioning and wellbeing. In addition, these secondary or subsidiary attachments can mitigate or compensate for the problems and ruptures with primary attachment figures – something that can be especially crucial under conditions of severe trauma and loss.

8

AUTHORITY AND ATTACHMENT IN ADOLESCENCE

Bowlby had a reputation of being most considerate of other people's work. This certainly was my experience of supervision with him. From 1986 to 1990 I did substantial locum work at Hill End Adolescent Unit (HEAU). That was an in-patient psychiatric resource for young people aged 11 to 16, located in the outskirts of London, with Peter Bruggen as lead consultant (see Chapter 1). The Unit's entire therapeutic programme took place in family or groups sessions; the concept of authority was thoroughly used. It was an innovative approach. It appeared to contradict some of the attachment ideas that I was learning at the time, on the surface at least.

Bowlby was aware of Bruggen's different philosophy but encouraged me to get on with it, as an important part of my professional development. Bowlby actually said to me that it was good for a junior psychiatrist to expand the repertoire of training experiences and integrate them. I rarely needed to discuss my work at the Adolescent Unit with him. I was feeling confident enough to explore a territory that was new but, in a way, also familiar. I had been an adolescent myself *not* too long ago.

Looking back, I can say that I very much enjoyed this post. The team was highly enthusiastic – with Bruggen as a charismatic and unconventional leader. The work was based on a modified *therapeutic community* mode – a term coined by Tom Main in his landmark paper "The Hospital as a Therapeutic Institution" (Main, 1946). It was painful at times to witness youngsters breaking down. Overall, however, seeing so many young people recovering, making progress and showing passion for life was a decidedly rewarding experience. In this chapter I shall explore key aspects of the work at the Unit, which provided a complementary perspective to my psychoanalytically oriented Tavistock training and my independent mentorship with Bowlby.

Bruggen was a creative and atypical consultant. I took pleasure in working and swimming with him – a pleasure that was reciprocal. He gave me a signed copy of his second book, *Helping Families: Systems, Residential and Agency Responsibility*, with a hand written dedicatory: "*To Arturo Ezquerro, with whom I have enjoyed swimming and working*" (Bruggen & O'Brian, 1987). I also had to accommodate the fact that he appeared to be in two minds about Bowlby. This is described vividly in *Castaway's Corner* (Bruggen, 2006, p. 307):

> As a priggish 1950s medical student, frozen and defended (I had seen the Robertson film 'A Two-year Old Goes to Hospital' and not felt a wisp of emotion), I was staying with my parents when they invited Burnley's new chief constable for dinner. Probed by my mother for the answer to rising crime and disorder, our guest mentioned John Bowlby's (1953a) 'Child Care and the Growth of Love' which had recently been published. I tried it and, although I found it difficult to read, I was curious.

Bruggen went on explaining that, in 1966, he actually met Bowlby as he himself was working his way into the Tavistock Clinic. The encounter took place at the Sixth International Congress of the Association for Child Psychiatry and Allied Professions, in Edinburgh. This was the culmination of Bowlby's four-year Presidency. He played a large leading role in the Congress and closed the proceedings by saying thank you to all the people who had worked so hard. But he did not give any name checks and then stepped back from the podium. The audience clapped enthusiastically for a long time.

Bruggen revelled in Bowlby's brevity, believing he was avoiding the usual tedious list of names; but subsequently experienced ambivalent feelings towards him when he stepped forward to the podium several times in short succession. Nonetheless, Bruggen considered attachment theory a beacon and "a sign post of orientation for clinical and caring workers" (Bruggen & O'Brian, 1987, p. 52). Recently, he and I watched together *Two Days, One Night*, a poignant but invigorating 2014 Belgian film drama, directed by the Dardenne brothers. As we discussed the film, he told me that he had admired Bowlby for being able to put his ideas in beautifully crafted plain English: "he was brilliant at cutting through jargon" (Bruggen, 2006, p. 307).

Exploration or experimentation?

The film Bruggen and I had watched together was attention-grabbing. It depicted, in powerfully simple images, a battle for survival – as Bowlby might have put it. Sandra, a young woman suffering from depression, lost her job in what appeared to be a case of discrimination against her in favour of her colleagues as the result of her mental health problems. Her fellow employees received an annual bonus from the money left after her dismissal. She could no longer cope and took an overdose.

Sandra's husband took her to hospital and she survived. He later encouraged her to fight for the job. She was hardly fit enough to pull herself out of bed, let alone wade into battle. But she was able to take heart from her husband's support and decided to visit each and every one of her colleagues in an attempt to reverse her redundancy. With each house that she visited, she became able to rediscover her appetite for life; she reconnected to the world. Who cared, in the end, that the odds were stacked against her and that she may well not get her job back?

Characters in fiction can transmit psychological reality in a powerful way – Freud had in fact suggested this. Sandra indeed conveyed to us that the fight for survival is always worth it, whatever the result. Even if she loses, she has already won. Like Bowlby and Bruggen, she put up a good fight. It may sound odd to draw an analogy between these two distinguished psychiatrists and a vulnerable fictional character such as Sandra. But they all share a need for secure attachments and a struggle for survival. And this struggle does not know of class, race, gender, sexual orientation, creed or status.

At the moment, much public confidence is being eroded by aggressive neo-liberal policies. The global crisis has made many vulnerable adolescents and young adults feel hopeless – especially in the light of high levels of youth unemployment. In a recent report outlined by Peter Walker in *The Guardian* on 20 October 2014, the Maternal Mental Health Alliance expressed concerns about the deterioration of care services for mothers, babies and young people. Substandard mental health care for pregnant women and new mothers is creating long-term costs of more than £8 billion every year, according to a pioneering study of the effects of maternal depression, anxiety and other illnesses. As reported by Walker, this piece of research was produced by the London School of Economics and the UK Centre for Mental Health charity.

With a modest budget, *Two Days, One Night* comes out as a psychologically delving and gently uplifting contemporary experience. While many people struggle to survive with little welfare support, in recent years, billions of pounds of British public money have gone to business, with Disney as one of the main beneficiaries. "They really are taking the Mickey", Aditya Chakrabortty remarked in *The Guardian* on 6 October 2014. In fact, the British government had since 2007 handed the Hollywood giant some £170 million to make films in Great Britain (last year alone nearly £50 million in tax credits).

This, I gather, is being considered a good investment in the long-term mental health of young people. In contrast to this, the same government has recently agreed to scrap the £347 million crises fund, which used to provide emergency cash for families on the verge of homelessness or starvation. While help for the poor and for people sleeping on the street is increasingly deemed unaffordable, the money given to the fantasy and lucrative world of Disney is considered well spent. I cannot help being concerned about the erosion of welfare, the rise of youth unemployment and the gradual loss of a secure society (Kraemer & Roberts, 1996; Ezquerro, 2000a; Gerhardt, 2010).

Bowlby had taught me that the quality of exploration is strongly linked to the experience of a secure enough base. That made a lot of sense. After the film, Bruggen intimated to me that he was one of the many thousands of children who were evacuated in Britain as a result of the war. He was received into foster care – a difficult experience for him. I can imagine that, in a way, he had to survive with a shakier base. But he built a more than good enough emotional resilience, as well as a glittering career as a psychiatrist and family therapist. Like Bowlby, he was helped by personal analysis, became a member of the British Psychoanalytical Society and developed his own independent thinking.

Both Bowlby and Bruggen had read Aldous Huxley's (1954) acclaimed book, *The Doors of Perception: On the Author's Sensations under the Influence of Mescaline*. Bowlby (see Chapter 5) chose to develop professional contacts with Sir Julian Huxley (Aldous' brother) and had little interest in mind-altering drugs. In his view, they can do more harm than good.

Bowlby was particularly concerned about the use of drugs for children and young people, as they interfere with the still developing central nervous system and the biochemistry of the brain. However, he occasionally accepted research funding from multinational pharmaceutical companies. On the other hand, Bruggen became angry with me when I organised a psychotherapy conference and told him that I would be prepared to accept such funding. Nevertheless, Bowlby's and Bruggen's main approach was drug-free psychotherapy.

Indeed, there were some differences. As a junior psychiatrist in the late 1950s, in contrast to Bowlby, Bruggen chose to have treatment with someone who used LSD:

> I had weekly therapy sessions and took LSD every few weeks, very carefully managed by a doctor giving me the drugs. It was still legal because the young had not yet started taking it for kicks, inspiring older people to try to stop them. I found it very helpful. I stopped taking sleeping tablets, started to pass my exams in psychiatry, to dream in colour and think in three dimensions, got on better with people and I settled down to live with someone else. The drug helped me and I'm sorry that is no longer available for others.
>
> *(Bruggen, 2006, p. 308)*

The *Single Convention on Narcotic Drugs 1961* made many (non-pharmaceutical) mind-altering substances illegal. A new war on drugs started, according to Bruggen, much to the delight of producers, pushers and the police. When I asked if he had been mischievous, he responded without hesitation that he was deadly serious on this:

> The truly mischievous were those who, having effectively lost their jobs with the end of alcohol prohibition in the USA, sought to fuel anxiety about other drugs in the press and legislature…. The subsequent prohibition of some of the mind-altering drugs has been followed by human alienation and suffering on a scale far greater than that wrought by the prohibition of alcohol alone in the 1920s.
>
> *(ibid., p. 308)*

If we use death as a metric for significance, now more than ten thousand deaths a year can be attributed to the illegal drugs trade in Mexico alone.

Most young people experiment with *drugs, sex, and rock 'n' roll*, as well as with relationships and authority. As they mature, this fascination diminishes. Working with disturbed adolescents who could hardly explore or experiment, or who had experimented too dangerously, became a major challenge for me. According to Bowlby, exploration is a creative and life-long learning process through which we examine something new systematically. Experimentation can also be creative and is widely used by scientists. However, in colloquial terms, it usually refers to a more transient process of testing external reality. In any case, adolescents search for new explanations: the childhood ones are no longer valid.

And so I decided to study this turbulent period in our life cycle. What follows is some of what I learned.

Is there a remedy for adolescence?

Etymologically, the word 'adolescent' comes from the Latin verb *adolescere*, meaning to grow, to blossom, to develop. Interestingly, the word 'adult' has the same origin. However, adolescent comes from the present participle *adolescentem*, meaning 'it is growing'; while adult comes from the past participle *adultum* meaning 'it has grown'. The Latin noun *adolescens* or *adulescens* was used in ancient Rome to designate a young person until approximately 25 years.

After this age, the person was called *iuvenis* until about the age of 40. In the second century BC, the Roman writer Marco Terencio Varrón recognised that *adulescentes ab alescendo sic nominatos* (adolescents are called like this because they are growing). In the Romance European languages, the terms *adolescent* and *adolescence* appear for the first time in France, in the thirteenth century and soon after this in Spain as *adolescente* and *adolescencia*. The term *adolescent* appeared in English in the fifteenth century; well before the first written record of the word *adult*, which appeared in 1531.

The start of a psychological study of adolescence is attributed to Granville Stanley Hall (1846–1924). He borrowed the concept *sturm und drang* (storm and stress) from German literature and applied it to young people. In Classical Greece, Plato held a view of youth as a time of marked emotional upheaval. Shakespeare portrayed teenagers as spending their time doing little more than *wronging the ancientry*. Most contemporary writers tend to agree with the idea of turbulence following the years of puberty: a disruption of peaceful child growth. In Hall's opinion, the emotional turmoil and rebelliousness of adolescence can be seen as defiance against establishment thinking. He also believed that adolescence contains the remnants of both an uninhibited childish selfishness and an increasingly idealised altruism.

Bowlby's language towards children was friendlier than Hall's. He thought that childhood is not a period of selfishness. This term has a negative connotation, and he preferred to reframe it with an understanding that proximity-seeking, attachment behaviour in children is habitually activated more often and in a more intense fashion than in adolescents or adults (Bowlby, 1988a, p. 82). From his evolutionary perspective, that is an instinct for social connectedness serving survival. He also considered that in adolescence the excursions from attachment figures become longer in time and space and that new attachment figures are likely to be sought (ibid., p. 62).

The general view today is to consider adolescence as a transition involving multi-dimensional changes: rapid bodily growth, dramatic psychosocial shifts, mood swings and emotional conflict or confusion. It could be said that conditions prevailing during this transitional life stage are sometimes unfavourable to rational thinking. Action is the key note, not only in the adolescent but also in those surrounding him or her; particularly those responsible for the care of young people in difficulty. However, in spite of the pressure for action, the provision of space and time for thinking is, in my view, critical for the adolescent, the parents and the care professionals. *Authority* during this period is a key issue for parents, for society and for the adolescents themselves.

Ordinary adolescent experimentation (or exploration?) is often 'pathologised'. However, adolescence is a normal developmental process. There can be many paths through adolescence constituting a range of normality. The adolescent journey seems to take a long time and yet it tends to be remembered as a short time. Unfortunately, some adults (and indeed some health professionals) come to regard adolescence itself as abnormal, owing to the strong feelings aroused in them by young people. As therapists, we need to be mindful that attachment and exploration needs can manifest themselves in a dramatically fluctuating manner during this life period, particularly in its early years. This may include risk-taking activities and aggressive rebelliousness against authority, as well as child-like demanding behaviour.

The ultimate goal of adolescence is to grow an adult. This is meant to be a natural course; but the trails by which a young person may traverse this phase show broad individual variations. While Erikson (1971) regarded adolescence as a normative process and not an affliction, Winnicott (1965, 1969) had often commented that there is no cure for adolescence and that the cure can only belong to the passage of time and the maturation process. In his view, this adolescent progression is largely a social phenomenon that takes time. Early adolescents can be pressed into sexual intercourse before they are emotionally ready for it – as if they were trying to get rid of the *sexual problem.*

Like Winnicott, Briggs (2002) also argues that a prolonged phase of adolescence might be needed to prepare for the demands of adulthood, in the context of our current turbulent society. In spite of its own turbulence, and partly as a result of it, I think adolescence is a delicate episode in our lives, in which there are both risks and opportunities. For the majority of adolescents, it should be considered a time of discomfort rather than disturbance. For a few, things can go wrong: manifestations of serious personality problems and mental illness can become prominent in this period. In order to reflect further on the interface between normality and pathology in adolescence, let us now consider some of the main features of adolescent development.

Adolescent ages and stages

In the twenty-first century, there is no worldwide agreement with regard to the time boundaries for adolescence. The United Nations Population Fund and the World Health Organization define adolescents as being between the ages of 10 and 19. However, the World Bank, the International Labour Organization and the World Programme of Action for Youth refer to adolescents as 'youth' who are between the ages of 15 and 24. Other agencies define adolescence differently, according to cultural beliefs and practices. In most countries, adolescence is broadly seen as a transition between childhood and adulthood, from dependence on family to autonomy. This means that, in some regions adolescence could terminate in one's late 20s, early 30s, or later.

A number of authors (for example, Blos, 1962; Miller, 1974; Steinberg, 1983; O'Connell, 1979; Coleman, 1985; Frankel, 1998) have suggested that it is useful to differentiate several sub-phases within adolescence. An overall description of these sub-phases could be as follows:

- Early adolescence or the period of turmoil: between, say, 11 and 14.
- Middle adolescence or the period of identification: approximately, between 15 and 17.
- Late adolescence: the time of settling into a role and an identity, from 18 to 20-something or older.

However, there are so many individual and group variations that the above should only be seen as a rough guide. As you can imagine, the tasks and behavioural patterns of these periods overlap and inter-mingle significantly, particularly those of early and middle adolescence.

Early adolescence

The rapid spurt of physical growth, including sexual organs, brings with it an inability to accurately estimate the new body space and self-image. It is difficult to digest this emotionally at the same pace to the one of the bodily changes themselves. The process reminds me of my first flight across the Atlantic. On arrival in South America from London, I had a strange feeling and I thought it was jet lag. However, one of my Latin American friends told me that the writer, and Nobel Prize of Literature, Gabriel García Márquez had suggested that when we travel by plane the body arrives first, while the mind is lost somewhere for a day or two until it can join the body again.

In the early adolescent, the physical and sexual changes are not matched by a psychological equivalent. A 13-year-old girl said in one the therapy groups: "I feel my body is ahead of my brain". This often generates a sense of inner turmoil and a sharp increase of aggressive drives. The young person dealing with these urges may feel bewildered – at times able to control them and, at other times, at their mercy.

This can lead to a rollercoaster of ups and downs. The same person is by turn assertive and submissive; industrious and lazy; charming and offensive; cynical and idealistic; arrogant and self-effacing; cruel and considerate; elated and downcast. In the same group, a 14-year-old boy said: "One minute I am on top of the world; next minute I am the most miserable person in the entire universe".

The increase in sexual and aggressive drives at this time, in addition to colouring the struggle for autonomy from the parents, may often lead to rejection of previously internalised attitudes. Parental values and standards can then be experienced as harsh and punitive; parents as less loved and less loving. With the partial withdrawal from the familiar parental love, the young person turns to a *special friend* who acquires an important significance for both boys and girls, in terms of the formation of an ego ideal.

This ideal would have to be gradually relinquished in order to develop a more realistic self-identity, which tends to characterise the sub-phase of middle adolescence. During this process, the young person may experience much pain and a sense of loss or inner emptiness and impoverishment. This may lead to a retreat to familiar positions, from which to make some plea for help from a parent or other authority figure to control the turmoil or disturbance. Alternatively, the young person may withdraw into a self-centred world or seek refuge in drug-taking.

Middle adolescence

During this sub-phase, in addition to continuing their struggle to adapt to the impact of their changing bodies and increased instinctual impulses, young people are moving towards establishing their identities as relatively autonomous individuals. This includes sexual identities and choices. In order to achieve a sense of individual uniqueness, the young person has to give up their unquestioned childhood acceptance of parental attitudes about the world, morals and society, and forge for themselves their own viewpoints. The loosening of the bond to the parents is, partly, compensated by an increased contact with peers. In middle adolescence, perhaps more than at other life stages, the influence of the peer group is critical.

Acceptance by their peers is a powerful antidote to the sense of loneliness and isolation experienced by many adolescents. Failure to achieve membership of a peer group (maybe due to personal inadequacy, emotional insecurity and fear of rejection) can drive the adolescent back to their parents. This might be experienced as a humiliating surrender. Parents would need to be understanding and sympathetic in order to help the adolescent to save face. Giving in to child-like demands for immediate gratification can be counterproductive at this stage: it can reinforce feelings of powerlessness and humiliation in the adolescent. This, in turn, may trigger anger and aggressiveness towards the parents. Sometimes the middle-aged adolescent feels trapped in a vicious cycle of anxiety, hostility and depression, as he tries to break away from the parents.

It is important that parents help their adolescent children regulate emotional distance and explore relationships with their peer group. For the future world of young people to develop harmoniously, it would have to be built in the company of their peers. This may involve friendship or rivalry; collaboration or competition. It is crucial for the adolescent to turn to others with similar uncertainties to their own. That is for mutual support; for exploration of related conflicts; for comparison and validation of sexual identity; for experimentation with social roles. Differing identities are tried out, frequently, on the basis of identification with significant adults or role models other than the parents, like teachers, footballers, pop stars or other celebrities.

These identifications may sometimes resemble the parent. At other times, they may well be oppositional – chosen to spite parents and contradict their values. The departure from parents involves not only the escape from their restrictions, but also the loss of their approval and support. This gap may partly be filled by a reactivation of 'narcissistic' libido; leading to a temporary egotistic state characterised by an overvaluation of the self, self-absorption and self-centeredness. The adolescent mental states can fluctuate between an inflated grandiose self and a deflated depressed self. This narcissistic stage is temporary and represents an intermediate position in development, between the giving up of the parental love objects and the gradual movement towards new external love objects of the opposite or same sex.

Late adolescence

This sub-phase is in some way open-ended. The physical growth is usually completed, but the adolescent is still facing the task of consolidating personal identity in the multi-relational context of an increasingly complex world. Society expects that the personality structure should now be quite firmly established. Optimally, the late adolescent would have achieved a reasonably stable sense of identity, as well as some constancy with regard to self-esteem, personal interests and relationships, which would help them navigate the stresses of everyday life.

At this point, however, there might be a resurfacing of those conflicts that were not properly worked through during the previous stages. This may generate problems with personal choices, friendships and love relationships; perhaps leading to an inability to cope with the increasing academic, social and work demands.

This *closing* sub-phase of adolescence is a testing one, throwing a heavy load on the integrative capacity of the young person. Important life decisions have to be made about examinations, career choice, long-term sexual relationships, living arrangements and social roles. Previous tenuously held adaptations will no longer suffice. Settling into adulthood may take a number of years for most late adolescents. It is not unusual to retreat into psychological defences that were previously useful but are no longer effective. This has been described by Erikson (1971) as a 'developmental moratorium'.

Thus, the time when adulthood itself is achieved remains diffuse, especially in the light of recent economic and socio-demographic changes. Some authors like Jacobsson (2005) have postulated that 'young adulthood' may have to be considered as a separate developmental stage in its own right. Thus, a new debate has started, and we may need to disentangle what belongs to late adolescents and what to young adults.

An innovative Adolescent Unit

Bowlby played a part in the process that opened the eyes of British society to the need of specific mental health services for adolescents, recognising the distinctive developmental needs and difficulties of young people. His message on adolescent disturbance was delivered timely to a country alarmed by war-time disruptions of family life and dismayed by the huge increases in juvenile delinquency (Bowlby, 1944). Specialist psychiatric services for this age group would soon be created in Britain. The first two in-patient adolescent units, at Bethlem Royal Hospital (London) and at St. Ebba's Hospital (Epsom), both opened in 1949. The Tavistock Clinic established its own Adolescent (out-patient) Department in 1959.

Bruggen's Adolescent Unit opened in St. Albans in 1969. Covering a population of over four million, the Unit primarily provided ongoing specialist consultation and support to families and professionals in the community, as well as short-term in-patient group treatment for troubled young adolescents. The intricacies of the therapeutic process were more or less as described in the following passages. At the point of referral, adolescents under 16 were assessed together with their family or the professionals in charge of their care.

The primary task of the assessment was to work with the family's resources and to support the authority of parents or professionals, with a view to keeping the young person living in the community. If this became no longer possible, the adolescent would join, at the point of admission, the hospital community group together with the other young residents and staff. Parents or professionals with parental authority were ultimately responsible for deciding on in-patient admission. This procedure has been meticulously defined (Bruggen & Pitt-Aikens, 1975; Bruggen, 1979; Bruggen et al., 1981; Bruggen & O'Brian, 1986).

Adolescents up to their 16th birthday are considered in most societies to be under legal age; in the UK they are described as *minors*. Before puberty, children have little option but to accept parental authority. Most of the major decisions in their lives are made by the adults. The relationship with authority alters significantly in adolescence. Among other changes, a physiological capacity to procreate is acquired; something that is largely beyond parental control. Parents may struggle with this; while the young person's emotional and psychosocial development cannot keep pace with the dramatic physical changes.

The authority of parents is gradually replaced by the authority of society. That is used for rules and regulations, with regard to legal age for remunerated jobs, consensual sex, getting married and voting at national or local elections. Authority also has a role model component, which is crucial for the adolescent's long search for identity and meaning.

After 16 adolescents have more legal rights, but full legal capacity is not usually obtained until the age of 18. Therefore, the decision-making structure employed by the Unit was consistent with society's legal framework. However, staff avoided using medical diagnoses as a reason for admission. In most, if not all, cases referred there was a link between the presenting problem and issues of authority in the family or the institutional home where the adolescent lived.

The majority of the young people referred were out of control and on the verge of being excluded from home. Care and control had both broken down. However, an admission to a psychiatric hospital was potentially detrimental to the image of a young person, since it might be interpreted as being mad, psychotic or psychopathic. This could negatively affect his or her range of opportunities in the future. As we saw earlier in *Two Days, One Night*, discrimination on the grounds of mental health problems is still present.

The Unit took the risk of stigma and discrimination seriously. Thus, the decision to admit a young person as an in-patient had to be justified beyond reasonable doubt. It would have to be a last resort and Bruggen literally meant this, even when it might not be politically correct. He and the team were so successful in keeping troubled and troubling adolescents in the community, that many of the 30 hospital beds remained empty. This achievement was not properly understood by the Department of Health's advisors who, within a year of the Unit being opened, recommended that he be removed from the job.

Like Bowlby, Bruggen was a good fighter. He managed to persuade the Health Authority to see merit in the *empty beds*, a concept that today we call care in the community. Additionally, having enough empty beds can help hospitals cope better in case of a sudden increase of illness, like in epidemics. In spite of the initial opposition, Bruggen kept his job for some 30 years until his retirement and provided a good role model for those who worked with him.

Work at HEAU was inspired by the Palo Alto Mental Research Institute (MRI) in California. Opened in 1958, MRI was one of the founding institutions of brief and family therapy. The latter had been introduced by Bowlby (1949) at the Tavistock Clinic. MRI gradually became one of the foremost sources of ideas in the area of interactional and systemic studies, applied to clinical work with individuals, families and groups. For many practitioners wanting to be at the cutting edge of psychotherapy research and practice, it was the go-to place. Many MRI members became leading figures in the field. Among them, Don Jackson, Jay Haley, Paul Watzlawick, Richard Fish, Irvin Yalom, Virginia Satir and Salvador Minuchin were prominent.

Fostering a climate of almost untrammelled experimentalism, MRI started the first formal training programme in family therapy, and produced some of the most seminal early papers and books in the field. While working at Bruggen's HEAU, I found it useful to read *The Situation is Hopeless but not Serious: The Pursuit of Unhappiness* (Watzlawick, 1983). The book provided me with original ideas for brief interventions with adolescents and their families, particularly those presenting themselves with dramatic scenarios where nothing seemed to be of help.

I was also influenced by the systemic family therapists of the Milan Group. In one of their books *Paradox and Counter-Paradox* (Palazzoli et al., 1978), it was possible to understand apparently contradictory messages in families coming to therapy for help to change while, at the same time, showing a resistance to change. In order to find a way forward, family relationships and interactions were not seen as *linear*, but as complementary and linked to one another: a system of somewhat *circular* feedback loops. The symptoms of the adolescent were no longer seen as being caused by, or causing problems to, another family member – but as a form of communication. The therapist's task was to tackle the family system differently; for example, to respond with the counter-paradox of *positive connotation*.

The anorexia of a girl or the delinquent behaviour of a boy were reframed as a powerful communication; which was in a way helping the parents to share a common worry and stay together rather than breaking up. Bowlby had been helping families using ideas on group dynamics, originally formulated by Bion and Rickman (1943). His work included talking with the family group about adolescent and childhood experiences in order to promote understanding and reduction of tension. In looking at the mutual influences that family members' communications had on one another, his approach could be considered systemic as well.

Bowlby was a pioneer in this but, having laid the foundations, he left to others the development and refinement of his early clinical work. This included the use of live supervision: one therapist would sit in the room but outside the circle and act as a consultant, exclusively, to the therapist conducting the interview. With the introduction of video cameras and one-way screens, the live supervision model gained new perspectives: observing the work from a meta-position.

When at one of the supervision meetings with Bowlby, in February 1998, I asked him for his views on systemic family therapy, he unassumingly responded that he had not kept up with the field and that he had been left behind by recent developments. He further explained that he was keen on generic systems theory and appreciated that the best way of looking at families was through the systemic lenses. After his response, he searched in his bookshelves and handed me something he quickly found. That was a copy of his most recently published paper *Developmental Psychiatry Comes of Age* (Bowlby, 1988b). The article is pretty systemic in its outlook. It uses concepts such as feedback loops, homeostasis and goal-corrected behaviour (see Chapter 6).

Towards the end of the session, Bowlby also gave me the gift of a brief piece of wisdom. This was a simple, short and powerful question that he used while working with families within which members found it difficult to communicate with one another: "*Who wants what?*" I found the question therapeutically effective: a shortcut that invited everyone in the family to think and try to understand other members' motives and expectations.

However, Bowlby was doubtful about the view of many systemic family therapists who regarded the child's or adolescent's symptomatology as being in some way beneficial to the stability of the parental couple. He did not look at the family dynamic in this way. On the contrary, he thought that, more often than not, the problem presented by the so-called *index patient* (usually the child or adolescent) was a reflection of an unresolved conflict in the relationship between the child and the parents.

Bowlby's comments in our supervision were consistent with what he had said in an interview the previous year, aged 80:

> I don't see the child's behaviour as in any way advantageous. I avoid the word 'functional' because that's used in so many ways. It doesn't seem to me there's any pay off in the child's behaviour. It is just an unfortunate outcome of a conflict that's going on elsewhere.
>
> *(quoted in Byng-Hall, 1987, p. 6)*

Bowlby would have enjoyed MRI's innovation and liveliness, I believe, if he had revisited it. His research into the consequences of early mother–child separation and the nature of the infant's early emotional bonds was absorbing most of his professional time and energy, during the period MRI took off. In fact, in 1957, he had taken a sabbatical to become a fellow at the Center for Advanced Study in the Behavioral Sciences at Stanford University, California. This Center was founded in 1954, just a few miles away from the place where MRI would later be located, and became one of the turning points in the unfolding of attachment theory (see Chapter 6). These two influential schools developed in parallel. The first volume of Bowlby's trilogy on *Attachment and Loss* was published in 1969, the year Bruggen's Unit opened.

In Paris, the previous spring, thousands of young people demonstrated and joined the global hippy revolution: a creative movement of love- and peace-making, which helped end the Vietnam War. These were the children of those who fought the Second World War – a twist in the adolescent rebelliousness that usually manifested itself towards established authority. Bruggen, like Bowlby, a committed pacifist supporting welfare rather than warfare, welcomed this tide of change. However, he was mindful of the needs for structure and limits brought about by his adolescent patients.

Bruggen discussed the management of adolescents with Derek Miller (1974), his supervising consultant at the Tavistock Clinic, and Winnicott (1969), his supervisor for the training at the British Psychoanalytical Society. Both supported him to use professional authority in his work with young people. In respect of his Tavistock training in adolescent psychiatry Bruggen said:

> My main supervisor and teacher was Derek Miller. He taught me to be clear, firm and tough with adolescents; a striking contrast to the permissiveness I had previously thought would work for everyone. His ideas helped me out of many tangles and, when I was subsequently appointed as consultant to an in-patient adolescent unit, this idea became one of my foundations.
>
> *(Bruggen, 2006, p. 309)*

HEAU's team developed an ethos through which parents, or carers, were invested with an unequivocal authority. The bottom line was about how to integrate authority and caring. Almost always, their decision-making on in-patient admission was based on their ability, or otherwise, to cope with their adolescent-children's difficult behaviour. Staff would always encourage parents to explore whether there might be anything else they or the adolescent could do differently in order to cope and prevent the in-patient admission. That was sorted out at the initial family consultation or at a follow-up meeting. The benefits of such consultations seemed more obvious when the people seeking help were close to despair.

Staff were cautious about using a formal psychiatric diagnosis: something potentially detrimental for the adolescent. Instead, they found it more useful to describe the problem in terms of the young person's complex and rapidly changing thoughts, emotions and behaviour – and how these sudden changes affected the adults living with them. The parents' ability to cope with the problems presented with their adolescent children was looked at and strongly supported. The team's availability for further consultations and guidance more often than not helped parents to rediscover and develop their own capacity to manage the adolescent at home. That was an ideal scenario: everybody staying at the coping level. But it was hard work.

A more usual scenario was parents complaining that they could not cope with the aggressive behaviour and dangerous lifestyle of the young adolescents who, when challenged, swore at them. This open hostility and lack of respect can be seen as a way of testing adult boundaries, which reinforces the idea that limit setting is an important part of therapeutic work with this age group:

> It is fashionable to say that authority can go too far.... For the younger adolescent (bursting with feelings of size and strength) individual liberty and authority are both important, but authority and the handling of it by older people who are prepared to receive hostility and confrontation without giving in, is especially important.
>
> *(Bruggen, 1979, p. 353)*

The authority of the adolescent

In a good number of the families referred to HEAU, the young adolescents decided if and when they went to bed, if and when they went out or came in; they often sabotaged any suggestion of being told what to do. In these family settings, the parents had abdicated their authority and responsibility for the care of the adolescent. A crisis had inevitably followed, leading sometimes to trouble with the law. In the circumstances, Bruggen and the team seriously valued the opportunity to support, rather than take over, the authority of the parents or those with parental responsibilities.

At the point of referral, the adolescents would never be seen on their own but together with those holding legal authority. As mentioned earlier, Bruggen was particularly adamant to emphasise that a decision to admit would always have to be made by the parents, or those holding legal authority, as part of a planned return to the family or children's home. In this way, the ineffectual parents may now stand up to their out of control adolescent children.

While evidently supporting the authority of the parents, the Unit also backed the developing authority of the adolescents themselves. A large proportion of them were troubled by contradictory forces and in need of a firm and caring boundary. Limit setting was initially difficult or unpleasant but, in turn, it enabled the young residents to take the message in: they developed a sense of inner authority that they could appreciate as their own. Young people learn fast.

When the Unit opened, the handover from the morning shift of nurses to the afternoon shift took placed behind the closed door of the nurses' office. After that, the daily community meeting took place; staff felt that it was important for them to be in control of the potentially out of control adolescents. The meeting was followed by a staff discussion group, in which propositions were gradually made about opening up communications and making them as transparent as possible.

As a result, a resolution was agreed neither to talk about colleagues in their absence nor to have secrets or gossip about work. Additionally, it was decided that the handover process itself, until then kept private, should be brought into the existing community meeting. Staff decided that, in order to become a true therapeutic community, this change was necessary for reasons of professional responsibility and common-sense management.

The staff handover acquired a new dimension that was easily understandable to all concerned: each person in the meeting had a role, either to talk to or listen to what was said about what had happened. The next suggestion came from the adolescents: one of them suggested that they themselves should give the handover. Staff met the proposal with certain degree of suspicion and concerns about the pace of change. At the staff meetings, some expressed anxieties that the adolescents might be too punitive, would not be objective, would exploit the opportunity to manipulate each other, disrupt the work or split the staff.

Indeed, one important responsibility of the staff was to protect the residents from how they may sometimes treat each other badly or unreasonably. However, the majority opted for giving the adolescents a try and, "when at last they were allowed to take over this role, the boys and girls were, of course, more fluent, more flexible, more imaginative and less punitive than the staff had ever managed to be" (Bruggen & O'Brian, 1987, p. 138).

The next natural step came when the adolescents suggested that they should take over the role of chairing the community meeting as well. Again, their handling of this piece of delegated authority was far more creative than the staff had ever achieved. Peer support and peer sanction were more sensitive and effective. With these two changes the community meeting became for boys and girls the most valuable experience of their brief stay at the Unit – four to six weeks on average. The factual information, feelings, dreams, wishes and fears shared at the meeting acquired new meaning; ideas and suggestions for further work or focus would arise spontaneously.

By all means, the adults retained the power of recapturing the authority that they had delegated, as and when this might be required. But this only happened rarely. Staff later introduced other therapeutic functions in the meeting such as:

"greeting new people, decision-making, saying farewell and monitoring staff" (ibid., p. 139). These additions to the therapeutic programme were usually harvested from courses, conferences and other events of continuous professional development.

In view of the far-reaching consequences of the changes introduced by the adolescents, staff had to rethink their own attitudes and prejudices. The staff meeting developed a self-reflective function where it was possible to mentally tidy up and to ventilate sentiments. In turn, each member was invited to comment on the running and handling of the community meeting, "whether the staff had distributed themselves evenly enough about the room, whether they looked attentive or not, and on the quality of their interventions" (ibid., p. 145).

People at HEAU, staff and patients alike, genuinely helped one another with honest and constructive feedback. Staff support contributed to quite a unanimous feeling of job satisfaction in the team. At Peter Bruggen's 80th birthday party, on 19 July 2014, I met again some 25 colleagues from HEAU. We all remembered our work at the Unit as a highly enjoyable and fulfilling professional experience.

Like Bowlby, Bruggen was a democratic leader who stimulated the development of our authority; we in turn encouraged the adolescents to develop their own authority. At this birthday party, I had a nice feeling of being connected to both Bruggen and Bowlby through the common memories shared with two of my consultant peers: Tony Jaffa and Tony Kaplan. We had worked together at HEAU as senior registrars and had attended the seminar on attachment that Bowlby had run at the Tavistock Clinic 30 years previously (see Chapter 1).

Staff support at the Unit provided also a healthy and balanced way of preparing the team to meet the minds and bodies of fast growing adolescents. Exercises involving the body were not uncommon. The day I had turned 30, I was literally rocked (baby-like) by my colleagues at the staff meeting: a unique birthday present and a good piece of insight – which may have otherwise taken a few months of personal analysis.

The attachment needs for physical and emotional closeness in the adolescents were differentiated from sexual feelings. Sometimes, staff members would give a distressed adolescent a hug that was not sexual. This would always happen in the presence of other people. Adolescents commented that staff affection helped them to feel wanted and accepted. The team developed attuned sensitivity to the feelings, views and growing authority of the young residents.

The late Matt Ellis, a young nursing assistant, commented at one point that live supervision for the staff meeting, similarly to how it was practised in the Unit's systemic family therapy programme, might also contribute towards professional insights and development. The proposal was unanimously accepted. From then on, a fair turn-taking rota was established and one member of staff would sit outside the group circle during the meeting – on a higher chair to catch a good view. Tony Jaffa (1987) described a first-hand experience of the benefits of this tool, which offered new opportunities for growth to younger and older members alike. The quality of the work and timing of staff interventions improved. The therapeutic community became more mature, which enhanced its healing potential.

Live supervision was later incorporated into the community meeting. This expanded the breadth of the work and gave a novel perspective to boundaries. Some of these could be negotiated flexibly, while others could not. The message delivered to the adolescents had to be clear, consistent and ongoing. Staff were in charge of the functioning of the Unit and paid to be so. They made decisions about how it would be run – but did welcome the views of the adolescents, usually consulting with them beforehand. Parents were in charge of where the young people under 16 would live. Adolescents were in charge of their bodies and their minds, their behaviour and their feelings (whether pleasant or unpleasant) and ultimately of their lives.

The adolescent peer group

Therapeutic group work was the backbone of HEAU. There is ample evidence indeed that adolescents can grow in therapy groups (Anthony, 1965; Evans, 1988, 1998, 2000; Behr, 1988; Lucas, 1988; MacLennan & Dies, 1992; Berkovitz, 1995; Tijhuis, 1997, 1998; Woods, 2003; Behr & Hearst, 2005). Of course, adolescents can also grow in individual therapy, but one-to-one therapy sessions were not available at the Unit. So, what happened when an adolescent became very distressed and felt in need of individual support?

The answer is this: they were offered the possibility of calling an instant group meeting. This would be attended by those staff and residents who were available. Allowing adolescents to exercise their own authority flexibly, to expose their vulnerability within an unambiguous boundary structure, paid off. At the ad hoc group meetings, there were moving episodes of open communication among the residents who were able to empower one another.

School work ran alongside therapy work at the Unit in order to keep up continuity of education. At the end of a school day, a 15-year-old boy called a meeting because a 13-year-old girl was looking very depressed and withdrawn. At the community meeting, earlier in the day, staff had attempted to support her to explore her feelings about her father's recent death. Some had asked her to talk about it but to no avail. At the extra meeting, the boy said that he was feeling sorry for her, while the girl looked at the floor silently.

I invited her to talk about good memories of her father. The rationale was that, in identifying the good parts of her father, she would be in a better position to mourn the loss of his goodness. This, in turn, might enable her to face the not so good side of her father and express her feelings about it, too. Suddenly, she shouted: "My father is dead! Why does everyone go on talking about him?" I was surprised by her exclamation and thought of saying that anger was part of a normal bereavement – an idea that I had learned from Bowlby. In the circumstances, however, such a comment would have been an expression of intellectual defensiveness rather than a helpful expression of sympathy to her feelings. The idea was correct; the timing wrong.

Fortunately, the same 15-year-old boy reacted more quickly than anybody else in the room: "They talk about your father because you don't, but I think you need to". This time, the girl listened to him intently and was able to accept his words – to my relief and that of my colleagues. In the next few days and weeks, she talked about how she was desperately missing her father who had usually been caring and supportive of her. Later, she also expressed anger about him who, at times, had not been emotionally available, due to his excessive drinking. This problem contributed to the cirrhosis that killed him. The girl was angry with his father who, in dying, had abandoned her.

Looking back, I could see a process through which adolescents at the Unit projected their incipient sense of personal authority onto their peer group. This investment proved to be an effective way, for most of them, to develop their own views and status. For these youngsters, it was easier to recognise in their peers the parts of themselves that they had projected onto them. The authority of the peer group was helping them to become assertive, rather than aggressive, and to regulate the distance from and to the authority of parents and other adults.

Quite often, parents have to learn to be *downgraded* and to encourage young people to develop autonomous thinking. As well as meaningful relationships with peers, adolescents need to study models of adulthood in addition to those of the parents (Harter et al., 1997). They need to feel that, around them, there are other adults (potential secondary attachment figures) who have already done what they, the adolescents themselves, are trying to do and whom they can use as models. For adolescents, it is also important to realise that reliable attachment figures at times of crisis are invaluable and will continue to be so for the rest of their lives.

The drugs question

Like most of the early therapeutic communities, the Unit tried to manage without using medication. Staff were particularly aware of the fact that the brain of young adolescents has not yet reached full physical and physiological maturity. Psychoactive drugs can deleteriously interfere with the metabolism of the developing brain. In any case, adolescents were encouraged not to *pharmacologise* pain and distress unnecessarily. A 12-year-old girl asked for painkillers to treat what she described as a "terrible headache". Staff advised her to try first some breathing exercises and a neck massage. It worked.

However, some adolescents were so much out of control that they were putting themselves or others at risk. This problem would be discussed at an additional meeting with the person concerned, his or her peers and the staff. The adolescent would be given an opportunity to change the dangerous behaviour to a safer level. This usually worked, although a few times staff needed to make a painful decision and use sedation.

In those occasions, when there seemed to be no other way to keep everyone safe, staff would put across a rather advanced piece of systemic thinking like this:

We have offered you opportunities to behave differently, but you have not changed. We are concerned that the situation is unsafe. We want everyone to be safe. We need to sedate you to treat our anxieties about what you might be doing next.

When an adolescent was sedated, we (the staff) tended to experience a sense of failure. In some way, this was similar to feeling expressed by many parents who could no longer cope with the out of control adolescent. At staff sensitivity meetings we talked about what we might have done to avoid sedation. We were pleasantly surprised one day, yet again, by the adolescents' creativity:

We had talked a number of times to an out of control 13-year-old boy. Eventually we said to him that we had run out of options and that would need to sedate him. But two fellow adolescents (a 14-year-old boy and a 15-year-old girl) intervened. They offered to keep an eye on the younger boy – and to try to protect him from behaving dangerously. We were reassured that they would call a meeting if necessary. The adolescents were able to use the authority given to them knowing that, if they *failed*, the staff had other resources.

This policy at HEAU had the advantage that it reduced the use of medication to a strict minimum, so the development of the young people's internal resources would be maximised. However, sedation was sometimes criticised outside the Unit as if it were a form of punishment. Additionally, as no one was in principle provided with regular medication, this generated a complex dynamic with those adolescents who needed it due to an organic condition. I can recall a 15-year-old boy who required anti-epileptic medication. In one of the therapeutic groups he commented that he was feeling singled out because he was the only adolescent in the Unit taking regular medication at the time.

The in-patient Unit as a secure enough base for exploration

I am aware that I have seldom elaborated on attachment ideas in this chapter. I have done it somewhat on purpose. During the four years I did locum work at HEAU, I rarely needed to present any problem to Bowlby – but it was reassuring to know that he was in the background, should need arise. Bruggen provided a model of group attachment for the staff that enabled my colleagues and I to work autonomously while he was overseeing our work. In addition, the therapeutic approach of short-term, crisis interventions with young people and their families proved to be cost-effective and inspired a number of adolescent psychiatrists (Kaplan, 2002; Kaplan & Racussen, 2012).

Although attachment language *per se* was rarely used at the Unit, Bruggen and his institution provided a secure enough base for me and others to explore and creatively develop brief therapeutic methods with adolescents and families. The short-lived nature of interventions did not encourage the youngsters to form significant attachments with the therapists, as was the case in longer-term therapy. Some colleagues considered this was a drawback in the Unit's programme.

However, adolescents were very much encouraged to think about attachments in their own lives.

In her book chapter "Attachment and other Affectional Bonds across the Life Cycle", Ainsworth (1991, p. 35) stated: "key changes in the nature of attachment may be occasioned by hormonal, neurophysiological and cognitive changes, and not merely by socio-emotional experience". Although beyond the scope of this chapter, those readers interested in exploring attachment in adolescence further may find it useful to look into some of the following: Papini & Roggman, 1992; Rosenstein & Horowitz, 1996; Moretti & Holland, 2003; Moretti & Peled, 2004; Markiewicz et al., 2006; Atger, 2007; Cassidy & Shaver, 2008; Perry, 2009; Allen & Miga, 2010; Flaherty & Sadler, 2011; Dubois-Comtois et al., 2013.

Most of these authors conclude, in different ways, that quality of attachment in adolescence will depend on both the young people and the parents' capacity to redefine their relationships. Co-constructing such relationships is a key element in achieving a secure enough attachment during this complex and rapidly changing developmental stage. Normal adolescents experience a need for an increasing distance from the parents. Physical proximity and spending time together are less necessary to ensure protection and comfort, and to promote exploration.

However, it is still reassuring for adolescents to know that their parents will be readily available, especially during stressful periods. Indeed, the young people's attachment history has a substantial influence on their ability to manage the challenges of adolescence:

> Adolescents who grow up without their home base providing the necessary support and encouragement are likely to be less cheerful, to find life – especially intimate relationships – difficult, and to be vulnerable in conditions of adversity.... It is fortunate, of course, that despite these handicaps some manage to struggle through.
>
> *(Bowlby, 1988b, p. 9)*

The young people admitted to the Unit often experienced a sense of community and peer group belonging. This gave them an opportunity to reflect on and renegotiate the relationships with their primary attachment figures, as well as exploring secondary attachments with peers and other adults. Staff often worked with the youngsters on what it was that they did to make it so difficult for their parents and, sometimes, for the staff. This provided a main focus of work and helped the adolescents take charge of their own behaviour. This, in turn, put them in a better position to accept the imperfect authority of the parents.

Once authority in the family was no longer disputed, anxiety went down and family members could start thinking, collaborating with each other and even feeling the affection that was previously lacking. This could sometimes happen with startling speed. After four weeks at the Unit, a 15-year-old girl wrote to her parents with a newly found sense of confidence and forward looking. I was moved by what she said:

Don't be afraid to be firm with me. I prefer it. It makes me feel more secure. Don't correct me in front of people if you can help it. I'll take much more notice if you talk quietly with me in private. Don't be too upset when I say 'I hate you'. It isn't you I hate but your power to thwart me. Don't make rash promises. Remember that I feel badly when promises are broken. Don't tax my honesty too much. I am easily frightened into telling lies. Don't ever think that it is beneath your dignity to apologise to me and an honest apology makes me feel surprisingly warm towards you.

(quoted in Bruggen, 1979, pp. 353–354)

For a large number of families, the initial meeting prevented the pressing necessity for admission. The knowledge that the Unit would be there as a safety net and that the staff would be available for further therapeutic consultations and guidance, enabled parents to cope with the adolescent at home. The support and assistance that the institution gave to families in crisis could be likened to that of a *secure enough base*. A group of caring and reliable professionals was accessible and responded promptly when needed. If parents could no longer cope, the in-patient admission provided breathing space for them and their offspring to *refuel*.

And that was it. Everyone would have to commit themselves to ensure that the length of admission would be as short as possible. So, change was negotiated via an active process of family therapy sessions and review meetings. Staff encouraged adolescents and parents to mutually agree on a *minimum change*. This, if achieved, should enable parents or carers to feel confident enough to cope again with the adolescent being back at home. Despite the brief nature of the work, at the point of discharge family members expressed a stronger wish for being together than at the point of entrance. It was also possible for them to communicate more openly and be less hostile with one another.

People who have travelled through the stages of adolescence have, inevitably, made many mistakes. So, young people need to take risks, make mistakes, get up and navigate through new experiences in order to grow. Of course, they have not yet had enough time to make the many mistakes that are required to learn about, and successfully manage, the complexities of life. Likewise, they have not had enough time to build up a reasonably stable inner structure, and to acquire the perspective that comes with the experience of overcoming many hurdles and surviving many battles.

It is easier for adolescents to develop healthily when there is a safe structure around them – which they can experiment, play, comply or rebel against: "the structure of standards of behaviour, of ideas, of times, of places and of limits. They need adults who are prepared to hold a point of view and to stand up for it" (Bruggen & Pitt-Aikens, 1975, p. 154). In attachment terms, they need a secure enough base without which the task of growing is harder.

We, the staff, also perceived the caring boundaries established in the structure of Unit as a professional secure base. We explored authority more openly than attachment thinking. Bowlby was interested in our work – and delighted to see me and Hill End Adolescent Unit growing in status. We all became less authoritarian but more authoritative.

9

ATTACHMENT ON THE EDGE

The Tavistock Clinic became the *maternity unit* where attachment theory was born. Pregnancy was difficult; labour and delivery hard work. Bowlby had to navigate through mountains of jargon in psychoanalytic texts and to face a hostile reception to his ideas, in the context of a largely Kleinian orientation that dominated the Clinic after the Second World War. This became a problem for him. But he had resilience and never gave up. His scientific mind conceived problems as neither more nor less than questions that have no easy answer. This attitude enabled him to face tricky questions and deliver tentative answers. This, in turn, helped him reformulate the questions, refine the answers and so forth. A virtuous circle or, rather, a revolutionary spiral developed.

The history of psychoanalysis is strongly linked, indeed, to sexuality (see Chapter 11). Initially, Freud was receptive to true stories of child sexual abuse and incest reported by his patients. But he could not cope with the consequences of his discovery and retreated. The stories somehow seemed unreal for him: a product of the patient's imaginations. Subsequently, he lost interest in real life events and concentrated on his patients' dreams and *phantasies* – a term generally used in the psychoanalytic literature to describe 'unconscious fantasies' (Makari, 2008).

Melanie Klein took this further and developed a theory, and a treatment technique, in which she gave primacy to the role of *phantasies*. Of course, she did not deny history but did not concentrate on it. In my early days at the Tavistock, I struggled to learn the language of the *Unconscious* (I still do). My patients were saying something, but Anton Obholzer was telling me in supervision that they were meaning something else. In Chapter 1, I described a mistake I made by talking to my first Tavistock patient as we were walking along the corridor, on our way to the consulting room. Following this, I decided to say nothing to my patients at the beginning of therapy sessions.

Obholzer made me aware that premature utterances would prevent the patient from spontaneously bringing 'uncontaminated' material to the session. He also directed me to personal analysis. After a first attempt that I shall describe below, I engaged in therapy four times a week with a Spanish-speaking, Mexican-born, training analyst – whom I shall describe as Dr Y. I gained a painful, new perspective of my own history. Almost exclusively, Dr Y used transference interpretations. In the 30 months of my treatment with him, he never greeted me verbally. However, I kept saying hello and goodbye before and after each and every session. He never started a conversation either.

On my arrival at the Tavistock, Obholzer had first recommended Ronald Britton, an experienced child psychiatrist who had recently obtained the status of training analyst. At 55, he was in his prime; soon he became a renowned international writer and lecturer who made major contributions to Kleinian thinking. He later served as President of the British Institute of Psychoanalysis and Vice-President of the International Psychoanalytical Association. I had not heard of him, as I knew little about British psychoanalysis. Obholzer talked highly of him and said that his training status should not imply that the Tavistock wanted me to train as a psycho-analyst. However, if I had eventually made that choice, I would have avoided the hassle of changing analysts.

The assessment was astonishingly straight. Britton received me with a silent handshake. Once in the consulting room he said: "We have 50 minutes. Tell me something about your mother". That, indeed, was an open question. As I was not sure if he wanted me to spend the whole '50-minute hour' on her, I asked: "For how long do you want me to talk about my mother?" He kept neutral eye contact but did not give a verbal response. And so I started a rather uncertain journey. A few times I paused and asked questions such as: "Have I said enough about my mother?" and "Do you want me to talk about something else?" But he was con-sistent with his approach and with his silence indicated, I thought, that he was waiting for me to carry on.

I was a bit lost and assumed that I was under a sort of psychoanalytic examination – but, strangely enough, did not feel anxious. Britton came across as smart and pro-fessional. Despite being a stranger to me, I felt I was in good hands. I trusted him and, while keeping an eye on my watch, ended up telling him all about my mother. In view of my poor English and mixed emotions, it was a difficult job. I stopped some five minutes before time. After a one-minute silence, he said: "Thank you. I think personal analysis would be good for you, but your English is not up to it". He paused and looked at me enquiringly, but I could think of nothing to say. He added: "I will talk to Dr Obholzer". I thanked him and said goodbye.

Looking back, I believe, I would have worked well with Britton. If I had learned English before French, I would have probably become attached to him and may (may not) be a Kleinian today. Louise Lyon, a Kleinian psychoanalyst, Trust Director at the Tavistock Clinic and a good friend, told me recently that the so-called chilly Kleinians of the past have evolved and are warmer nowadays.

Margot Waddell (2002) provided an excellent, comprehensive and user-friendly account of contemporary Kleinian thinking and practice at the Tavistock.

Indeed, Britton's recommendation was that I should have analysis in my *mother* tongue. So, here I was working with Dr Y. For the most part of the first two years, I enjoyed it. I had never before talked to anyone in such detail and for so long about my parents and siblings. He did not pay much attention to the major losses and bereavements that I had experienced as a young child. But he interpreted that I must have felt dethroned by my younger brother and jealous of my brain-damaged sister, who needed a great deal of attention from my parents. That was a discovery and liberation. However, there was an extraordinary lack of warmth in his approach, which I did not take personally but attributed to the rigorous requirements of his technique.

In spite of this, I looked forward to attending all the sessions and felt reasonably attached to Dr Y, without experiencing much anxiety or discomfort. I often talked to him about my work at the Tavistock, which helped me separate what belonged to me and what to my patients. I was eager to learn about them as well as about myself. Bowlby supported my Kleinian analysis: "You can learn from it", he said. But he warned me that the Kleinians put a strong emphasis on the negative side of the transference. I could cope with that. However, as I shall explain later, some *contextual* issues in the third year of analysis became difficult to handle.

Can we make sense of life and death?

As I struggled to make *transference interpretations* in the work with my Tavistock patients, Obholzer gave me a copy of Melanie Klein's classic paper "The Origins of Transference" (Klein, 1952). This is a key publication, beautifully written. I treasure it especially as it was a gift from my somewhat idealised Kleinian tutor, with whom I was feeling ambivalently attached. It came across as a caring gesture at a time when I needed it most. It helped me to understand basic aspects of psychoanalytic theory and technique and, also, to feel more secure in my relationship with Obholzer. I gather Joan Riviere (Bowlby's analyst) must have played a part in the final version of the paper, as she often edited Melanie Klein's writings in English.

Klein's article starts with a reference to Freud's position in 1905 regarding his conception of *transferences*:

> They are new editions or facsimiles of the tendencies and phantasies which are aroused and made conscious during the process of the analysis; but … they replace some earlier person by the person of the physician. To put it another way: a whole series of psychological experiences are revived, not as belonging to the past, but as applying to the physician at the present moment.
>
> *(quoted in Klein, 1952, p. 433)*

It is interesting to note some ambiguity in Freud's use of the term 'psychological experiences'. It leaves an open door to interpreting it as either real life events or imagined occurrences. In respect of sexual abuse, it appears that what really mattered in his view was the psychological perception – whether based on external reality or fantasy (see Chapters 10 and 11).

Like Freud, Klein suggested that some form of transference operates throughout life and influences all human relations. I think not many people would argue with that. In the psychoanalytic treatment situation, as it opens up roads into the patient's unconscious, the past is gradually being revived – both in its conscious and unconscious aspects. According to Klein, the patient transfers early experiences, object relations and emotions, and re-experiences them in relation to the analyst. Like Klein, Bowlby also thought that the deeper we penetrate the *Unconscious* and the further back we take the analysis, the greater our understanding of the transference.

However, Bowlby disagreed with Klein's prime statement about the earliest stages of development:

> The first form of anxiety is of a persecutory nature. The working of the death instinct within – which according to Freud is directed against the organism – gives rise to the fear of annihilation, and this is the primordial cause of persecutory anxiety.
>
> *(Klein, 1952, p. 433)*

Bowlby could not find scientific evidence for such an instinct, nor could he think of a research method to investigate it either. He told me that, if we had been born with a death instinct, we would not have come this far on our evolutionary path. His opposition to Klein's views on this contributed, in a way, to his determination to search deeply into our fights for survival – including the need for aggression, as well as affection. This in turn led to the birth of attachment theory: truly, a life instinct.

In further contrast to Bowlby, Klein made it clear that she was not concerned with either pre-natal or evolutionary processes. Her interest started from birth onwards. There were some connections between these two psychoanalytic giants, but their divergences were greater:

> These persecutory feelings from inner sources are intensified by painful external experiences …, frustration and discomfort aroused in the infant the feeling that he is being attacked by hostile forces. Therefore the sensations experienced by the infant at birth and the difficulties of adapting himself to entirely new conditions give rise to persecutory anxiety.
>
> On the other hand:
>
> The comfort and care given at birth, particularly the first feeding experiences, are felt to come from good forces.
>
> *(Klein, 1952, p. 433)*

Bowlby appreciated the fact that Klein took the environment into account, but regretted her way of conceptualising it – particularly her use of the term 'bad breast' to explain hostile forces and 'good breast' to illustrate the comforting ones. Additionally, he believed that Klein was overemphasising the importance of the breast and feeding experiences. In his view, that was insufficient to explain the strength of the infant's demand for contact with the mother.

Klein's use of the term 'object relations' was based on her argument that the infant has, from the beginning of post-natal life, a relationship with the mother – something with which Bowlby agreed. However, he objected to her contention that the infant focuses primarily on the breast: "The core of the superego is thus the mother's breast, both good and bad" (Klein, 1952, p. 434). Incidentally, that statement was also a departure from Freud's emphasis on the role of sexuality in development – and his idea that the superego has its origin at a later stage, in the resolution of the *Oedipus complex* (see Chapter 11).

Bion, Bowlby's colleague within the Tavistock group during and after the Second World War, elaborated on Klein's ideas:

> Normal development follows if the relationship between infant and breast permits the infant to project a feeling, say, that it is dying, into the mother and to reintroject it after its sojourn in the breast has made it tolerable to the infant psyche. If the projection is not accepted by the mother the infant feels that its feeling that it is dying is stripped of such meaning as it has. It therefore reintrojects, not a fear of dying made tolerable, but a nameless dread.
>
> *(Bion, 1967b, p. 116)*

Bowlby was thoroughly exposed to Kleinian ideas, first hand, through 10 years of personal analysis with Joan Riviere (1927), and supervision by other Kleinian analysts including Melanie Klein herself. Klein had learned directly from the analysis of very young children and put more emphasis than Freud on early relations – and less on sexuality: "object relations are at the centre of emotional life. Furthermore, love and hatred, phantasies, anxieties and defences are also operative from the beginning and are *ab initio* indivisibly linked with object relations" (Klein, 1952, p. 436).

However, the prominence Melanie Klein gave to aggression led to the development of a technique that paid much attention to the negative side of the patient's mental life: "I became convinced that the analysis of the negative transference, which had received little attention in psychoanalytic technique, is a precondition for analysing the deeper layers of the mind" (ibid., p. 436).

Bowlby was inspired by the Freudian axiom that the child is father to the man, meaning that the roots of our emotional life lie in infancy and early childhood, and valued the fact that Freud "sought to explore in a systematic way the connection between events of early years and the structure and function of later personality" (Bowlby, 1979a, p. 1). Despite his dissatisfaction with the Freudian emphasis on sexuality as the main determinant force in child development, Bowlby appreciated what Freud wrote in 1938 (the year before his death) about the power of the early mother–child attachment:

unique, without parallel, laid down unalterably for a whole lifetime, as the first and strongest love-object and as the prototype of all later love relations – for both sexes.

(quoted in Bowlby, 1958a, p. 369)

Though Bowlby used Freudian and Kleinian concepts, he emphasised more positive ideas about the child's needs for a favourable environment, including good parental skills, and refused to see the mother as a 'part-object'. In his report *Maternal Care and Mental Health*, he wrote:

> During infancy and early childhood ... the child is dependent on his mother.... She orients him in space and time, provides his environment, permits the satisfaction of some impulses and restricts others. She is his ego and his superego. Gradually he learns these arts himself and, as he does, the skilled parent transfers the roles to him.... Ego and superego development are thus inextricably bound up with the child's primary human relationship.
>
> *(Bowlby, 1951, p. 53)*

For as long as I can remember, I was aware of contradictory forces both within and around me. Indeed, my school education divided the world up between good and evil forces – something similar to what American and other politicians do nowadays when they depict some countries as forming part of an 'axis of evil'. I must confess I have never felt comfortable with this perception of the world, as we all contain conflicting or contradictory forces within us. During my exposure to Kleinian analysis and supervision, I became more aware of subtle, unintentional or unconscious manifestations of my own anger.

Klein described a further form of anxiety, which develops during the second quarter of the first year: *depressive anxiety*. This type of apprehension is generated from states in which love and hate, and correspondingly good and bad aspects of the mother, are being integrated. At this stage,

> the infant increasingly perceives and introjects the mother as a person. Depressive anxiety is intensified, for the infant feels he has destroyed or is destroying a whole object by his greed and uncontrollable aggression. Moreover, owing to the growing synthesis of his emotions, he now feels that these destructive impulses are directed against a loved person.
>
> *(Klein, 1952, p. 434)*

Bowlby was permeable to these ideas, but formulated aggression in the context of adverse experiences in the child's environment – not as an uncontrollable side effect of the death instinct. While discussing some of the violent fantasies in the child's mind after prolonged separation from the parents, he described "the intense depression that humans experience as a result of hating the person they most dearly love and need" (Bowlby, 1951, p. 57). He postulated that hatred and aggression result from threats or perceived risks to our survival. In his early publications, he had already suggested that aggressive and delinquent behaviours are often linked to traumatic ruptures (Bowlby, 1938, 1944).

In his report for the World Health Organization, his view on the most basic ingredient for growing up mentally healthy is clear: "the infant and young child should experience a warm, intimate and continuous relationship with his mother (or permanent mother substitute) in which both find satisfaction and enjoyment" (Bowlby, 1951, p. 13). I think nobody would disagree that such positive parent–child experience is beneficial, although it does not give permanent immunity – certainly not; other external and internal factors are required. On the other hand, disruptions in the early relationship with the mother (or mother figure) can be compensated later by favourable relationships – such as therapy. But the relationship with the therapist may sometimes hurt.

The clash

After two-and-a-half years in analysis, I was hit by a number of unfortunate events in short succession. My analyst, Dr Y, had started repair works in his home (where his consulting room was located) and the noise made it difficult for me to hear him properly. Lying on the couch deprived me of the possibility of using lip reading as an aid. I told him that the noises were excessive and that I struggled to hear his voice. I asked if it would be possible to change the time of the sessions. Dr Y ignored my request and said instead that I was being distracted by my own internal noises. I could hardly digest his comment and was unhappy with it.

I arranged an audiology test at the Royal Free Hospital, which showed that I had a bilateral hearing loss. Therefore, I was more vulnerable to external noises than most people. The news was a blow. A few days later, I was still ruminating my undigested mixed emotions on my walk to a therapy session. As I approached the edge of a zebra crossing, a sporty red Mercedes passed very fast. The driver was my analyst. It transpired that he was rushing to our session (in our nearly three years together, he was always punctual) and that he did not see me. I was walking slowly and had almost started crossing. It was a near miss: I felt this could have been a fatal accident.

I reported the incident in the session and said that it had made me feel frightened. Dr Y used a transference interpretation and said that I was expressing 'castration anxiety' as, in his opinion, I was bringing to the present the childhood unconscious feeling that my father was sexually more potent than I. Well …, it was tricky to recover from that one. After the session, I shared my disappointment with a friend who tried to cheer me up and said: "You nearly ended on the local newspaper's front-page: An analysand taken to hospital by his own analyst". My friend's support and humour helped me feel lighter, but that was short-lived.

Obholzer had previously introduced me to the work of Bion. At this difficult time, I revisited his theory of thinking:

If the infant feels it is dying it can arouse fears that it is dying in the mother. A well-balanced mother can accept these and respond therapeutically: that is to say in a manner that makes the infant feel that it is receiving its frightened personality back again but in a form that it can tolerate – the fears are manageable by the infant....

(Bion, 1967b, pp. 114–115)

If the mother cannot tolerate these projections, the infant would inevitably become more anxious and frightened. Looking back, I believe my dread was one of death – a survival anxiety, rather than a fear of castration.

At this watershed time I also recalled something that Bowlby had recently said to me in supervision; namely, that therapists need to tolerate extended periods during which they may feel ignorant and helpless, without becoming defensive. In this sense, as a student, I was privileged: I had licence not to know. And, in accepting not knowing, I was willing to know. My working relationship with the other main supervisor, Obholzer, was good enough. However, at this critical point, I did not feel comfortable enough to talk to him about the difficulties I was experiencing with my analyst. So, I told Bowlby that I did not know to what extent such difficulties might be affecting the psychotherapeutic work with my patients.

Bowlby was reassuring and encouraged me to be especially vigilant and receptive to the stories that my patients were sharing with me. I told him I was anxious that I might not be able to follow the technique I was learning from Obholzer, who had introduced me to Bion's (1967a) idea of approaching each session 'without memory or desire'. In the back of my mind I was trying to hold on to the following strategy:

Discard your memory; discard the future tense of your desire; forget them both, both what you knew and what you want, to leave space for a new idea. A thought, an idea unclaimed, may be floating around the room searching for a home. Amongst these may be one of your own which seems to turn up from your insides, or one from outside yourself, namely, from the patient.

(Bion, 1980, p. 11)

Bowlby also tried to approach the sessions without prejudices, but gave priority to forming an attachment relationship. He was content to follow the lead of the patient and allow each session to unfold in its own way, raising as it may do memories of previous sessions and pointing the way to future work – without giving a particular agenda. However, he would bear in mind some therapeutic tasks such as assisting his patients with their explorations and encouraging them to consider past and current relations, including the relationship with him as their therapist. As an active listener, he would develop hypotheses and test them through sensitive questioning. At one point I heard him saying that psychotherapy is a caring method of enquiry.

I was trying to integrate Obholzer's Kleinian approach with Bowlby's emphasis on attachment. In spite of the differences, I found common ground:

> Unless a therapist can enable his patient to feel some measure of security, therapy cannot even begin. Thus we start with the role of the therapist in providing his patient with a secure base. This is a role very similar to that described by Winnicott as 'holding' and by Bion as 'containing' ... a secure base from which to explore and express his thoughts and feelings.
>
> *(Bowlby, 1988a, p. 140)*

I want to highlight that at no point did Bowlby criticise the work of my other supervisors. In fact, he offered suggestions that would help me value and understand the work of others. He also alerted me to publications, often not his own, which would assist me in dealing with problematical situations. He advised me to read a recently published book, *On Learning from the Patient*, by Patrick Casement, a psychoanalyst of the Independent Group:

> For each person there are always two realities – external and internal. External reality is experienced in terms of the individual's internal reality, which in turn is shaped by past experience and a continuing tendency to see the present in terms of the past. Therapists, therefore, have to find ways of acknowledging both realities and the constant interplay between them.
>
> *(Casement, 1986, p. 2)*

Inspired by Casement's approach, I became gradually able to build new bridges between the Tavistock's Kleinian tradition and Bowlby's attachment path – a kind of 'binocular vision', as Bion (1980) put it:

> The analyst can learn to follow with one eye those aspects of a patient about which he knows he does not know, while keeping the other eye on whatever he feels he does know. There is a creative tension between this knowing and not knowing.
>
> *(quoted in Casement, 1986, p. 5)*

I found the use of Bion's (1974) ideas in the *On Learning* book particularly enlightening:

> Instead of trying to bring a brilliant, intelligent, knowledgeable light to bear on obscure problems, I suggest we bring to bear a diminution of the 'light' – a penetrating beam of darkness.... Thus, a very faint light would become visible in maximum conditions of darkness.
>
> *(quoted in Casement, 1986, p. 223)*

Freud himself had explored the issue of darkness and light. I was moved by his touching observation:

I have to thank a three-year-old boy whom I once heard calling out of a dark room: 'Auntie, speak to me! I'm frightened because it is so dark'. His aunt answered him: 'What good would that do? You can't see me'. 'That doesn't matter', replied the child, 'If anyone speaks, it gets light'. Thus what he was afraid of was not the dark, but the absence of someone he loved; and he could feel sure of being soothed as soon as he had evidence of that person's presence.

(Freud, 1905, p. 224)

To my mind and my heart this is a beautiful, simple description of our need for attachment.

Further context and trauma

I was still in the dark in my own analysis when, it happened, I started working one day a week at an in-patient psychiatric unit for late adolescents and young adults, aged 18 to 25, in South London. At a clinical meeting, a couple of weeks after the fast car incident, a colleague presented the case of a 19-year-old boy who had recently been admitted due to a psychotic breakdown. When details of his divorced father were presented, I was shocked to learn that this person was Dr Y. I said to the chairman of the meeting that I had a stomach upset, apologised and left the room. But it was too late. With my new hearing aids, I had already heard the part in which my colleague had reported that this young man was feeling badly treated by his father.

This accidental piece of information was highly disturbing for me, as it resonated with the way I was currently feeling treated by Dr Y. At the next session, I conveyed my shock and distress to him. I added that I was feeling unsafe and that I could no longer continue my analysis with him. I gave one month's notice. The rupture was traumatic. Having said that, I must also confess that deep inside I had experienced ambivalent feelings towards my analyst from the outset. That might have indeed been 'transference', in part.

In my own time, I tried to reflect on my feelings. I realised that I had initially felt seduced and seriously contemplated the possibility of undergoing full training at the Institute of Psychoanalysis – for which five times a week personal analysis was a requirement. But my ambivalence made me cautious about this. I in fact decided to undertake only four times a week analysis – more than enough to become a psychoanalytic psychotherapist, which only requires three times a week. On the fifth day, rather than being immersed in analysis, I submerged in the local *Swiss Cottage* swimming pool, a short walk away from the Tavistock, for a '50-minute hour' of physical and mental exercise.

It happened that Peter Bruggen, my research tutor, had just lent me a paper: "How to Swim with Sharks", written by Voltaire Cousteau, not long before he died in Paris, in 1812. Little is known about this author. He may have been a descendant of Francois Voltaire and an ancestor of Jacques Cousteau. Apparently the essay was written for sponge divers. It was translated from the French and published by the journal *Perspectives in Biology and Medicine* in 1987 – the year I got into trouble with my analyst. And, incidentally, the year María and I got married.

At first, I thought that Bruggen was being funny but, no, he was deadly serious and told me not to bleed! In the paper, I did certainly learn this is a cardinal principle: if you are injured you must not bleed. Bleeding prompts an aggressive attack from sharks and might often provoke the participation of docile fish. Not to bleed when injured is difficult. This may indeed seem impossible. However, diligent practice will permit the experienced swimmer to sustain a serious laceration without bleeding or even exhibiting any loss of composure. Unless you learn to control your bleeding you should not attempt to swim with sharks, for the peril is too great.

I thanked Bruggen and was haunted by reading:

> The control of bleeding has a positive protective element for the swimmer. The shark will be confused as to whether or not his attack has injured you and confusion is to the swimmer's advantage. On the other hand, the shark may know he has injured you and be puzzled as to why you do not bleed or show distress. This also has a profound effect on sharks. They begin to question their own potency.
>
> *(Cousteau, 1987, p. 487)*

Of course, when survival is at stake, swimming with sharks is like any other skill: "It cannot be learned from the books alone; the novice must practice in order to develop the skill" (ibid., p. 486).

Context, in a sense, refers to the general conditions and circumstances in which an event takes place. And so it is usually related to understanding. In order to understand an event better, I think, it is important to locate it in time and space – or is it? Context can also refer to the parts of a text that precede and follow a particular passage. According to Earl Hopper (2003), psychoanalyst, sociologist and group analyst, such parts should be sufficient to establish the meaning or meanings of the passage. Indeed, my understanding of the situation was incomplete. I was angry and puzzled but felt that ending my analysis was reasonable, in the circumstances. When I told Bowlby he said that my decision was sensible. He added that, unfortunately, Kleinian technique did not usually take context into account.

Bowlby then gave me a copy of a paper in which Guntrip (1975) described in detail his experiences of analysis with Fairbairn and Winnicott. The latter provided a caring human relationship – something that Guntrip had not been able to experience from the former, who was cold and distant, no matter that his interpretations might have been accurate. Interpretation alone is not enough, particularly if it is experienced as the therapist maintaining a protective distance from what the patient needs to communicate. Guntrip felt that his warmer and more secure attachment with Winnicott helped healing.

With regards to the therapist's attitude, Sebastian Kraemer (2011, p. 92) referred to Bion's experience of analysis with Melanie Klein after the Second World War.

By the time the war had ended Bion had, on the same day in February 1945, become both a father and a widower. His wife Betty died of either a pulmonary embolus or septicaemia within hours of delivering her baby daughter, while he was serving as a military psychiatrist at the Front in Normandy. Subsequently, Bion found that his analysis with Klein was quite an ordeal: her "insensitivity seemed to him to border on inhumanity" (Bléandonu, 1994, p. 100).

Bowlby also encouraged me to directly explore Winnicott's seminal work *Playing and Reality*:

> If the patient cannot play, then something needs to be done to enable the patient to become able to play, after which psychotherapy may begin. The reason why playing is essential is that it is in playing that the patient is being creative.
>
> *(Winnicott, 1971, p. 54)*

In Bowlby's view, playing and being creative are key components of exploration for which a reasonable level of secure attachment is required.

I was not in the mood to try another analyst for a while. In fact, it took me nearly a year to feel that I could trust somebody else. The context appeared to have become a contest! Dr Y contacted Obholzer, my boss, without my consent or my knowing. Obholzer arranged a meeting to let me know that some of his consultant colleagues in the Adolescent Department had strong feelings that I should not continue the Tavistock training, without being in personal analysis.

This was not an official requirement for my training in child and adolescent psychiatry, although it was strongly recommended. It was, in some way, a part of my unspoken job description. In his managerial capacity, nonetheless, Obholzer decided to allow me to continue with my psychotherapy training at the Tavistock. He said: "You are talented. When other trainees make the mistakes you make, they lose their patients. But you get away with it".

I wanted to understand better the feelings that I was experiencing as therapist towards my patients and, also, the feelings that my analyst might have experienced toward me. I asked Bowlby and he gave me a copy of another landmark publication: "Hate in the Countertransference" (Winnicott, 1949). From this paper, I learned to dig deeply into the patient–therapist relationship and realised that countertransference can be problematical when it remains unconscious.

According to Winnicott, countertransference feelings should be seen as a complex and broad phenomena. These include relationships and identifications that are under repression in the analyst, as well as tendencies belonging to his personal experiences and development. Winnicott differentiated these aspects from what he called objective countertransference – a term he used to describe the analyst's love and hate in reaction to the actual personality and behaviour of the patient.

Bowlby agreed with Winnicott's idea that psychoanalytic treatment might become impossible unless the analyst's own hate is well sorted out and conscious. Otherwise, it might not be possible for the analyst to provide a secure base:

> An analyst has to display all the patience and tolerance and reliability of a devoted mother to her infant; has to recognise the patient's wishes and needs; has to put aside other interests in order to be available and to be punctual and objective; and has to seem to want to give what is really only given because of the patient's needs.
>
> *(Winnicott, 1949, p. 74)*

The infant has to be held physically and emotionally in order to grow; the patient often needs to be held psychologically in order to be healed.

Ryu Suzuki, a Japanese colleague at the Tavistock Clinic, had just completed an internal piece of research on adolescent 'drop out' from psychotherapy. His presentation occurred at the time when my position at the Tavistock was precarious. Suzuki contended that *countertransference* played a part in premature or unplanned treatment endings. He meant that the feelings of the therapist towards the patient, particularly those related to the therapist's own unresolved issues, in some way contributed to the *unilateral* decision of the adolescent to end treatment. Of course, that largely happens at an unconscious level. And, indeed, countertransference is only one factor of the many variables in the work with adolescents (see Chapter 8).

Suzuki's hypothesis offered food for thought. Of the more than one hundred adolescents referred to the Tavistock, in the previous three years, nearly two thirds had left in an unplanned manner without the agreement of the therapist. At the time of the research's report, only two of all the patients referred had been in therapy for more than two years. I talked to Bowlby about the fact that these two adolescents were still coming to see me for twice-weekly therapy; I asked him: "What have I done wrong?" He smiled sweetly and replied: "They have become attached to you".

Bowlby on the Unconscious

We do not control our unconscious selves and, in consequence, we have to give up the occasional comforting or defensive fantasy of a self that is fully integrated and complete. Even when we are secure in our relationships with other people, we need to accept that we are unaware of a large part of reality around us and within ourselves. Despite criticism that he did not pay attention to the Unconscious and the internal world (see Chapter 4), Bowlby was an advocate of the understanding of unconscious processes. In his 1956 lecture on Psychoanalysis and Child Care (Bowlby, 1958c, 1959), delivered as a part of the commemoration of the centenary of Freud's birth, he stated:

> Time and again we hear it said by teachers and others that a child is suffering because of the attitude of one of his parents, usually the mother.... But what the critics have usually failed to take into account is the unconscious origin of this unfavourable attitude. As a result, all too often the erring parents are subjected to a mixture of exhortation and criticism, each as unhelpful and

ineffective as the other. A psychoanalytic approach at once casts a flood of light on the origin of the parents' difficulties and provides a rational way of helping them.

(Bowlby, 1979a, p. 17)

Psychoanalytic therapy aims to make conscious some of our unconscious material. As a therapist, Bowlby followed this path. Indeed, he was concerned with the mechanisms through which real life experiences and perceptions might have been excluded from consciousness. He would often start with the conscious thoughts of the patient and, then, look into the unexamined assumptions that underline these thoughts.

In a way, the technique he used was a flexible integration of psychoanalytic and cognitive approaches. Like Freud and Klein, Bowlby accepted that the ego is not a complete master in its own home – since a large part of us will always remain in the dark. However, he was more interested than Freud and Klein in employing an active method of exploration of historical facts, in order to enable his patients to reconstruct their internal world. Only by acceptance of the past will we become able to put it behind us and to make its meaning more bearable, particularly when the experiences have been traumatic.

Bowlby's approach was one of enquiring into the relational experiences of his patients; he was especially careful in his explorations when he suspected that these experiences had led the patient to believe in a distorted reality. With characteristic modesty, he considered his approach far from original. His patients would often perceive or interpret current situations from the perspective of past emotionally significant experiences that they had shut away from consciousness. In such circumstances, Bowlby discerned that the patients would be prone to cognition, affect and behaviour maladapted to the current situations.

In his paper "On Knowing what you are not Supposed to Know and Feeling what you are not Supposed to Feel", Bowlby (1979b) provided evidence that adverse experiences during childhood play a large part in cognitive disturbance. He referred to situations where children observe scenes that parents would prefer they did not observe and form impressions that parents would prefer they did not form. According to him, the children are sometimes pushed to conform to their parents' wishes and put such information out of their consciousness. As a result, some of these young people appeared unaware that they had observed such scenes or formed such impressions. Their normally spontaneous curiosity and appetite for learning might be inhibited; their capacity to trust people seriously affected.

In *Separation: Anxiety and Anger* Bowlby (1973) explored situations where the pressures on the child are unequivocally direct. Some parents or carers threaten to abandon a child as a means of control. This can be a powerful weapon, particularly with young children. A child subjected to such a threat is often pushed to conform to the parents' or carer's wishes, and may exclude from further processing the event or events he knows they want him to forget. Threats of abandonment often underlie mental states of acute and chronic anxiety.

Apart from psychoanalysis, Bowlby studied a number of disciplines including cybernetics and information processing (see Chapter 6). In ordinary information processing, a large proportion of the inflow coming through our senses is excluded. This exclusion takes place in order to protect us from being overloaded. In a healthy individual the more relevant information gets through and the less relevant information is excluded. Almost all of this processing occurs so rapidly that it is outside conscious awareness.

The *decision* of excluding or accepting information tends to serve the person's best interests under normal circumstances. If someone is hungry, the ordinary course is to give priority to sensory flow concerned with food. However, when there is something dangerous or threatening the inflow concerned with safety would take priority, at the cost of excluding other information.

Throughout our lives we are constantly accepting in or shutting out flows of information. These processes apply to perception of new sensory inflow, as well as to information already stored in memory. Some of what has been excluded or repressed from consciousness may reappear, in different forms at other stages. For children who have been subjected to repeated threats of abandonment it is not unusual that, later in life, they may respond to bereavement or loss with chronic depression, a condition in which one of the distorted beliefs could be that of having been deliberately abandoned by the dead person as a punishment (Bowlby, 1980).

This filtering process habitually occurs without the individuals concerned being aware of what is going on. Many of the experiences that have been forgotten or repressed continue to be influential, to a greater or lesser degree, in affecting an individual's feelings, thoughts and behaviour. During the early years, a child's mind is especially sensitive to external influences. Therefore, young children are particularly vulnerable to parental threats of rejection or abandonment. This vulnerability tends to diminish after a child has reached adolescence.

When traumatic damage has been extensive in the early sensitivity periods, the vulnerability is usually carried with more intensity and weight to the adult years. This may result in psychosis and major personality problems, including 'multiple personality' or 'dissociative identity disorder' (Bowlby, 1988a; Sinason, 2002, 2011; Southgate, 2011). Different parts of the personality or different identities might develop disconnected from one another. Each of these parts could be trying to perform a different function in the shattered life of the patient. For instance, some people may hear voices to act as 'companions' after experiencing the isolating effects of severe trauma, such as child sexual abuse (see Chapter 10).

According to Bowlby, it is crucial that therapists treating patients with these problems give full credence to the childhood experiences reported. Therapists also have to give a sympathetic recognition of the patients' unreturned yearning for love and care – and of their rage towards the people who grossly neglected or abused them. Some of these unresolved feelings might be displaced and directed at the therapist, either at the beginning of the treatment or at later stages.

If yearning for love and care has been shut away, it would usually continue to be inaccessible from consciousness. When anger is repressed, it would frequently be redirected at other targets. Thus, therapists will need to monitor carefully their own feelings towards the conflicting transference that these patients normally bring with them. In my view, supervision in psychoanalytic psychotherapy is crucial – for all analyst/analysand pairs (see Chapter 11).

Attachment theory helps us understand the irresolvable state of affairs, in which an abused child is placed in respect of an abusive parent or carer. When the source of a child's potential security is also a supply of pain and danger, the relationship becomes a self-perpetuating conflict, as suggested by Main and Weston (1982):

> The situation is irresolvable because rejection by an established attachment figure activates simultaneous and contradictory impulses both to withdraw and to approach. The infant cannot approach because of the parent's rejection and cannot withdraw because of its own attachment. The situation is self-perpetuating because rebuff heightens alarm and hence heightens attachment, leading to increase rebuff, increased alarm, and increased heightening of attachment.
>
> *(quoted in Hopkins, 1990, p. 19)*

In other words, by abusing the child, the parent simultaneously 'attracts' the child – and generates a highly anxious, disorganised/disoriented attachment pattern.

One of the therapeutic tasks described by Bowlby (1988a) consists of helping patients discover the true targets of their yearning and anger, which will help them to see more clearly the sources of their anxieties and fears. In turn, this will put the patients in a better position to reappraise their responses and, if necessary, to undertake the challenge of personality restructuring. Before this reorganisation can take place, patients will need to spend time pondering how the original adverse experiences have continued influencing them, usually through unconscious biases. Such reappraisal has to be done by the patients themselves. However, unless therapists enable patients to feel some measure of security, therapy might not even start.

Before Bowlby, psychoanalysis had paid little attention to the concept of security as potentially therapeutic. Joseph Sandler, a Freudian analyst, had suggested a notion of 'safety' as a feeling quite distinct from sensual pleasure. He wrote in 1959: "patients might thwart analytic work by regression to childhood relationships associated with punishment or pain, because the security associated with these relationships made them more rewarding than the insecurity and isolation associated with new ventures" (quoted in Hopkins, 1990, p. 19).

Bowlby felt uneasy about the pejorative connotation implicit in this theory of 'regression' and did not find it useful. He differentiated security from safety with unique precision. In his view, an infant held in his mother's arms in the middle of a dangerous storm is *unsafe* but, at the same time, could be feeling *secure* (see Chapter 6). Without such perception of a psychological or emotional secure base, patients may find it difficult or impossible to think about, reconsider or analyse, very painful and traumatic aspects of their lives – many of which have become unconscious, through defensive exclusion or repression (as different from regression).

The criticism that Bowlby did not pay attention to the Unconscious and the internal world cannot honestly be upheld. Part of the problem came from the fact that he changed some of the language and terminology of psychoanalysis; another part came from his deviance from orthodox psychoanalytic technique. He was unsatisfied with the extended used of the term 'internal objects' among his psycho-analytic colleagues in their descriptions of the internal world. This, in his view, unfortunate term did not reflect clearly enough the reality that the mental life of the child is shaped by the ongoing internalisation of his relationships.

In the first volume of *Attachment and Loss*, Bowlby dealt with the question of how a child gradually builds up his internal world and proposed the term 'internal working models' to replace that of 'internal objects':

> Starting, we may suppose, towards the end of his first year, and probably especially actively during his second and third when he acquires the powerful and extraordinary gift of language, a child is busy constructing working models of ... how his mother and other significant persons may be expected to behave, how he himself may be expected to behave, and how each interacts with all the others. Within the framework of these working models he evaluates his situation ... and makes his attachment plans.
>
> *(Bowlby, 1969, p. 354)*

Internal working models are mental representations of relationships – primarily of attachment-related experience (Main, 1991; Pietromonaco & Barrett, 2000). These models help us all understand and make sense, as much as it might be possible, of a constantly changing environment. Within this understanding, it is normally easier to develop a psychological sense of felt security and to select appropriate survival-promoting behaviours. In the second volume of Attachment and Loss, Bowlby elaborated further on his concept of the internal working models:

> It is plausible to suppose that each individual builds working models of the world and of himself in it, with the aid of which he perceives events, forecasts the future, and constructs his plans.... A key feature is his notion of who his attachment figures are, where they may be found, and how they may be expected to respond. Similarly, in the working model of the self that anyone builds a key feature is his notion of how acceptable or unacceptable he himself is in the eyes of his attachment figures.
>
> *(Bowlby, 1973, p. 236)*

In short, when the attachment figures are sensitively responsive and consistently reliable, the child will perceive them as a 'secure base' and will naturally develop a pattern of 'secure' attachment with good self-esteem. If the attachment figures are predominantly dismissive and emotionally distant, the child will usually develop a strategy or pattern of 'avoidant' attachment in which closeness will tend to be avoided – in order to protect himself from disappointment. If the attachment figures are significantly inconsistent, the child will typically develop an anxious pattern of 'ambivalent' attachment, as he will be unsure about what to expect. If the attachment figures are abusive or struggling with major unresolved trauma, the child will characteristically develop a pattern described as 'disorganised/disoriented' attachment.

Early patterns tend to persist but can be changed and, of course, there are variations, overlaps and combinations of these main patterns of attachment (see Main, 1991; Cassidy & Shaver, 2008; Howe 2011).

Most attachment theoreticians suggest that you give what you have received:

> To be attentive one has to be attended to. In any kind of danger, support close by is needed. Being resilient in one's work (as opposed to compulsively self-reliant) depends on a lively sense that help is at hand, perhaps at the end of a telephone or at the end of a shift, but there nonetheless.
>
> *(Kraemer, 2015, p. 144)*

Attachment patterns have a counterpart: "A pattern of attachment behaviour related to compulsive self-reliance is that of compulsive care-giving. A person showing it may engage in many close relationships but always in the role of giving care, never that of receiving it" (Bowlby, 1977, p. 207). This pattern is over-represented in the helping professions, which may partly explain why for doctors or therapists it is difficult to be a patient: "being the care-giver, with the fantasy of being invincible and having no thoughts about one's own needs" (Garelick, 2012, p. 81).

Bowlby, as discussed earlier, had indeed described the concept of a secure base in the relationship between patient and therapist too. He did it in terms similar to what Winnicott depicted as the therapist's capacity to 'hold' the patient's needs in mind, and to what Bion defined as the therapist's capacity to 'contain' the anxious and hostile projections of the patient. However, Bowlby put a greater emphasis on the need that patients often have to perceive the therapist as a trusted companion who provides support, encouragement, sympathy and, on occasion, guidance. And it was this emphasis which impinged on the technique of psychoanalysis that led to disagreements with psychoanalytic colleagues.

Note

Writing about Dr Y has been emotionally difficult. I have tried to be fair within my subjectivity. I have disguised details and changed circumstances to protect anonymity. The narrative should not be taken literally but as an aid to illustrate my experience of being professionally on the edge. My secure attachment with Bowlby helped me to survive and to grow. While writing this chapter, I recalled that he shared with me something he had learned from Bruno Bettelheim: that which cannot be put into words cannot be let to rest.

10

ATTACHMENT AS RECOVERY FROM CHILD SEXUAL ABUSE

Sexuality is built into every aspect of our being: it transcends the biological function of procreation to also become a vital force in human relationships and creativity. Sexuality is about both creating life and feeling alive. But it can go terribly wrong. Bowlby has been criticised for writing relatively little about sex. He was of course aware that sexuality is indispensable for human survival and development. But he was sceptical about the value of the *Oedipus complex*, one of the cornerstones of psychoanalysis, as a universal sexual principle governing mental life. Discovering and validating attachment as an essential relationship and a primary instinctual force in its own right was at the core of his professional life. It was well worth it.

Bowlby (1969, pp. 233–234) saw attachment and sexuality as two distinct systems that "are apt to impinge on each other and to influence the development of each other". In his view, the introduction of attachment as a discrete organisation "in no way imperils the fruits of psychoanalytic insight". He further stated that "a great research effort is required to unravel all these overlaps and the influences of one class of behaviour on another".

Such a research is not within the remit of this book. However, I would direct the interested reader to a number of authors who have explored the interface between sexuality and attachment (for example, Fonagy, 2001; Holmes, 2001, 2010; Widlocher, 2002; White & Schwartz, 2005). Peter Fonagy and Jeremy Holmes extended their exploration beyond sexuality. They in fact straddled the worlds of attachment theory and psychoanalysis.

The developing trend is one of non-prejudice, inclusiveness and fluidity in respect of human sexuality, which is good news (Nitsun, 2006). But we need to be aware that there has been much *pathologising* in the past and, although there is a positive climate of political correctness, we have to be mindful about possible negative attitudes – internalised over generations, operating in subtle ways. There are increasing administrative requirements to tick boxes disclosing sexual identity and orientation as well as gender. Of course, this is meant to be used to prevent any form of sexual or gender discrimination. But there is a risk of over-compartmentalising sexuality, which may end in abusive practices. What about just saying: I am only a human sexual being. Optimally, a securely attached sexual being?

The only time I saw Bowlby angry in the six years of our work together was when I asked him about child sexual abuse. He raised his eyebrows and said with a sense of regret that Freud's change of heart on this matter had been a disaster! Until 1897, Freud believed that the stories of childhood sexual abuse reported by his patients were true and caused long-term damage. In his 1896 paper on the aetiology of hysteria, he had referred to child sexual abuse and had stated: "Injuries sustained by an organ which is as yet immature, or by a function which is in the process of developing, often cause more severe and lasting effects than they could do in mature years" (quoted in Zulueta, 1993, p. 140).

But Freud then retreated and postulated that his patients' emotional problems were caused by *unconscious phantasies* or delusions of seduction that had not actually occurred (see Chapter 11). Bowlby considered that Freud's disbelief or denial of childhood sexual abuse contributed to a dreadfully ignorant and unhelpful clinical practice with the victims. The denial also held back a much needed social awareness of the problem for more than half a century.

In the final interview given by Bowlby on 15 February 1990, conducted by Virginia Hunter at the Tavistock Clinic, he stated: "I have to say as a student I was almost forbidden to give attention to real life events. Well, I'm talking about the 1930s ... and there's still, I think, excessive emphasis on fantasy" (Hunter, 2015, pp. 139–140). He then went on to report that, only four years before, whilst he was at a case conference in a very well-known clinic in the USA, a psychoanalyst presented the case of a woman who reported that she had been sexually abused by her elder brother. Nevertheless, the analyst was convinced that this was a fantasy.

Bowlby had no doubt that the woman's account was true, as her problems were typical of what you might expect as an outcome of child sexual abuse. He then asked the analyst whether he had read the literature on sexual abuse in childhood and its consequences. Bowlby was rather astounded to learn that this analyst was totally unfamiliar with any literature on the subject and added: "Well I mentioned this, you see, because this was only four years ago. So this reluctance to believe that what a patient tells you is true is still around and I think it's not only un-therapeutic, it's anti-therapeutic" (Hunter, 2015, p. 140).

Besides psychoanalytic practitioners, the majority of professionals within mental health and social institutions maintained a *dignified* silence. Denial was in fact present at all levels in the society. The strength of this defensive mechanism was masterfully described by Friedrich Nietzsche (2000, p. 270): "'I did that', says my memory. 'I could not have done that', says my pride, and remains inexorable. Eventually, the memory yields".

In the 1950s, a number of social scientists started to conduct large-scale survey studies of sexual practices, especially in the USA. Kinsey et al. (1953) documented that between 20 per cent and 30 per cent of the women interviewed reported having had a sexual experience as a child with a male; between 4 per cent and 12 per cent reported a sexual experience with a relative; and 1 per cent reported a sexual experience with a father or stepfather.

The prevalence of childhood sexual abuse was substantiated in these studies but, paradoxically, the reality of the phenomenon continued to be denied by both the professionals and the public. For example, most of the sexually abused women in the Kinsey study reported being disturbed by the experience and, yet, the researches indicated that the women's distress resulted not from the sexual act itself but from their social conditioning. It seems that Kinsey and his colleagues, in their attempt to encourage enlightenment and tolerance of sexual attitudes, failed to distinguish between essentially harmless acts, committed by consenting adults, and frankly exploitative acts – such as the prostitution of women and the molesting of children.

In the 1970s and 1980s, the feminist movement contributed to bringing the problem of child sexual abuse into the open, along with other taboo issues such as rape and gender violence. In the summer of 1987, the Cleveland Report had a powerful shaking effect in all the social strata in the UK. In the spring of that year, 121 children from the then county of Cleveland – an area of some 583 square km that included the economically depressed towns of Hartlepool, Redcar and Middlesbrough – were taken into temporary local authority care on suspicion of having been sexually abused. The majority of the children had been abused and some were re-abused by an unprepared child protection system. Cleveland was the first known case of child sexual abuse in Britain that involved multiple victims and multiple perpetrators.

Other shocking reports from Rochdale, Orkney and Broxtowe followed on in quick succession. The magnitude of the problem was such that it could no longer be ignored. The media gave ample coverage. There was unanimous concern about the welfare of the victims and psychological treatment programmes developed. Unfortunately, the criminal justice process itself added much pain and distress to the victims' trauma. Children were summoned unnecessarily and given little information; they were also kept waiting for long periods and subjected to tough cross-examinations. In February 2013, the UK media reported the suicide of Frances Andrade after giving evidence in the criminal trial of her abuser. This tragic event highlighted the re-traumatising nature of the legal process.

New *fires* have continued erupting until the present day. On 7 July 2014, the UK Home Secretary at the time and now Prime Minister, Theresa May, told the media that she had decided to set up a national inquiry into child sexual abuse. The announcement followed the revelation that 114 Home Office files on alleged abusers, during the period 1979 to 1999, had been lost or destroyed. This implies that the evidence must have been suppressed by people in positions of power. The now ongoing investigation includes public bodies, the private sector and wider civil society with a duty of care to protect children in England and Wales, from 1970 to the present. This full national inquiry may help address the wider social and political context in all its complexity. The first three Chairs of this ongoing inquiry have already resigned.

In the summer of 2014, yet another scandal of child sexual exploitation and its subsequent cover-up came to light: a massive case of child sexual abuse perpetrated by organised gangs in the town of Rotherham in South Yorkshire between 1997 and 2013. An initial report condemned the failure of the authorities to act effectively to protect many children from the abuse or to even acknowledge that it was taking place. The number of sexually abused children in England and Wales could be as high as 600,000. The estimation comes from the National Household Survey of Adverse Childhood Experiences. The concern of the police is that it is not gangs that are the biggest problem but home: 90 per cent of such abuse is perpetrated by people children already know.

Childhood sexual abuse is far too often a hidden crime; it is shockingly pervasive and occurs throughout all layers of society. Being a bystander and remaining silent is tantamount to colluding with the abuse. Unfortunately, prevailing power structures often intimidate and overwhelm witnesses who then feel emotionally paralysed. Based on her professional experience of more than 30 years, Sue Richardson (2013) considers that recognition of child sexual abuse is characterised by cycles of discovery and suppression.

Richardson further thinks that it is important to identify the needs of victims for someone who can recognise their suffering and advocate on their behalf. More therapeutic initiatives for survivors are needed; for example, free counselling and psychotherapy services to operate within an open door policy. She further suggests that it is necessary to go beyond the consulting room and address the problem effectively in the social, cultural and political arenas.

Bowlby became aware, in the late 1970s, of the huge prevalence of child sexual abuse. He had retired at 65 from his NHS consultant post, in 1972. In my supervision with him, he talked about a feeling that, as a clinician, he had not developed enough expertise to approach the problem confidently enough. He said that most of the time during his career child sexual abuse was rarely referred to by anyone and that, on those rare occasions, the abuse was considered to be all in the mind and not a real event.

Bowlby strongly advised me to believe my patients when they reported stories of abuse in their childhood and adolescence. He also advised me to be especially mindful about using physical touch for support, as this might be perceived as something sexual (see Chapter 11). In his view, it is particularly important to be impeccably ethical, caring and sympathetic for the victims to feel safe. Ever since, in my clinical work with individual and group patients, I have tried to bear his advice in mind (Ezquerro, 1998a, 1999, 2010; Ezquerro & Bajaj, 2007; Ezquerro & Canete, 2012).

Bowlby (1979a) joined the voices of those who were alarmed by the high incidence of incest and its damaging effects on children. He clearly named this as sexual exploitation of the children and considered that, in the most severe cases, it could lead to psychosis or problems of multiple personality (see Chapter 9) – something that is now being described as 'dissociative identity disorder' (DID). He remarked that the experiences that give rise to such disorders have probably been repeated over several years of childhood, "perhaps starting during the first two or three but usually continuing during the fourth, fifth, sixth and seventh years, and no doubt often for longer still" (Bowlby, 1988a, p. 113).

The Campaign for the Recognition and Inclusion of Dissociation and Multiplicity, organised by the Paracelsus Trust in recent years, is a praiseworthy endeavour for continuous awareness of the problem of child abuse. The Trust is aiming to improve understanding of the devastating consequences of the problem and to develop effective interventions. The Bowlby Centre is under the umbrella of the Trust and has played an active part in this campaign. Kate White, Editor of *Attachment: New Directions in Psychotherapy and Relational Psychoanalysis* (the Bowlby Centre's journal), has been particularly proactive in the process of championing survivors of abuse.

Child sexual abuse is much more than a problem. I believe it is a social illness and we need to approach it as such. The greater the awareness and understanding of it as an illness, the greater the chance to improve prevention and treatment. The societal response has often been one of denial, minimisation or rationalisation. Fundamental changes in society are required to fight this illness and enable survivors to be open about their experience – and still be able to participate in society as equals, without the fear of shame, judgement, marginalisation or stigmatisation.

In attachment terms, Richardson (2013) believes that the problem can only be tackled by moving towards a more secure society – a secure base to which we can return. Maintaining such a secure base would require the continuous repair of loss of agency, and of public, professional and political ruptures. A complete prevention of child sexual abuse is not an achievable goal in the foreseeable future. However, each one of us (politicians, professionals and ultimately all citizens) should aim towards it. This is a task or battle that will have to be sustained generation after generation.

In order to further explore child sexual abuse and ways of recovering from it, I would recommend a very readable book: *Attachment, Trauma and Multiplicity*, edited by Valerie Sinason (2002). The book investigates the still largely unaddressed and unexplored subject of DID; it includes clinical accounts and personal stories of people who are affected by this condition. Sinason believes talking about this is particularly important: until quite recently, most major psychotherapy and psychiatric training schools in the UK did not accept the existence of child sexual abuse and its long-term harm.

Bowlby (1988a) left us an important reflection that we cannot know what we cannot bear to know. Deeply rooted in attachment knowledge, Sinason (2011, p. 10) advocates a model of the mind that may help remove the stigma that is often placed on people suffering from DID, so that everyone can bear it in a more optimistic light: "if the mind is seen as a seamless collaboration between multiple [group] selves, a kind of 'trade-union agreement' for co-existence, it is less threatening to face this subject". I shall now try to illustrate this.

From denial to therapeutic evidence

I met Jacqui Dillon in September 2013 at a London Conference on *Attachment and Psychosis* organised by the International Society for the Psychological and Social

Approaches to Psychosis. She presented her own experience of recovery from child sexual abuse to an audience of professionals and users of mental health services. Her story is disturbing but invigorating, enraging but full of hope. As a survivor she has learned directly from her abuse, from her psychological defences and survival strategies, from the mistakes made by some professionals and from her attachment-based psychotherapy. Her insights are points of light from which we can all learn. She has become a true expert.

When I decided to write a chapter on childhood sexual abuse, I asked Jacqui Dillon for consent to use her story. My chief aim was two-fold: first, to give hope to many victims; second, to invite professionals and the public to reflect further on this huge problem. Dillon has not been one of my patients; she has been under the care of colleagues whom I do not know. The boundary is clear. She had already chosen to put key aspects of her story in the public domain. She has written movingly about her traumatic experiences, her recovery and her ongoing work (Dillon, 2010a, 2010b, 2012; Dillon & Hornstein, 2013; Dillon et al., 2013).

I had considered the possibility of asking some of my patients for permission to write about their experiences of being survivors of childhood sexual abuse. But I decided not to do so. I had in the past asked patients for their formal consent, which they gave to me. But I have never been really certain about how they might have been emotionally affected if they had read their stories in a professional journal or book chapter. As I am entering late middle age, I am becoming more cautious. I do not wish to risk any form of emotional repetition of the patients' original intrusive abuse. Having said that, my patients know they will have my full support if they decided to speak out.

From now and further on I will address Jacqui Dillon by her first name. I am privileged that she trusted me with her story in the many conversations we held in December 2014 and January 2015. The passages and quotes that will follow are based on these conversations. She has read and approved my final draft.

Jacqui was born and grew up in Hackney, East London. She can recall looking up into her mother's eyes when she was a little girl. She starved for attachment and love, desperately needing a reflection of herself to know that she was real and safe in a scary world. But she was met with a cold, hostile stare. The mother seemed to have been distracted by the problems she had herself had as a child with her own mother. When she looked at Jacqui, she could only see a reflection of her own traumatic memories, unmet attachment needs and rage; she was unable to see her own daughter for what she was. Jacqui felt trapped. She wanted to escape but also needed to be protected and extended her shaky arm trying to touch her mother, who laughed and bit Jacqui's hand – just as her own mother had done to her.

An unspeakable ritual abuse – physical, emotional and sexual – started very early for Jacqui. She can recall hearing voices by the age of five. Both her parents were involved in the abuse as part of a gang of sadistic paedophiles. The abuse continued until she was 15. She was repeatedly intimidated by the abusers who told her that if she ever talked to anyone about what was happening she would be put in jail because, they said, she had done terrible things. Moreover, they told her that no one would ever believe her and that everyone would think she was mad; as a result, the doctors would lock her in a mental asylum forever and would throw away the key. The abusers also threatened Jacqui with violence and left her with a persecutory feeling that they could hunt her down and kill her.

The consequences of such extreme and sustained abuse were devastating; the effects all consuming, encompassing every aspect of Jacqui's life. She was betrayed and exploited by those who should have provided care and protection for her. This experience left her with a profound sense of terror, seclusion and shame. Her internal world was filled with highly disturbing and scary images that literally shattered her into pieces. However much she yearned for it, she had no place of safety, no saviour to come to the rescue – and no reliable attachment figure to turn to.

Jacqui felt terribly isolated and tried to survive the best way she could. She inhabited a dual reality. In one world, she pretended to be a normal schoolgirl with ordinary parents. She was in fact perceived as a gifted child who won writing and drawing competitions, played with her friends and liked wearing clips and ribbons in her hair. In the other world, she was a dirty little bitch, evil and unlovable, treated with cruelty and contempt by anyone who could get their hands on her. She felt she deserved everything she got.

Jacqui developed a special relationship with the voices in her head: "They talked to me, talked about me to each other…; they comforted me, protected me and made me feel less alone". One of the early voices that has been there for her throughout her whole life is the voice of a 'great mother'. This is very powerful maternal figure, who is beautiful and kind; a beneficent person who has often been there comforting and soothing her. Jacqui believes that the voice of the 'great mother' has helped her survive and has encouraged her to develop loving and compassionate feelings towards her own daughters.

Jacqui's body became a recipient of her revulsion at an early age. Secretly, she started to self-harm: cutting herself, banging her head against the wall and tearing her hair out. She soon discovered that her physical pain mitigated her distress and emotional pain. This dynamic had been explored by Zulueta (1993, p. 154):

> Identifying with the aggressor, even at the expense of her own body, gives the incest victim a sense of control and power which she desperately seeks. But such an identification … also implies that the child is wicked and deserves to be punished.

Zulueta was following Fairbairn's (1952, pp. 65–66) idea that the abused child's "outer security is purchased by her taking on the badness of those on whom she depends".

In addition, understandably, Jacqui developed a complex relationship with food: overeating, forcing herself to vomit, and starving herself. She felt that manipulating her food intake and self-harming were both giving her an illusory sense of control over her body: "For once, I could do what I liked to it. I was mistress of my own universe".

Creativity played a large part in Jacqui's survival during her childhood and adolescence. She loved writing stories and poems, drawing and painting. She also read many books. These allowed her to access other worlds. The stories and characters captivated her imagination, and made her feel less lonely. The world still held some magic and wonder for her. She dreamt that one day she would be safe. And free. And loved.

Although the sexual abuse ended when Jacqui was 15, its consequences lived on for many years. Her world continued to be split in two parts. These two realities co-existed with some degree of success. On the surface, she managed to live independently and to develop a fruitful career in the media. But she went on struggling with feelings of despair, hearing voices and harming herself. She knew that what the abusers had done to her was very wrong, but their threats continued echoing in her mind. She was often frightened and remained silent.

Jacqui was 25 when she gave birth to her first daughter. The pregnancy was planned and she much longed for this child: one the happiest events in her life. However, in the post-partum period, she felt overwhelmed by memories of the abuse. The voices in her head multiplied and intensified — saying things that were extremely disturbing and terrifying. She began seeing horrific images of abuse, torture and death. Marks and bruises appeared on her skin, like stigmata. Self-harming spiralled out of control and she became paranoid. She did not leave the house because of the fear that she and her daughter would be abducted and killed.

The split of Jacqui's world in two parts became rapidly more dramatic. She felt she was going mad. On the one hand, she was a devoted mother, forming a close and intimate bond with her baby daughter, and breastfeeding her on demand. On the other hand, she was convinced that she was contaminating the baby with the poison that swirled around in her own mind and body. She would be changing her daughter's nappy and suddenly she would be covered in blood. She would blink and the blood would disappear. She could now see no escape from the horrors of the past and considered that the only way out would be to end her life. In desperation, she called her GP who urgently referred her to a consultant psychiatrist. She was admitted to an acute psychiatric ward on that very day. She felt it was the end of the world.

Separation from her daughter was a traumatic experience for Jacqui. She was desperate to get back home to be reunited with her. She *knew* that her breakdown was a consequence of her childhood sexual abuse and decided to talk about it to the psychiatrist who assessed her. She was shaking as she talked to him and, after a few sentences, he interrupted her to say that other in-patients had reported similar incidents. But, he added that when family members were interviewed it became clear that the patients' reports were symptoms of their mental illness. Looking intently at Jacqui, he said: "These things didn't really happen; they are delusions, a part of your illness".

Jacqui can recall looking at the psychiatrist in astonishment, while feeling strong palpitations and a rush of adrenalin in her body. She would have liked to be able to lift the filing cabinet behind him and drop it on his head. Instead, she told him that she did not feel well. She left the consulting room and locked herself in the toilet. She banged her head against the wall in utter frustration and despair. She could only think of getting out of the hospital and decided to lie: "I returned to a familiar world of pretence and smiling while I felt I was dying inside".

In the next few days, Jacqui avoided talking about the abuse. She tried to appear calm and co-operated with the staff. She told them that resting in hospital had helped her and that she was feeling much better. Her request to be discharged back home was accepted. Looking back she thinks that being white and articulate helped her. Most of the other patients on the ward were black.

The message Jacqui received at the hospital was that she was ill, and that everything she said and did was a consequence of her illness. Staff tried to persuade her that the abuse never happened and that she needed to take medication. Her reluctance to take that in was also interpreted as a symptom of her illness. However, she disagreed with the diagnosis of psychosis. This had been delivered to her as meaning a potentially life-long illness – something that she was not prepared to accept. She felt that the mental health system was adding insult to her injury.

Jacqui's first in-patient psychiatric admission, in 1993, was her last. She believed that the hospital environment was so un-containing emotionally that it could have become lethal: "Isn't it ironic that a place that was meant to provide sanctuary for me became a place that nearly drove me over the edge?" This experience was traumatic for her in its own right. In some way, it also became mixed with the very complex trauma of being a victim of parental abuse. She had been unable to trust her parents. She was now left with an even stronger feeling that people who were meant to protect her, and to care for her, could not be trusted.

Jacqui's attachment needs were largely unmet. Her repeated childhood abuse was damaging to her emotional development. She was very talented and sustained a precarious equilibrium until the demands of becoming a parent disturbed it. The realisation that she could not trust the hospital professionals in charge of her care was painful. She was deeply hurt by the fact that they did not believe her. But, in her fight for survival, she was still longing for a secure enough attachment. After careful searching, she decided to see an attachment-based psychotherapist – whom I shall call Fred. The initial arrangement was three sessions per week.

At this stage, Jacqui was unable to trust anyone and it was critical that the therapist believed her. After the initial 'softening up' period, she gradually gained a new perspective of her problems. She began to understand that what the abusers had done to her was sick, a brutal manifestation of their own traumatic experiences – and that her symptoms were a natural and understandable response to the abuse. She realised that she would need to work hard over a number of years to achieve a more solid and long-lasting equilibrium.

Fred's priority was to provide a secure base from which Jacqui could explore and contain the many traumatic memories that were surfacing. He empowered her to be in control of the therapeutic process and to go at her own pace. Building trust takes time. Fred was patient, consistently responsive, reliable and sensitive to her feelings. He, slowly but surely, became a trusted companion who enabled her to feel confident enough to undertake the task of coming to terms with her traumatic past. He had the courage and integrity to witness her truth, which Jacqui appreciated: "Having an empathic witness who was willing to hear and see my suffering made me feel real and, for the first time, as if I mattered".

The ghosts of the past were scary but Jacqui discovered that she was not alone, as she had always been. The attachment to her therapist gave her strength to confront her traumatic memories without feeling persecuted or fearful. She rediscovered her curiosity and appetite for reading. She read about attachment theory and came across the work of Judith Herman (1992) on *Trauma and Recovery*. Making links between what she was reading and what she was going through in therapy became a meaningful and powerful experience for her, which changed her understanding of life.

Herman is a distinguished American psychiatrist, who has made important contributions to the treatment of victims of incest – as well as other complex and repeated traumatic experiences. She outlined a three-stage sequence of trauma treatment and recovery. The first involves regaining a sense of safety, for which a therapeutic relationship is usually required. The second phase involves active work upon the trauma using a number of therapeutic strategies. This work can take place when a therapeutic secure base has been established. It should include an exploration of the trauma – remembering and mourning that which was lost as a result of such trauma. The third stage focuses on a reconnection with the world in order to begin a new post-traumatic journey.

These stages are not normally completed once and for all. Richardson (2011) elaborated on them from an attachment-based perspective. Jacqui had felt helpless and isolated for so long that, at times, she was anxious to be reassured by her therapist that he would not let her down. As the full magnitude of her trauma started to unfold, she needed to formulate a few questions to him. Will you be able to understand me? Will I be too much for you? Do you really want to hear what I have to say? Are you going to get me? Can you admit when you get it wrong? Are you going to see me not for my symptoms but for who I am? Are you prepared to go with me all the way?

Well …, her therapist survived – which helped Jacqui understand and accept his support as an act of commitment to health and, ultimately, to life. Only then did she become able to truly grieve her losses.

In order to have a sense of safety in between sessions, Jacqui became active in the process of constructing a symbolic safe place at home – something that she had not experienced as a child. She put together cushions, blankets and soft toys, which provided a retreat where she could turn to when overwhelmed by intrusive traumatic memories. This retreat also helped her to mourn the loss of an ordinary childhood in a healthy family – something that had been cruelly taken away from her. The secure enough base with her therapist enabled her to feel safer in her *new* home, assembling the fragments, integrating the experience and mapping the world.

The therapeutic relationship with Fred assisted Jacqui with the next task: reconnecting with the world and forming new attachments. Fred had in fact become an internalised attachment figure, who was helping her assuage her turbulent internal world and change her perception of the external world. The latter was a dangerous place filled with barely concealed threats and sinister people, where she felt trapped by a feeling of impending dread. She decided to stop having contact with people who undermined her and her therapy. She slowly developed relationships with people who understood and accepted her: "I created a sanctuary for myself which allowed me to safely work through the traumas that I had experienced".

With some ups and downs, overall progress was steady. A big turning point for Jacqui was when she began working directly with her *voices*. Up until this time she had been largely terrified by them. It was crucial that her therapist was willing to *listen* to these voices, and to support her in making sense of what they were trying to communicate. The voices were more than just voices. They were 'dissociated' selves, with different names, ages, experiences, feelings, and identities; which were created in an attempt to handle the trauma. The voices held memories of the abuse from the perspective of perpetrators, deniers, blamers, victims, comforters and protectors – including the 'great mother'.

Rather than trying to eradicate these different parts of herself, Jacqui tried to transform her relationship with them: "Each was part of the whole of me. I learned that I needed to listen to them and understand them and the context in which they had emerged and to greet them with compassion and understanding". She began to honour the voices as they had helped her survive. She tried to put them together, each one working towards supporting and understanding each other. In this inspiring way, she became able to integrate her *psychotic* symptoms into a coherent life experience. This increased her sense of connectedness and wholeness: a true work of art.

This outcome made Jacqui think that her experience of recovery might be of help to other people. In 2001, she joined an innovative community mental health project in East London and became involved with the UK Hearing Voices Network. Founded in 1988, this is a part of a wider international movement that had started in Holland, in 1987. Hearing Voices Networks are formed by people who hear voices (typically diagnosed as auditory hallucinations), as well as their supportive family members, mental health practitioners and activists. Jacqui put it squarely: "Like many psychiatric survivors, active participation and social action was and remains an important aspect of my healing and recovery" (Dillon & Hornstein, 2013, p. 287). Indeed, the personal is political. And healthy secondary and group attachments are instrumental for our survival too.

Jacqui has served as chairperson of the UK Hearing Voices Network and has provided training for other voice hearers, in the last 12 or so years. She is not against mainstream psychiatric services, but she is committed to the promotion of an alternative approach. In these networks voices are seen in a positive light: not as signs of mental illness, but as meaningful and understandable responses to trauma and loss. Jacqui has felt at home here and has become a secure base for many survivors of childhood sexual abuse with a diagnosis of psychosis. Recovery is not necessarily about getting rid of voices but about understanding them and changing the relationship with them, so the traumatic voice can become harmless or even helpful.

The risk of not coping with the sexual abuse and its consequences is greater when the child has been coerced not to talk about it, under the threat of violence and the admonition that no one would believe the story of the abuse (Bowlby, 1979b, 1988a). Regrettably, professionals have often made things worse by not believing their patients' stories. Bowlby fought all his professional life against the main current of psychoanalytic practice that put the emphasis on the patient's fantasies. He took seriously the real traumatic events reported by his patients.

Bowlby also taught me to encourage patients to believe in the self-healing properties of the human mind, like those of the human body. And in the possibility of recovery from trauma through the formation of new attachments across the life cycle, even in later life (Ezquerro, 1989, 2000b; Ezquerro & Canete, 1999, 2000, 2004; Ezquerro et al., 2000, 2004). Bowlby's view was shared by other relational psychoanalysts like Guntrip:

> A problem created in childhood is 'never too late to mend'.... Age does not necessarily bring loss of capacity for emotional change and relief of longstanding tension.
>
> *(quoted in Hazel, 1996, p. v)*

Bowlby, no doubt, would have been moved by Jacqui's struggle to become attached, survive and grow. She had a major breakdown after giving birth to her first child. And I can imagine that she might have felt anxious during her second pregnancy. However, this experience turned out to be a major breakthrough. When she gave birth to her second child at home, the two midwives who cared for her and the new baby were surprised by how calmly, quietly and effortlessly she went into labour and delivery. They asked for her secret and Jacqui replied: "dissociation".

11

PROFESSIONAL SEXUAL ABUSE: A PERVERSION OF ATTACHMENT?

A challenge closely related to child abuse is that of fighting sexual abuse of patients perpetrated by professionals.

Towards the end of his life, Bowlby referred to this problem as a "*hot potato*" (quoted in Hunter, 2015, p. 154). Indeed, attachment and care-giving are often expressed in terms of physical touch. And touch, although not inevitably, is also connected with sex. As we shall see below, Freud was quite alarmed when he realised that therapeutic encounters did sometimes involve sex.

Bowlby was not totally against the occasional use of physical touch in therapy as a caring gesture, because in certain circumstances it can have therapeutic value. But, he said, touch has to be used with quite a lot of discretion. In his opinion, all therapists should be aware of the patient's attachment history, handle sexuality with ethical care and be particularly mindful in some dyadic situations. For example, in the therapeutic encounter between a middle-aged man and a young attractive girl, touch "could so much easily mean sex than anything else" (quoted in Hunter, 2015, p. 154).

Current estimates indicate that at least 10 per cent of male and 3 per cent of female psychotherapists violate sexual boundaries with their patients (Tschan, 2014). What today is documented as professional sexual abuse was not an uncommon occurrence in the early days of psychoanalysis. The traditional therapeutic couch became a place where sexual affairs took place. Indeed, before the actual physical involvement, the intra-psychic boundary was the first to disintegrate. For a long time, it seems, there was no clear understanding of professional boundaries – or was there?

The problem is still substantial; all of us in the profession should be very alert and collaborate with the aim of eradicating it. We have a duty to protect vulnerable people and to help them feel safe. Bowlby told me in supervision that it is important to understand the strength of unmet attachment needs that patients often bring to therapy. He had pointed out several times that Freud himself had missed the centrality of attachment (Bowlby, 1958a, 1969).

Some psychotherapists seem to misinterpret the patient's strong needs for attachment as sexual seductions; some of these therapists also give in and act out their own sexual feelings. That is sexual exploitation of a vulnerable person by someone who is in a position of power. I do not need to go into the incestuous meaning of this – and the parallel with child sexual abuse.

The correspondence between professional abuse and child abuse is implicitly reflected in the following:

> In the past three decades we have begun to appreciate the prevalence of childhood sexual abuse and emotional abuse, how these lead to dissociative states and complex post-traumatic syndromes. Had I had that knowledge in the early 1970s, I believe that I could have held to the boundaries of the analytic situation with a young woman patient whose problems I now see more clearly as having emerged from such a complex traumatic syndrome. The traumata were re-enacted in the analysis.... Though I had been able to help colleagues and trainees with difficult countertransference situations, I could not do that for myself and did not accept for myself imperative need for further personal therapy.
>
> *(Pines, 2000, p. 295)*

Freud abstained from sexual liaisons with his patients. He several times stated that analysts have to continually work on abstinence from sexual relations in their clinical practice (Tschan, 2014). Despite his instructions, many of his followers (including his inner circle) transgressed the professional boundaries. In a letter to Carl Jung in 1906, quoted in *Freud and Man's Soul* by Bruno Bettelheim (1984), Freud made a double-edged remark that psychoanalysis is in essence 'a cure through love'.

Unfortunately, Jung appeared to have interpreted this the wrong way and ended having an infamous sexual affair with one of his patients, Sabina Spielrein. When the affair ended she felt that she had been used and was deeply hurt. Besides Jung, other foremost psychoanalysts had sexual relationships with their patients, including Sandor Ferenczi, Ernest Jones, Frida Fromm and Karen Horney (Tschan, 2014). And there were more.

Freud himself struggled with sexual boundaries and initially appeared to have wanted to keep the problem secret within the profession. In his letter to Oskar Pfister of 5 June 1910, Freud observed that "the transference is indeed a cross" (Meng & Freud, 1963, p. 39). And in his letter to Jung, on New Year's Eve of 1911, Freud commented: "We must never let our poor neurotics drive us crazy. I believe that an article on 'countertransference' is sorely needed; of course we could not publish it, we should have to circulate copies among ourselves" (McGuire, 1974, pp. 475–476).

In a further letter to Jung about sexual experiences with patients, Freud stated:

> Such experiences, though painful, are necessary and hard to avoid. Without them we cannot really know life and what we are dealing with. I myself have never been taken in quite so badly, but I have come very close to it a number of times and had a 'narrow scape'... weighing on my work and the fact that I was ten years older than yourself ... have saved me from similar experiences. But no lasting harm is done. They help us to develop the thick skin we need to dominate 'countertransference', which is after all a permanent problem for us; they teach us to displace our own affects to best advantage. They are a blessing in disguise.
>
> *(ibid., pp. 230–31)*

Freud's feelings about professional sexual boundaries seemed to fluctuate. This gave a sense of ambiguity that was not in the patient's best interests. Like Jung, he on occasions appeared to blame female patients for the sexual boundary transgressions of psychoanalysts: "The way these women manage to charm us with every conceivable psychic perfection until they have attained their purpose is one of nature's greatest spectacles" (ibid., pp. 230–31).

Glen Gabbard (1995) suggests that the sexual transgressions perpetrated by the analytic pioneers contributed to a legacy inherited by several generations of psychoanalytic practitioners. Moreover, Gabbard thinks that institutional resistance to addressing these difficulties in contemporary psychotherapy practice may partly relate to the ambiguities surrounding boundaries in the training analysis itself. Freud's correspondence with Sandor Ferenczi and Ernest Jones provides further clarifying details of the problem of boundary violations in the early days of psychoanalysis.

Ferenczi, via an invitation received from Jung, met Freud in February 1908 and became deeply attached to him. Ferenczi related to Freud as a father figure, with admiration and affection. The following sequence of events and quotes I refer to in the next paragraph are taken from Haynal and Falzender (1993, p. 364):

On 14 July 1911, Ferenczi wrote to Freud to let him know that he had taken into analysis Elma Palos, the daughter of his mistress Gizella Palos. Ferenczi had started an affair with Gizella in 1900, which continued through her marriage with Geza Palos. In 1910, Ferenczi took Gizella into analysis for a few months, after which she asked him to treat her daughter Elma. During the course of the treatment, Ferenczi fell in love with Elma and, on 3 December 1911, wrote to Freud to say: "I cannot maintain the cold superiority of the analyst". That was followed by some *resolutions*. On New Year's Day 1912, Ferenczi asked Freud to urgently take over Elma's therapy, to which Freud replied on 2 January 2012: "I am obliged to do so".

Gabbard (1995) gives further details about this blurring of boundaries. During the three months of Elma's analysis with him, Freud made regular reports to Ferenczi regarding Elma's thoughts and feelings. Freud also sent confidential letters to Gizella about Ferenczi, who took Elma back into analysis later in 1912. Despite this messy situation, or maybe as a result of it, Freud took Ferenczi into analysis between 1914 and 1916, a process that was disrupted by the First World War. Elma married an American suitor in 1915. Under Freud's insistence, Ferenczi eventually married Gizella in March 1919.

Oddly enough, on the day of the wedding, Geza Palos (Gizella's former husband) died of a heart attack – although there were rumours that he committed suicide. Coincidentally as well, in March 1919, Ferenczi was appointed at the University of Budapest as the first professor of psychoanalysis in the world. A few months later, following a secret committee meeting, Freud pushed Ferenczi to resign from his presidency of the International Psychoanalytical Association – to allow Ernest Jones to take over and move the headquarters from Budapest to London.

Ferenczi had written to Freud on 23 May 1919: "from the moment you advised me against Elma, I developed a resistance against your person, that even psychoanalysis could not overcome, and which was responsible for all my sensitivities" (quoted in Dupont, 1988, p. 311). Subsequently, Ferenczi engaged in other problematical boundary issues. He wanted to believe that self-disclosure of the analyst could be an important therapeutic reparative force.

Ferenczi's idea was that by actively including the therapist's personality in the therapeutic situation, the encounter with the patient would be more genuine. So he was prepared to make a self-disclosure, as long as it would be relevant to his patients' therapy. He in fact experimented with 'mutual analyses' in respect of four women patients. He analysed them for one hour (or at least he tried) followed by another hour in which he would let the patient analyse him. According to Gabbard (1995, p. 1125), entries in Ferenczi's diary showed "his confusion of his own need to be healed with that of his patients".

Swan (1974) pointed out that there are good grounds to believe that, to different degrees, a number of leading early psychoanalysts (including Sigmund Freud, Melanie Klein, Carl Jung, Otto Rank, Wilhelm Reich, Sandor Ferenczi and others) were sexually abused as children. Ferenczi wanted to give to his patients the love they had not received from their parents and developed a technique in which he attempted to repair his patients' childhood damage. His technique included kissing and hugging the patient as an affectionate mother who "gives up all consideration of one's own convenience, and indulges the patient's wishes and impulses as far as in any way possible" (quoted in Gabbard, 1995, pp. 1125–1126). It seems that, as a victim of mistreatment, he over-identified with his patients. This dynamic was not foreign to other analysts.

Freud became openly critical of Ferenczi and, on 13 December 1931, wrote:

A number of independent thinkers in matters of technique, will say to themselves: why stop at a kiss? Certainly one gets further when one adopts 'pawing' as well, which after all doesn't make a baby. And then bolder ones will come along … resulting in an enormous increase of interest in psychoanalysis among both analysts and patients.… Father Ferenczi gazing at the lively scene he has created will perhaps say to himself: maybe after all I should have halted my technique of motherly affection 'before' the kiss".

(Jones, 1957, p. 164)

Freud was also involved in another major boundary issue when he undertook the analysis of Loe Kann, the common-law wife of Ernest Jones, in 1912. Jones had moved to Canada in 1908 and Kann joined him there. His reputation was marred by rumours that he was recommending masturbation and the use of prostitutes to his patients, and even showing obscene postcards to them to stimulate their sexual feelings. A former patient threatened to charge him with having had a sexual relationship with her and Jones paid her $500 in blackmail money to prevent a scandal, although he said that there was no truth to her claim. At one point she had attempted to shoot him and he employed an armed detective to protect him (Gabbard, 1995, p. 1127).

On 28 June 1910, Jones wrote to Freud disclosing that Kann had first come to him as a patient: "Now I have always been conscious of sexual attraction to patients; my wife was a patient of mine" (quoted in Gabbard, 1995, p. 1127). Kann had a number of somatic symptoms and a problem of morphine addiction. Anxious that he would lose her, Jones asked Freud if he would analyse her. Freud accepted and seemed to be taken by Kann, to the point that he needed to share his feelings in his letter of 23 June 1912 to Ferenczi: "I will be pleased to expend much Libido on her" (ibid., p., 1127). And, at Freud's behest, Jones underwent a period of analysis with Ferenczi.

The bond between Freud and Kann grew stronger as the treatment continued and he invited her to spend Christmas Eve with his family. Freud made regular reports to Jones, breaching the confidentiality due to the patient, as he had done with Ferenczi. Jones seemed to have felt increasingly excluded and became sexually involved with his maid Lina (Appignanesi & Forrester, 1992). Freud perceived Jones as sexually impulsive and was concerned about possible sexual boundary violations with patients. On 14 January 1912, Freud wrote to Jones: "I pity it very much that you should not master such dangerous cravings" (Paskauskas, 1993, p. 124). The relationship between Jones and Kann ended in 1913.

Joan Riviere, Bowlby's analyst, had a complex relationship with Jones and Freud. Born in 1883 to a well-off family in Brighton, Riviere married in 1907 to a barrister (son of a Victorian painter) and had one child. She suffered a breakdown on the death of her own father, which occurred around that time. Her ongoing emotional distress led to her starting personal analysis with Jones, in 1916. However, she had several admissions to a psychiatric sanatorium during the course of 1916 and 1917. With Jones' help, she made a good recovery and became very interested in psychoanalysis as a profession. Jones was impressed by her understanding of psychoanalytic theory and made her a founding member of the British Psychoanalytical Society, of which he was the first President in 1919.

However, the analytic relationship between Jones and Riviere became difficult. On 1 April 1922, Jones wrote to Freud about his analysis of Riviere: "It is over twelve years since I experienced any [sexual] temptation in such ways, and then in special circumstances" (Paskauskas, 1993, p. 466). The analysis reached an impasse and Jones recommended Freud to her for further analysis. Riviere moved to Vienna in 1922, where she had treatment with Freud for about a year. She had met Freud and Melanie Klein at the Hague Conference in 1920.

Riviere asked Freud at this conference about the possibility of going into analysis with him. Apparently, Freud could not make room for her analysis at the time. However, he negotiated her position as translation editor of the *International Journal of Psychoanalysis* with Jones, securing her nomination against Jones' resistance (Bakman, 2008). From 1921, Riviere worked with Freud and his daughter Anna Freud, as well as with James and Alix Strachey and Ernest Jones, in a committee responsible for translating Freud's work into English. She supervised the translation and editing of several volumes of Freud's Collected Papers, and has been considered his best translator – that "tall Edwardian beauty with picture hat and scarlet parasol" (Gay, 2006).

On her return to London, after her analysis with Freud, Riviere became actively involved in the work of the British Psychoanalytical Society. She met Melanie Klein again in Salzburg in 1924 and became a key supporter of her ideas. In September 1927, Freud complained to Ernest Jones about Riviere's criticism of his daughter Anna Freud. In his reply, Jones referred to Riviere's views as having been "expressed in her characteristically uncompromising and rather vehement fashion" (quoted in Kahr, 2012, p. 36; and in Steiner, 1985, p. 34).

Riviere became a training analyst in 1930, a few months after Bowlby had started his analysis with her. She was also the analyst of world renowned figures like Susan Isaacs and Donald Winnicott and supervised prominent Kleinian analysts like Hanna Segal, Herbert Rosenfeld, Henry Rey and others. James Strachey, general editor of the *Standard Edition of the Complete Psychological Works of Sigmund Freud*, considered her to be a professional of complete integrity and a very formidable person.

Personal and professional lives were intertwined in almost every conceivable way during the early developmental stages of the psychoanalytic movement. Most on the boundary issues were of a non-sexual nature (Gabbard, 1995). I shall briefly mention a few incidents relating to these. Freud analysed his daughter Anna, who would later indicate that she felt exploited by many aspects of this process, including her father's publications of her dreams, and daydreams, without her consent. She also felt uncomfortable with her father's use of her own clinical material for teaching after she had become a psychoanalyst.

Ernest Jones apparently had a tentative (platonic) romance with Anna Freud, which did not survive the disapproval of her father! Karen (1998, p. 108) pointed out that Anna Freud was never able to form a significant attachment to another man or a sexual connection with anyone, male or female, and suggested that to some degree she was stuck in her father's emotional orbit.

Melanie Klein also analysed her own children. Besides, she encouraged patients to follow her during her holidays and provided analytic sessions for them while they laid on the bed in her hotel room. Moreover, Melanie Klein analysed Ernest Jones' children and his wife. Winnicott held Margaret Little's hands through long periods during many therapy sessions while she laid on the couch and, at least on one occasion, broke confidentiality by telling her about another patient he was treating at the time – including his countertransference reactions towards that patient. Other analysts gave papers they had written to their patients for them to read. (Gabbard, 1995, p. 1131).

I am aware that it has been suggested that 'professional boundaries' are a relatively recent notion and that psychoanalytic technique, like other learning processes, had to develop via trial and error. It has also been suggested that one way of under-standing these historical boundary violations is "to see them as the inevitable labor pains accompanying the birth of a new field" (ibid., p. 1131).

But hang on a minute! Are we denying something here? Born between the third and second centuries BCE, could the Hippocratic Oath have been used as a sym-bolic midwife for the psychoanalytic baby more than 2000 years later? This ancient body of medical writings contains simple, common-sense thoughts. Any physician is expected to promise to treat patients keeping them from harm and injustice, "remaining free of sexual relations with both female and male persons, be they free or slaves".

The Hippocratic Oath also had a rather advanced and clear-cut concept of the physician's duty to the confidentiality of the patients:

> What I may see or hear in the course of the treatment or even outside the treatment in regard to the life of men, which on no account one must spread abroad, I will keep to myself holding such things shameful to be spoken about.

This piece of wisdom was guarded in the Library of Alexandria in Egypt, the greatest library of the ancient world, but still far away from the source of the River Nile – of which more later.

Sexual offences against patients by their psychotherapists went largely unrecog-nised until the late 1960s. It was around this time, under the influence of the feminist movement, that the awareness of sexual exploitation and its association with existing patriarchal structures started to come into the public eye. But social change was slow. This allowed quite a few *professionals* to continue their exploita-tive practice, selling the idea that having sex with their patients would help the patients to overcome their sexual and emotional difficulties. In a paper entitled "Overt Transference", James McCartney (1966) claimed with no modesty that his sexual engagements with his female patients were beneficial for them.

Professional sexual abuse was sometimes unashamedly recommended as 'therapeutic'. The therapists, of course, claimed the sex was not only consensual but psychologically indicated – a statement that went essentially unchallenged for far too long. In his book *The Love Treatment: Sexual Intimacy between Patients and Psychotherapists*, the New York psychiatrist and psychotherapist Martin Shepard (1971) asserted that having sexual intercourse with his patients was of great help for them. And he encouraged his colleagues to use this treatment modality as, according to him, a sexual involvement can indeed be a useful part of the psychotherapeutic process. Such was the tenor of the times that a number of magazines and newspapers instigated a debate by presenting headlines such as: "Should you sleep with your therapist?"

Equally to most cases of child sexual abuse, professional sexual exploitation is a complex traumatic experience, which includes a breakdown of trust in the person who is meant to provide a safe haven. Survivors are far too often not believed or respected. Their pain can be trivialised and sometimes not even acknowledged. It is not unusual for the abuse to take place in front of the eyes, noses and ears of people who do not want to know, as if these witnesses were neutral observers.

Tschan (2014, p. 32) ponders that attachment theory is crucial for understanding the suffering of the survivors of both childhood and professional sexual abuse, which in his view are "always a relational crime". Indeed, due to their role, care professionals must be considered as significant attachment figures with a substantial power differential over their patients.

In its *Guidelines for Medico-Legal Care for Victims of Sexual Violence*, the World Health Organization (WHO) stated that "appropriate, good quality care should be available to all individuals who have been victims of sexual assault" (WHO, 2003, p. 17). And survivors should have a say about any therapeutic intervention following the abuse.

Glen Gabbard (1996) points out that every psychotherapy institute and society has seen the ravages of severe boundary violations. And it can be quite tempting to attribute these abuses to a small handful of corrupt colleagues. But this way of thinking would mislead us to defensively disavow our vulnerability to boundary transgressions, and to see them as the province of a few who have nothing in common with the rest of us. The facts are otherwise: when professionals who commit professional sexual abuse are compared with professionals who do not commit boundary violations there are not so many differences as expected. On the contrary, they seem to have more in common than there are differences.

Believing that 'this would never happen to me', assuming that the offender belongs to a different species, can be dangerous. Awarded and well-regarded professionals have committed professional sexual abuse. Any of us could be an offender and supervision of our clinical practice should be mandatory. Indeed, psychotherapy institutions have often been paralysed in their efforts to take action when such cases surface, particularly when the analyst charged is a well-respected practitioner in the field. The needs of the victims, which should be paramount, are often neglected. So, protecting children and patients from sexual victimisation should be the primary goal of any support or treatment for perpetrators (Gabbard, 1994; Gabbard & Lester, 1996; Tschan, 2014).

Similarly, to the unconscious intergenerational transmission of trauma (Coles, 2013), there can be an unconscious transmission of attitudes about boundaries from one psychoanalytic generation to the next. However, this chapter's small review of boundary violations in the early history of psychoanalysis in no way should be used to justify current transgressions, or to blame our analytic parents. On the contrary, it is aimed to offer an opportunity to reflect and learn from past mistakes. There should be no more secrecy and ambiguity about professional sexual abuse.

For far too long professional bodies exhibited greater concern for the protection of the transgressing therapist than for the patient. Fortunately, this attitude has been changing in recent decades. However, there still is a long way to go. I believe some cases warrant a retrospective institutional apology and greater reparative gestures for the survivors to overcome professional exploitation at an emotional level.

It would appear that some psychotherapy institutes are reluctant to consider giving an institutional apology, as they may fear the legal implications. Though understandable, defensive attitudes perpetuate the suffering of victims. Saying sorry is a way of expressing regret about something that should not have happened, as well as sympathy and reassurance for the victims that it was not their fault. In the Madrid Declaration on Ethical Standards of Psychiatric Practice, the World Psychiatric Association (1996) left no room for doubt: "Under no circumstances should a psychiatrist get involved with a patient in any form of sexual behaviour – irrespective of whether this behaviour is initiated by the patient or the therapist".

The source of the Nile

The early history of psychoanalysis is indeed linked to sexuality, particularly to the concealed existence of child sexual abuse which, in late nineteenth-century Europe, particularly in the most conservative elements of society, was hidden behind a wall of respectability, modesty and collusive silence – if not outright lies. In 1885, the 29-year-old Freud obtained a grant to study with Jean-Martin Charcot, a leading neurologist at the Salpetriere, in Paris, and was haunted by his clinical presentations of patients with 'hysteria' – the neurotic condition *par excellence*.

Hysteria is a Greek word for uterus. In ancient times physicians believed that the disease was caused by 'body wandering' of the uterus It was Charcot's co-worker, Pierre Janet, who first described the traumatic origin of hysterical symptoms and laid the foundation for a new understanding of traumatic events' impact on mind and body. Charcot postulated a link between a remote traumatic accident, like a bad fall, and some of his patients' current symptoms. In his view, however, the patients did not suffer from residual physical effects of the accident, but from the idea they had formed of it.

In the late nineteenth century, it was fashionable among European physicians and psychiatrists to attribute medically unexplained symptoms to various forms of sexual activity or the lack of it. For example, 'neurasthenia' was attributed to masturbation and sexual overindulgence. Neurasthenia was a psychiatric diagnosis that had been introduced by George Beard, an American physician, in 1869. It consisted of a range of largely unspecific ailments, where nervous exhaustion and lethargy were the prominent features.

The diagnosis of 'anxiety neurosis', on the other hand, tended to be applied to people who were considered to be sexually frustrated, such as virgins, abstainers and those who practised coitus interruptus. Neurosis was a term originally used by the British physician William Cullen, in 1769, to describe symptoms for which a physical cause could not be found. It was seen as a vague general affliction of the nervous system. When patients suffering from hysteria reported experiences of sexual abuse, the largely male medical establishment dismissed credibility as they considered that women were quite easily impressionable, suggestible and emotionally unstable.

Freud's first attempt to explain hysterical symptoms appeared in the book *Studies on Hysteria* that he co-authored with his mentor Josef Breuer, in 1895, based on their clinical observations about a number of patients with a diagnosis of hysteria. Breuer saw the symptoms as reactions to emotional trauma. Freud went further than that and considered that repressed memories of sexual-related trauma may play a part in the formation of the hysterical symptoms.

Breuer struggled with the management of one of his patients, Anna O, who at one point imagined that she was pregnant and called him to assist her with labour as an emergency. But Breuer managed to disentangle himself from the treatment before disaster occurred and referred her to Freud. Breuer and Freud agreed that patients can fall in love with the therapist and may expect reciprocal feelings. Incidentally, Anna O introduced the term 'talking cure' to describe her psychotherapy with Breuer. This term is now used profusely in the definitions of psychotherapy, in many languages across the world.

Freud continued gathering information from patients who were reporting to him incidents of childhood sexual molestations. On 21 April 1896, he presented his controversial paper "The Aetiology of Hysteria" to the Society for Psychiatry and Neurology of Vienna. He detailed the stories of eighteen patients, twelve women and six men (Partridge, 2014, p. 144). He made more direct links than in the *Hysteria* book between the patient's symptoms and childhood sexual trauma, perpetrated mainly by fathers but also by other close relatives, older siblings and carers. His so-called *seduction theory* was born but it would be short-lived.

After the meeting, Freud wrote to his loyal friend Wilhelm Fliess to express his concerns that his lecture had been met with an icy reception and that Richard von Krafft-Ebing, who chaired the meeting, had commented that the presentation sounded as a scientific fairy tale. At the end of his letter to Fliess, as quoted in Zulueta (1993, p. 139), Freud complained: "And this after one has demonstrated to them a solution to a more than thousand-year-old problem, a 'source of the Nile'!"

What Freud postulated was that the abusive experience had been repressed and remained latent for years, before the hysterical symptoms erupted with the emergence of strong sexual urges in adolescence and young adulthood. A latency period was consistent with medical conditions such as syphilis:

> Our view then is that infantile sexual experiences are the fundamental precondition for hysteria … they do not do so immediately, but … only exercise a pathogenic action later, when they have been aroused after puberty in the form of unconscious memories.
>
> *(Freud, 1896, p. 212)*

Zulueta (1993) further reported that Freud was so keen on his 'discovery' as to suggest that the pathogenic role of childhood sexual experience was not confined to hysteria, but held good equally for 'obsessional neurosis' and perhaps, also, for the various forms of chronic paranoia and other functional psychosis: "The new method of research gives wide access to ... events ... which have remained unconscious.... Thus it inspires us with the hope of a new and better understanding of all functional psychical disturbances" (Freud, 1896, p. 221). In view of the complexity of symptoms presented by the victims of child sexual abuse, including dissociation and multiplicity of 'individual selves' in the patient's personality, it is a pity that Freud's attempt to understand the nature of the problem was dismissed.

Many of Freud's colleagues did not accept that childhood sexual abuse in the family could have actually occurred; some even accused him of putting these ideas into his patients' minds. Breuer defended him from these accusations but his support was limited, as he felt that Freud's discoveries might have been overstated. Breuer accepted that sexuality was an important factor in the aetiology of neurosis, but did not agree with Freud's hypothesis that hysteria was always a deferred consequence of a pre-puberty sexual shock.

Freud wrote to Fliess on 4 May 1896: "I am as isolated as you could wish me to be; the word has been given out to abandon me, a void is forming around me" (quoted in Sinason, 2011, p. 12). As symptoms of hysteria were so widespread, not even sparing his siblings or himself, Freud had to infer that maybe his own father was guilty too. But he then appeared to exclude the fathers as main perpetrators, and concentrated more on relatives, carers and older siblings – although in the latter case, Freud implied, the older child had been seduced previously by an adult.

We may say that Freud surrendered to external pressure from his peers and the bourgeois society of the Austro-Hungarian Empire, as well as the internal pressure of his own doubts. He repudiated his initial belief and affirmed instead that his patients' frequent reports of childhood sexual abuse were illusions or fantasies. In September 1897, Freud wrote to Fliess again to let him know about the difficulties he was experiencing in the treatment of incest victims and about the rationale behind his retreat from his seduction theory:

> The continual disappointment in my efforts to bring any analysis to a real conclusion.... Then the surprise that in all cases the father, not excluding my own, had to be accused of being perverse.... Then, third, the certain insight that there are no indications of reality in the unconscious, so that one cannot distinguish between truth or fiction.... Accordingly, there would remain the solution that sexual fantasy invariably seizes upon the theme of the parents....

And Freud ended the letter on a highly personal note:

> The expectation of eternal fame was so beautiful, as was that of certain wealth, complete independence, travels, and lifting the children above the severe

worries which robbed me of my youth. Everything depended on whether or not hysteria would come right.

(quoted in Zulueta, 1993, pp. 157–158)

I can imagine that for Freud the abandonment of his *seduction theory* probably was as disturbing as its discovery. He had enthusiastically compared his findings with the discovery of *caput Nili*, but he was then pushed to retreat. In addition, he was going through a personal painful period (Krull, 1979). Freud was deeply shaken when his father died on 23 October 1896, after being ill for four months. Three days later, he wrote to Fliess: "I find it difficult to write just now … The old man's death has affected me profoundly" (quoted in Festic, 2009, p. 20). But his creativity survived and, within three years, he produced his masterpiece *The Interpretation of Dreams* (Freud, 1900). This, he said, was a reaction to his father's death: "the most important, the heaviest loss in one's life" (ibid., 2009, p. 20).

Freud's self-analysis also put him in touch with other traumas of his own child-hood. Freud's brother Julius died when Freud was 22 months old. His maternal uncle, also called Julius, had died the previous month. Freud's mother became pregnant at the time with his sister Anna and might not have been emotionally available for him. Additionally, according to Simon Partridge (2014), there is strong evidence that before his third birthday Freud was sexually stimulated by his nursemaid (the 'old woman') in a completely inappropriate way until her dismissal, without warning, for alleged theft.

Freud wrote to Fliess at the end of 1897:

> I can only indicate that the old man [father] plays no active part in my case … in my case the 'prime originator' was an ugly, elderly woman…. If I succeed in resolving my hysteria, I shall have to thank the memory of the old woman.
>
> (quoted in Partridge, 2014, p. 141)

In his book *The Assault on Truth*, Masson (1985) suggested that the inappropriate sexual activity that Freud's nanny had with him was another factor that might have in some way played a part in his suppression of the *seduction theory*. Marcel (2005) looked further into Freud's traumatic memories and proposed a re-examination of Freud's choice of the Oedipus myth.

The role played by nannies and nursemaids has recently been explored by Katherine Holden. She is a historian, visiting research fellow at the University of the West of England, and daughter of Hyla Holden (see Chapter 3). Her book *Nanny Knows Best: The History of the British Nanny* (Holden, 2013) provides a thorough review drawing from real stories extending for over a century of demonised and idealised nannies.

Similar to what Bowlby had suggested about Freud's difficulties in understanding attachment needs, other eminent psychoanalysts have looked into Freud's early history from an attachment perspective. Louis Breger, Professor Emeritus of psycho-analytic studies at the California Institute of Technology, stated that Freud's "avoidance of the centrality of attachment is the most pernicious effect of his failure to come to terms with his own history of traumatic losses" (Breger, 2009, p. 108).

An original champion of incest victims, Freud indeed took flight. But he did not completely deny the stories of incest of his patients. It seems that he tried to adopt a convenient *neutral* position suggesting that, at the end of the day, what really matters is the psychic life of the patient. So, it was no longer important whether or not the events had occurred. In a way, child sexual abuse retained a diminutive share in his thinking and in his clinical practice; it was virtually absent in his subsequent writings.

While Freud kept mainly quiet about child sexual abuse, Ferenczi became able to talk openly about it – as he had no doubts that many of his patients had been sexually abused as children. Ferenczi decided to *exhume* the seduction theory that Freud had buried and presented its *rediscovery* to a large audience of psychoanalytic colleagues in Wiesbaden in 1932. That was an honest and disturbing paper, in which he used both his personal and professional experience: "Confusion of Tongues between the Adults and the Child" (Ferenczi, 1932, 1949).

One example of the confusion of tongues is when the child yearns for closeness with a parent who, from a disturbed perspective, *misinterprets* the child's need in terms of an 'adult sexual tongue' (a language the child does not know) and then forces the child to conform to it. For instance, a father touches his daughter in a sexually inappropriate manner, while she speaks her innocent 'child tongue'. Additionally, the father tries to persuade the daughter that lust on his part is really the love for which she yearns. This is not 'infantile sexuality'; this is plainly child sexual abuse – something that can be described as a *perversion* of the attachment relationship.

Ferenczi also tried to provide an explanation of the process through which the abused child, who wishes to recover a state of tenderness, is emotionally paralysed and unable to talk about the abuse: "Through the identification, or let us say, introjection of the aggressor, he [the aggressor] disappears as part of the external reality, and becomes intra- instead of extra-psychic" (Ferenczi, 1932, p. 162).

Similar to Freud's reasoning in his 1896 "Hysteria" paper, Ferenczi argued that adult trauma develops as a result of the sexual seduction of a child by a parent or authority figure. He elaborated his idea of trauma in terms of emotional neglect, physical maltreatment, and empathic failure, which are usually present in child sexual abuse. And he linked early sexual trauma to neurotic character, as well as borderline and psychotic disorders in later life.

Ferenczi's paper was strongly rejected by his colleagues, particularly by Freud – who 36 years previously had been subjected to a comparable rejection when he talked about child sexual abuse. Isn't it ironic that Freud appeared to have lost any sense of empathy towards Ferenczi in spite of his own experience of rejection? In fact, Ferenczi was excommunicated from the psychoanalytic movement; which, according to Partridge (2014), might have contributed to his early death the following year – aged 59.

The "Confusion of Tongues" paper was not allowed to be translated into English for nearly two decades. The paper contains criticisms of the professional hypocrisy that is hidden and never revealed. It also draws attention to scenarios in which the professionals (including himself) create a situation that is unbearable as it imposes on the patient "the further burden of reproducing the original trauma" (Ferenczi, 1949, p. 227).

Oedipus revisited

The void and persecution that usually surrounds whistle-blowers had unfortunately suffocated Freud's findings of early sexual trauma and confined them into the realms of the occult (Herman, 1992). But his curiosity did not go away. A successful production of *Oedipus Rex*, the tragic Greek myth play of Sophocles, was staged in Vienna at the time. Watching the play had a strong impact on Freud. He wanted to believe that the plot was as relevant on the modern stage as he supposed it had been for the Athenians of 425 BCE.

Based on a very partial reading of the myth, Freud interpreted it as evidence of a trans-historical and trans-cultural archetype of sexual motives in humankind. Put it at its most simple, every child has a desire for the parent of the opposite sex along with a wish to displace or kill the same-sex parent. This generates a conflict, described as the *Oedipus complex*, whose resolution is key to healthy psychosexual development. Bowlby regretted that the emphasis on the Oedipus complex led to a cover-up of the truth and to the establishment of 'unconscious phantasy' as the main objective of psychoanalytic study.

Freud has been rightly criticised for his male chauvinism, for seeing the passage through the oedipal conflict mainly from a masculine perspective: the boy, because of the loving wish for the mother and the hostile wish against the father, feels threatened by the father, which Freud described as a fear of castration. However, the boy also loves his father; and so experiences a fear of losing the father as well. In consequence of these two fears, the child's sexuality comes to grief and is altogether suppressed: and the so-called 'latency period' sets in, around the age of six, but is dramatically broken with the onset of puberty.

In traditional psychoanalytic theory, entering the latency period implies a 'resolution' of the Oedipus complex: the fantasies about the objects that are both desired and feared are given up, and become replaced with identifications that are formative in later sex-role behaviour. This also leads to the introjection of parental attitudes and the beginning of the superego or conscience.

Indeed, there is far more to the story of Oedipus than Freud chose to present. Oedipus was the son of King Laius and Queen Jocasta of Thebes. Laius was only one year old when his own father died. He was left in the care of his mother, and his uncle usurped the throne. Later, Laius was forced to leave both his mother and the city of Thebes. When he is next seen as an adult in Pisa, he kidnaps and sodomises Chrysippus, the beautiful illegitimate son of his host, King Pelops, who very infuriated curses Laius.

On learning from an oracle that he is to be murdered by his own son, Laius abjures sexual intercourse with his wife Jocasta until she, moved by her frustration, intoxicates and seduces him into the conception of their fateful son, Oedipus. Laius, mindful and fearful of his curse, tightly binds the feet of the baby and asks Jocasta to kill him. She felt guilty at the thought of doing it herself and ordered a servant to commit the murder. The servant took the infant to the top of a mountain for him to die. A shepherd rescues the baby, names him Oedipus (meaning swollen feet) and takes him to Corinth, where Oedipus was raised by King Polybus and Queen Merope.

As a young man, Oedipus hears a rumour that he is not the biological son of Polybus and Merope. When he questions the King and Queen, they deny it; but, still suspicious, he asks the Delphic oracle who his parents really are. The oracle seems to ignore his question and tells him instead that he is destined to mate with his own mother – and to shed with his own hands the blood of his father.

Desperate to avoid his foretold fate, but overlooking the fact that the oracle had not answered his initial question, Oedipus leaves Corinth still in the belief that Polybus and Merope were his true parents. He assumed that, once away from them, he will never harm them. On the road to Thebes, Oedipus meets Laius, his true father. They quarrel over whose chariot has preference of passage, apparently unaware of each other's identities. Oedipus throws Laius down from the chariot and kills him, thus fulfilling part of the oracle's prophecy.

Shortly after, Oedipus arrived in Thebes and found the city was terrorised by the Sphinx who was killing anyone unable to guess her riddle. The Sphinx asked him: "What is the creature that walks on four legs in the morning, two legs at noon, and three in the evening?" Oedipus replied that it is man, who crawls on all fours as an infant, walks upright later, and needs a walking stick in old age. The distraught Sphinx then threw herself off the cliff-side. Oedipus's reward for freeing Thebes from the Sphinx's curse is the kingship and the hand of Queen Jocasta, his biological mother. The prophecy is thus fulfilled, although none of the main players knows it, or do they?

Freud concentrated on what he imagined Oedipus' internal world might have been, but withheld the story of Laius – the perverse father who was full of filicidal rage. Freud also ignored the family dynamics and the collusive Jocasta. Many of his disciples, whether out of loyalty or fear, certainly turned a blind eye to the inconsistencies of the 'father' of psychoanalysis. Those who questioned the centrality of unconscious phantasy were usually excluded from the psychoanalytic establishment. Hence, for a long time, many psychoanalytic practitioners overlooked the roles that the parents were playing in the story of Oedipus – and in the stories of their patients.

Freudian oedipal assumptions have been increasingly challenged in recent decades, as there has been a greater awareness of child abuse. From an attachment perspective, a different reading of the myth could be made taking into account Laius traumatic experiences as a child, which would have contributed to his sexual violence towards young people like Chrysippus, and to his murderous feelings towards his own son Oedipus.

Malcolm Pines (1998) acknowledged that parental seduction and violence are not situations of fantasy; they are real. In his opinion, we have lived through an era where the politics of the family, and the exercise of power over children, were almost totally unnoticed. Many practitioners tended to see traumatic childhood experiences in terms of externalisations of the child's own innate sexual and aggressive drives – ignoring the desire and hatred of the adults.

In the Kleinian Group, John Steiner (1993) highlighted how Oedipus, with the prophecy of the oracle still ringing in his ears, kills a man old enough to be his father and marries a woman old enough to be his mother. So Oedipus turns a blind eye as does Jocasta and all the key players in the tragedy, including the citizens of Thebes – which is a mechanism present also in institutional and societal collusion.

Steiner suggested that 'turning a blind eye' conveys enough ambiguity as to how conscious or unconscious the knowledge is. He further elaborated that, in the course of the play, the characters on the stage and people in the audience are 'persuaded', by the skill of the dramatist, to ignore the truth put before them. An insightful theatre director put it this way:

> I am sorry to say this, but no one has understood before now that Oedipus is not about the revelation of truth but about the cover-up of truth. Everybody knows who Oedipus is from the start and everybody is covering up. Just like Watergate. Just like all through history – the lie is what societies are based upon. And it has nothing to do with the Oedipus Complex because Oedipus never had a complex.
> *(Pilikian, quoted in Steiner, 1993, p. 122)*

Most significantly, Oedipus himself attacks his eyes, "which are his link to the reality he cannot bear, and he tries to annihilate the source of his pain by destroying his capacity to experience and perceive" (ibid., p. 124). Steiner's position on this is consistent with Bowlby's previous suggestion that we cannot know what we cannot bear to know (see Chapter 10).

Bowlby regretted Freud's shift from seduction theory to a rather speculative theory of infantile sexuality, based on a highly biased reading of the Oedipus myth:

> Ever since Freud made his famous, and in my view disastrous volte-face in 1897, when he decided that childhood seductions he had believed to be aetiologically important were nothing more than the product of his patients' imaginations, it has been extremely unfashionable to attribute psychopathology to real life experiences.
> *(Bowlby, 1988a, p. 78)*

Freud went along with a collective cover-up and used a myth, which is not a lie but an imagined reality, to construct a theory of development centred on what he perceived as the primacy of infantile sexuality. Bowlby challenged this and replaced it with a new developmental perspective grounded on the instinctual need for meaningful attachment relationships.

In this chapter, I have tried to show that the risk on the part of therapists to re-enact their patient's abuse increases when no proper consideration is given to the importance of attachment. Bowlby (1969) taught us that one of the main functions of attachment is protection. Some sexually abused women in particular are at a greater risk of being trapped in a 'confusion of tongues'. Their needs for an intimate, secure and protective attachment relationship have often been taken as sexualised behaviour – which has put these women at a greater risk of being further abused by the very people who should be protecting them but exploit them instead: a perversion of the therapeutic attachment relationship.

Gwen Adshead (1998), a forensic psychiatrist and group analyst, advocates an understanding of everyone's need for attachments, particularly at times of stress. She is mindful about the problem of a sexualised or eroticised attachment which is often present in forensic settings. A significant sub-group of forensic patients have experienced sexual abuse as children. Some of these patients, through projection, may wrongly perceive that the principal nurse or other member of the nursing staff is attracted to them, or even loves them, proclaiming that if they had met under different circumstances a romantic attachment would develop between them. Therefore, a key feature of relational and therapeutic security is "the making and maintaining of professional boundaries in the relationships between staff and patients" (Adshead & Aiyegbusi, 2014, p. 206).

Bowlby's work was based on honesty, empathy and compassion. As a clinician and supervisor, he provided a secure base which had a flawless protective component. An increasing number of psychotherapy, mental health and care institutions have introduced an obligation for all their registered practitioners to have some form of individual or group supervision – no matter how experienced or senior they might be.

There are new schemes for continuous professional development that include the requirement of regular peer group meetings or peer supervision, in which consultants and other clinicians can share concerns about their work. In my view schemes of this nature should be extended to all therapists and carers, in order to maximise healthy personal growth and protection for all patients and clients. We have come a long way but still have a long way to go.

12

THE WIT AND WISDOM OF JOHN BOWLBY: PERSONAL REFLECTIONS

Thank you for embarking with me on this journey through the life and work of John Bowlby – a great man, mentor and friend. The world of mental health, social care and the wider health economy owes a great deal to the originality and clarity of his thinking; to his vision, perseverance, compassion and encouragement; to what many have described as his genius; to his humanity. But his life was not spent wading through a grey porridge of political posturing. Indeed, outside the consulting room he was a sparkling and witty character.

John Bowlby's human side became clearer to María and to me from a travel log that he had posted to his wife Ursula about his first adventure through Spanish-speaking Latin America: the last of his many long expeditions. Ursula had to stay at home just before departure.... She wrote to us, within a few months of his death. It happened to be the only undated letter of the thirty or so that she sent to us: a metaphor for an encounter with John – a truly timeless experience.

Dear Arturo and María,

I thought you might like to read the enclosed (no need to return). It was with the collection of John's letters to me (1939–1980) which after he died I gave to the Wellcome Foundation's 'contemporary medical archives centre'. They have sorted them and put them (mostly) in order, but some need to be dated and that's what I am doing now. I asked them to make photocopies and give them to me, and this they have done.

I copied out extracts from John's 1980 letters to circulate round the family (who certainly couldn't cope with his hand writing) – from Bogotá he went onto the States to Charlottesville (Mary Ainsworth) and Berkeley (Mary Main). In all he was away for 4 weeks (Jan/Feb 1980), a longer trip than usual. I was to have come with him but at the last minute a family commitment dictated that I stay in England. It was a difficult decision. John was very good about it, but he minded.

He was 73 without a word of Spanish (bound for Lima), and only just mobile following a repair operation for a ripped Achilles tendon. In addition there was a blanket of silence over Peru. No-one could enlighten us – not the Peruvian embassy, not the British Council. We have no way of communicating with Lima. It was hard to watch as John limped away into the blue, into this complete silence. While he was away I spent the time down in Herefordshire giving moral support to our eldest, Mary, and her two young sons.

Yours,

Ursula

PS. Because of the postal strike in Peru, John posted a lengthy letter when he reached the States.

The following travel passages were handwritten by Bowlby.

Aboard National flight to Miami, Jan: 28, 1980.

The plane, a big DC10, is barely 1/3 full so conditions are good. I am stretched out over two seats with my back to the window and feet up ...: lunch at 2.30, as I expected, meant I was glad of my porridge [which I, Ursula, had insisted he had for breakfast].

Quito, 9 a.m. Jan: 29, 1980.

Arrangements at Miami were slow, but I got my Telexed ticket for Lima [arranged by Jo Sancha, to our great gratitude] and changed around my U S tickets to cater for my changed itinerary (a major undertaking I could not do in London) and continue to get a bus and two spells in a bed (2 + 4 hours) before catching the stopping-plane for Lima (2 ¾ hours to Panama and 1 ½ on to Quito). Coming in here we had an exciting view of the lower Andes, with some of the highest peaks standing up snow-covered, above banks of broken clouds ... a fair number of American tourists aboard and some businessmen with quite a sprinkling of local Indians who are much in evidence at the airport ... we continue to cook on the tarmac. We are of course bang on the Equator here – just remembered.

Lima, 9 a.m. Jan: 30, 1980.

A hot rather humid morning which despite the thinnest clothes makes me sweat doing nothing. Max [Hernández] greeted me at the airport and from then on the scene became one of enthusiastic welcome and non-stop discussion. All the trouble [our inability to communicate with Lima] was due to a post and telephone strike. Max himself spent hours trying to get through and had the same experiences as we had – the bell 'ringing' and no answer ... my numerous hosts are preoccupied with discussing shop, showing me around and talking politics ... supper with Roberto Lerner and his wife, who leads the Bowlby Study Group here – from 8–10 p.m. my first meeting with them.

They are an intelligent well-read lot and speak fairly good English. Origins extremely diverse. Mostly educated in Europe. Four out of the 5 analysts here (including Max) were trained in London, in the Independent Group (Winnicott, Rycroft, Pearl King, etc.) so they are open-minded and congenial. This evening is the Foundation of the Psychoanalytic Society of Peru to which I am invited – 8.45 signing the documents with dinner afterwards. Hate nights galore!

The preliminary study-group last night was largely occupied in planning my 5-day engagements. I insisted on keeping Saturday and Sunday clear... I also insisted that 3 professional engagements a day were enough. I am staying at the Hotel Country Club – a low-spread Edwardian establishment in this green suburb of San Isidro. Green lawns, oleanders and other flowering shrubs, a tall palm or two reminiscent of India (except no rushing parrots to keep me company) – all very congenial. Even the taps on my bath are the same pattern as ours at home, tell Pia [younger daughter] ... I feel more at home in these rather passé surroundings than in some hyper-efficient tourist hotel in town. ...

More than anything I am struck by the mixture of ethnic groups. The study-group comprises Spaniards, several international Jews, two tall blond girls, Anglo-Saxon or Scandinavian and other less easily identifiable. Everywhere local Indians doing the menial jobs, and mezos [mestizos] the in-between ones ... . The mezos look very much like Chinese [In fact he discovered later they were Chinese].

... The lady in whose parent house the study group meets turns out to be the offspring of Palestine Arabs, refugees from Israel, named Allegri Majlus – no wonder I found the surname difficult. The celebration on Wednesday evening started at 9.30 and after appropriate ritual and speeches to which I was asked to contribute. The senior six of us went to a restaurant in an old Spanish Colonial house downtown which proved most congenial and delicious food tho' far too much of it. It was a thoroughly enjoyable event at the price of bed at 2 a.m.

Yesterday I had discussion groups and case conferences 10–12 and 1–2.30, after which I got in a couple of hours sleep before giving a lecture in a crowded and very hot hall from 7.30–9 p.m. Translation makes these events doubly tiring but the people I talk to are intelligent and well-informed and also most appreciative ... It stays extremely hot but I'm sleeping well. I do all I can to keep my leg up, especially as I am getting some swelling at times. Otherwise no trouble.

There is much about Lima that reminds me of India ... The same contrast between spacious suburban houses with masses of colourful bougainvillea ... the anonymous concrete blocks of flats and offices... and an endless wasteland around the perimeter of factories and shanty-towns, huge bill-boards, tricycle rickshaws and rubbish. All roads pot-holey, trucks and buses ancient and noisy, small elderly cars often without the silencer, Indian children hawking fruit or magazines, driving impulsive and disorderly tho' fortunately not very fast, stopping at red lights regarded as eccentric, not a seat belt in sight ...

Cuzco, 7 a.m. Sunday, Feb: 3, 1980 [I think about 8,000 feet up]

You will be surprised to see I'm really in Cuzco … A lovely sunny blue and white day … Cuzco is a beautiful small agricultural town with very extensive old Spanish Colonial houses and all quite unspoiled. In the square are two huge churches, one the cathedral. Everywhere Indians with huge bundles on their backs and children of all ages. The women are all extremely broad in the beam, and squat. They trot about with a curious rolling gate …

The hills around Cuzco remind me of Sariska [Rajasthan], but quite green. On examination one sees endless small plots of cultivation, mostly potatoes. A thin scatter of sheep, scrawny cattle and llamas graze here and there … Height is only a minor problem I think. I walk very slowly and go uphill and up steps only one step at the time.

Before leaving Cuzco I was able to visit the cathedral, a splendid seventeenth-century building massively constructed of great stone blocks. Considering some very severe earthquakes, especially in 1950, it is astonishing that it stands intact. This is attributed to Inca foundations and, I presume, stone masonry by the Inca descendants.

Lima, Sunday 2 p.m.

Back at Lima airport about 1 p.m. we were met by Saúl Peña, the senior analyst here … a jolly man who seems very appreciative tho' I suspect he has read next to nothing I've written. Books are scarce and expensive here and I plan to send a lot after returning home. All hospitality and living expenses are being paid for, so I'll express my gratitude in free copies. Very hot down here in Lima, but more oxygen!

Monday, Feb: 4, 1980–6 p.m.

… Yesterday afternoon and evening I spent with Saúl Peña and his wife Louise and their two small sons. We drove due east to the river Rimac, gushing down from the snows and altho' we only went 30 miles we were already 3,000 feet up in the most desolate gorge I've ever seen, not excepting Death Valley. Whereas at Cuzco the sierra are green, here they are totally bare, large steep brown slag-heaps, tumbling brown rock and moraine …

But birds are extremely scanty (unlike India), partly lack of water I presume and partly, I suspect, killing them for food. Two good spots, one a charming little vireo, similar to California. The other a diminutive falcon, ruddy back and dark wings … I am very fit and the Achilles tendon giving no trouble.

Wed, Feb: 6, 1980

In half an hour I am to board an Avianca flight (Colombian Airlines) to BOGOTA and LONDON! Nostalgic + + + … Max came in as I was breakfasting and felt that my visit had crystalized support for the various child-development, family-therapy and community-psychiatry plans he is fostering. On these occasions one acts as a catalyst for one's friends' schemes, which is very satisfying. To Max's satisfaction I have been able to shake confidence in traditional and dogmatic psychoanalysis and to say things no-one else could easily say …

Plane to Bogota: What Bogota holds, apart from thieves and brigands about whom everyone warns me, is unclear. In Lima I saw plenty of psychologists, social workers and only a handful of moderate analysts. In Bogota I am the guest of the Psychoanalytic Society of Colombia and anticipate conflict with some of them.

Monday, Feb: 11, 1980

Thursday and Friday were two heavy days, starting at 8.15 a.m. and ending at 11.30 p.m. after very late and very dull dinners. Saturday and yesterday were much better, especially yesterday which I enjoyed. Bogota is a city of 5 million strung along under high hills to the East and a wide fertile plateau to the West. All together more prosperous than Peru. A green landscape with mixed farming and attractive woodlands. Incidentally, enormous planting of Australian eucalyptus everywhere. The plateau is 8,000 feet up, but I don't think it bothers me more than very slightly.

Yesterday we set out at 9 a.m. for a 70-mile drive to the coffee plantation belonging to the family of a psychoanalyst. This meant driving West across the plateau and then down a tremendous gorge to a broad and fertile valley, flanked by hills of anything between 5 and 8,000 feet. On the lower slopes are the plantations – coffee with banana trees as shade, a very pleasant combination. The day was warm, high 70's, the sun overhead pretty hot, but a light air kept us from cooking. Company was good and English adequate. I was especially pleased to see lots and lots of birds in the 500 acres of plantations – including some blue and green love-birds and a little finch with the most brilliant scarlet head, breast and shoulders. Up in the sky a few black vultures – very common here even around the airport.

… On Friday evening I addressed a large professional audience of some 500 people for which my Spanish slides prepared by Carlos [son-in-law] were most useful. The analysts here were appreciative and a recurring refrain was: "Will ye no' come back again?" I think they feel a bit lost. Disillusioned with 'Kleinianism' they are searching around. To my surprise a handful had read Attachment and Loss, tho' others had never heard of it. After my seminars, however, one of the elder went out and purchased two volumes of the Spanish edition … In Bogota, like Lima, I wore thin clothes and had got quite sunburned … A couple of days rest and catching up with life is what I want most of all.

Ursula explained that Bowlby got his wish, flying on from Bogota, via Miami and Washington, to Charlottesville (Virginia), from where this diary-letter took four days to reach the Rectory Farmhouse where she was staying.

Bowlby wrote about what he saw and what he heard; he wrote about what he knew – a basic principle of successful writing. He was reliable and supportive of the people who worked with him. Freda Martin, widely renowned as an innovative thinker, teacher and clinician, rightly regarded as the mother of attachment theory in Canada, studied and worked with Bowlby for 15 years at the Tavistock Clinic after which she wrote: "You could count on him in every way" (Martin, 1991, p. 66).

Bowlby was consistently responsive, straight-forward and witty. At a recent meeting, Anton Obholzer told me that, before being Chairman of the Tavistock Clinic, he had attended as a junior doctor the very seminar on attachment theory where I met Bowlby some 20 years later. Obholzer shared with me an anecdote that, on one occasion, his peers were late for the seminar, so for a few minutes he was alone with Bowlby and asked him the question of what parenthood might be about – to which he smiled with tenderness while saying: "Dr Obholzer, parenthood is about regret".

I also met Colin Murray Parkes recently. He is a distinguished British psychiatrist, as well as an author of numerous books and publications on grief. The Queen had made him an Officer of the Order of the British Empire for his services to the community and his support to bereaved people. He worked with Bowlby over several decades at the Tavistock and considered him to be the best supervisor he ever had and a dear friend. Parkes in some way reminded me of Bowlby. I had a delightful time with him. I enjoyed his gentle, reflective manner – his Britishness.

Parkes told me that Bowlby had a formidable intellect and was a lovable person who, despite being emotionally difficult to reach and not expressing affection verbally, gave him a feeling that he was close. Parkes is not a psychoanalyst and sometimes felt that his Tavistock colleagues did not consider him as one of them; but he always felt at home with Bowlby who had high expectations of him. The first time Parkes gave Bowlby a paper for his comments, he wrote that it was half baked and encouraged him to get on with it. Parkes added that he learned a lot from Bowlby about good writing.

Parkes also shared with me some of his privileged knowledge about John Bowlby's family. He said that John loved his children very much but he left Ursula to play the maternal role entirely. She was emotionally very intelligent. She was in charge of the home. Mary, their eldest daughter, had said to Parkes that she was sometimes angry with her father because, each time she had an argument with mother, father would always take mother's side! Parkes added that John and Ursula were very close and John supported her authority as a mother unconditionally. Parkes felt he was fortunate to be one of Bowlby's close friends and always felt valued by him.

With regard to Bowlby's personal relationships, Ursula had said: "John wasn't curious about people, about 'how they ticked', and he was very incurious about himself. This seems an absurd statement, considering his career, but anyway it is true" (quoted in Karen, 1998, p. 428). All this, of course, is a hallmark of an avoidant pattern of attachment. But, no doubt, he managed many successful and fulfilling relationships. His well of feeling, shapeless and unarticulated as it may have been at times, could be touched by others.

Factors which almost certainly played a part in making Bowlby sensitive to separation were his life experiences, particularly the influence of his social environment during childhood and adolescence. He grew up in a typical upper-middle class family where the right-wing Tory principles of 'King, Country and Empire' were cultivated. His change in political persuasions before the war, from Tory family tradition to his own left-wing Labour choice, can be understood in the light of his commitment to help vulnerable children – which in turn contributed to his growing social consciousness.

In his late years, Bowlby's main concern seems to have remained what it was for him as a young man; that is, the well-being of children and society: "I am the kind of person who identifies a typhoid bacillus and says, look, if you let the typhoid bacilli get into the water supply, there'll be trouble. That's been my job in life" (quoted in Byng-Hall, 1991b, p. 267). His colossal efforts at theory building were mainly in the service of social change: Tory by nature but socialist by nurture!

When Bowlby died, an outpouring of reminiscences paid tribute to the affection, loyalty and respect that he had engendered. There was some mention, too, of his confident assertiveness – which might help explain how a young man like him so new to his chosen field achieved such a powerful status. He was often considered aloof and emotionally distant, a trait that some people attributed to shyness or awkwardness (Holmes, 1993). Others like his close friend Eric Trist and his first boss at the Tavistock Jock Sutherland (1990) ascribed this quality of Bowlby to a protective shell that made it difficult for him to express personal feelings.

Barbara Kahan, a social worker who played a pivotal role in the development of residential care for children and young people, felt fortunate to have been taught by Bowlby and gave a more complete and balanced portrait of him:

> He had a severe and serious appearance, tall and spare, with a penetrating gaze sometimes, momentarily relaxing into a delightful smile which started with his eyes and swiftly illuminated the rest of his face. Too reserved with too much integrity to be a cult figure, the influence he exercised and the contribution he made were unparalleled.
>
> *(Kahan, 1990)*

Bowlby was known to say that social workers were easier to convince than his own psychoanalytic colleagues.

Victoria Hamilton, a psychoanalyst who was supervised by Bowlby at the Tavistock Clinic in the 1970s, described his presence as

> penetrating but responsive eyes beneath raised eyebrows which to me expressed both interest and a slight air of surprise and expectation... a remarkable ability to listen to the thoughts and beliefs of others, combined with a capacity for objectivity and a rare facility with the English language. He could step back from an idea and reformulate it in a succinct articulate way.
>
> *(quoted in Holmes, 1993, p. 33)*

In contrast to this confidence in his professional role, Ursula said that he rarely spoke of his personal feelings and that he was "completely inarticulate when he tried" (quoted in Karen, 1998, p. 29).

Those who came to work with Bowlby at the Tavistock, having heard in advance about his haughtiness and stubborn, sometimes pugnacious, adherence to his views, were often surprised by his gentle availability and deep fund of affection (Karen, 1998). Intellectually he was efficient, focussed and formidable. Ursula was to describe him as "the most formidable man I ever met" (ibid., p. 30).

In old age, Bowlby admitted to having been a rather arrogant young man, to which Ursula added: "he was also an arrogant middle-aged man and an arrogant old man – he knew he was right in fact" (ibid., p. 30). Yet, he was very straight and honest too, admirably, almost touchingly, incapable of being devious – and he possessed an unshakeable integrity. Karen (1998, p. 30) added: "He was also very well-mannered and had an unusual ability to maintain relations with those who held opposing views. He was in almost every respect an old-fashioned English gentleman".

When Bowlby was in his prime, he appeared to have become the sort of person who never wastes time, and who is able to understand and integrate everything he has read or studied. Ursula thought of his mind as "a smoothly functioning Rolls Royce". But it was a Rolls Royce with artillery.... He fielded questions from unfriendly members of an audience with shrewdly pointed replies (ibid., p. 30).

In Bowlby's generation, a Rolls Royce was a symbol of status and British excellence. However, his car was a large family Volvo – a symbol of security and protection in the eventuality of a road accident. Gill Bryant, a social worker at the Tavistock Clinic, sent an email to me on 13 February 2014 confirming that Bowlby's car was indeed a big Volvo, and that she often saw him struggling with long manoeuvres to place it in the small parking bays of the Tavistock. Was this a symbolic reflection of the difficulties he experienced for his theories to be accommodated within the psychoanalytic community?

Bowlby had at one point said: "Mine was a very stable background" (quoted in Scarf, 1976, p. 151). But this should not be taken to mean warm, secure, and emotionally responsive or any of the other qualities that he believed were so important to a developing child. His parents were conventional upper-class people of their day, with a belief in intellectual rigour and a stiff-upper-lip approach to all things emotional. Although Bowlby never discussed the matter and seemed to have put it out of his mind, he did not have a happy relationship with either of his parents (Karen, 1998, p. 30).

Bowlby's mother, according to Ursula, was a sharp, hard, self-centred woman who never praised the children and seemed oblivious to their emotional lives; his father, although rarely present, was something of an inflated bully (ibid., p. 31). Both parents set themselves utterly apart from their children, handing over their care to nannies and a governess. The children ate separately until the age of 12, when they would be permitted to join the parents for dessert. Although Bowlby would never criticise his parents, his views on the needs of young children could be seen as an indictment of the type of upbringing to which he had been subjected and to the culture that had fostered it (Karen, 1998; Van Dijken, 1998).

Bowlby's training analysis with Joan Riviere started in 1929 and was unusually long (nearly 10 years). Riviere's physical beauty and professional views were causing a sensation in British psychoanalytic circles. Many colleagues, Kleinian and non-Kleinian, considered that her theorising was ahead of her time. She was also known by some who knew her well to be something of a bully (Grosskurth, 1986). Bowlby seemed to have taken objection to the behaviour of Riviere about something and he wanted to change to another analyst in 1935, but his senior colleague Susan Isaacs persuaded him to stay and complete his analysis (Van Dijken, 1998).

Pia Durán, Bowlby's younger daughter, said to me humorously at a recent social gathering that her father had ended his analysis with Riviere soon after he married her mother, in 1938, as he could not afford a wife and an analysis at the same time. Ursula had confessed some 20 years earlier: "The only thing he told me about her [Riviere] was that she was a lady" (quoted in Karen, 1998, p. 33).

Bowlby became the *new boy* who emerged in the British psychoanalytic scene in the late 1930s. He was brilliant, confident, energetic, impetuous at times, and decidedly off-putting on occasion – with a terrific sense of purpose and no reverence for prevailing theories or their makers. In the coming years he would get under a lot of people's skin (Karen, 1998). He was also as precise as a Swiss watch and consistently methodical throughout his professional life.

In the nearly six years I worked with him I did not have to wait for him – not one single minute. He was impeccably reliable and consistent. At one point, he advised me to have a moderate scepticism when a new idea lit up in my head. He shared with me his own method: he would write down the new idea and would let it rest for a couple of days before revisiting it. This is seamlessly consistent with what his secretary, Dorothy Southern (1990, p. 15), said about him:

> For all his written work Dr Bowlby's method of writing was first to draft a section, put it on one side for 48 hours, re-read and revise, and then bring it in for typing. He loved the language and his clarity of writing has been a great influence.

On 16 September 1990, two weeks after Bowlby's death, Ursula sent me excerpts of a poem by Anthony Thwaite. The poem had been published in *The Times* on 11 February that year and, she said, reminded her of some of her husband's writings:

> He writes what he remembers, innocent, though now he is no longer innocent: What he remembers, what he tries to write is how things were. He cannot get it right…. But in the morning, reading what he wrote last night, the only words he finds he wrote are on the surface. And the page below is blank as things he did not want to know.

The only time I ever saw Bowlby slightly anxious was a couple of weeks prior to his 80 birthday conference at the end of June 1987. In supervision, just before this celebratory event, he talked to me about his psychoanalytic colleague and friend Margaret Mahler and her sudden death aged 88. He recalled with a hint of sadness on his face that she had died the month before a major international conference, held in Paris in November 1985, which was planned to be a homage to her long and productive professional career. The event turned into a memorial to pay tribute to her life.

Bowlby's 80 birthday conference was attended by more than 400 delegates from many countries. He was immensely happy and fulfilled. The occasion was full of intellectual and emotional meaning. Shortly after the conference, whilst speaking at another celebratory event at the beginning of July, he collapsed and his breathing stopped:

> The medics in the audience pronounced him dying and the audience dispersed in a dazed state. The news quickly spread. The whole of the Tavistock (at least the part I had contact with) was swept into a state of grieving which I had not anticipated. It seemed that we did love him even if we did not always behave as if we did.
>
> *(Byng-Hall, 1991a, p. 5)*

The family went home as he was deeply unconscious in hospital with no apparent chance of survival. A few hours later, he sat up and asked for his spectacles … .

A Tavistock myth developed that Bowlby had then wanted to dictate the next chapter of the book he was writing. The story did not prove to be strictly accurate. However,

> like all myths it conveys a certain truth …, this story… epitomized the man. John Bowlby had a burning mission to get the really important jobs done. Not even 'death' could stop him in his tracks. And certainly not merely old age.
>
> *(Byng-Hall, 1991a, p. 5)*

No doubt Bowlby wanted to write a new chapter in his life.

While waiting for further news about his health, I found a note in my Tavistock's pigeon hole from his secretary:

> Dear Dr Ezquerro
> You may like to know that Dr Bowlby is well again and would be able to see you for a final supervision before the holiday on this coming Thursday, 30th July at 2.45 p.m.
> Could you let me know if this is possible please?
> Dorothy Southern
> [Memorandum, 29 July 1987].

This is an example of Bowlby's commitment to his work, and to the progress of his trainees and supervisees! When he died, more than three years later, Dorothy Southern wrote a moving appreciation:

> I became Dr Bowlby's secretary on the 12th February 1951, so I have been with him almost 40 years... He was exceedingly generous with his time (writing time too) ... and a great 'putter-in-touch'.... I was asked by the Tavistock if I could be considered a secure base for Dr Bowlby. My answer was undoubtedly yes... He was also the founder of the Tavistock Library... we now have the John Bowlby Reading Room to remember him by and which he was able to enjoy. I had long hoped there would be some recognition for him at the Tavistock.... It has been a privilege and a pleasure to have worked with Dr Bowlby ... and to have known the many colleagues and researchers who have been close to him.
>
> *(Southern, 1990, pp. 14–15)*

The recognition of Bowlby's life-long service at the Tavistock, and his unique contribution to human health, had been summarised by Obholzer in his letter of 18 February 1987 to the Prime Minister's office at 10 Downing Street – of which Bowlby's wife Ursula gave me a copy:

> Dear Sir,
> Re: Dr John Bowlby, C. B. E. [Commander of the Most Excellent Order of the British Empire]
> I am writing to ask you to submit Dr John Bowlby's name for the Birthday Honours List. He was awarded the Commander of the British Empire in 1972 and we would like the Prime Minister to consider recommending that her Majesty bestow a Knighthood on Dr Bowlby to coincide with his 80th birthday this year.
> Dr Bowlby was one of the team of psychiatrists working for the War Office – World War II, who developed the procedure for the selection of the Officer Selection Board which was later adopted by the Civil Service.
> After the war, Dr John Bowlby became Chairman of the Children's Department at the Tavistock Clinic, then a private clinic which joined the National Health Service in 1948. He held this office from 1946 to 1968. With characteristic energy and foresight John Bowlby developed the three areas of work which have brought this Clinic world renown in the field of mental health: clinical services, research and training of psychiatrists and other mental health professionals. As a child psychiatrist, his contributions in training and research have been outstanding and he is regarded by many as the most distinguished British child psychiatrist of this century, having developed insight into the foundations of mental health in childhood, which has resulted in preventive measures as well as enhancing the therapeutic treatment of emotionally disturbed children.

Dr Bowlby, who continues to serve as an Honorary member of our teaching staff, has gained recognition world-wide. I take the liberty of enclosing supportive letters of recommendation from the Rt. Hon. Baroness Sear and a number of eminent British scientists. These provide a picture of Dr Bowlby's wide raging achievements in the field of mental health.

Dr Anton Obholzer

Chairman, Professional Committee

I think Bowlby's life exudes a contagious optimism. In the last part of his journey, a time when he had gathered most resources and experience to draw from, he was happy, confident, actively creative and well prepared to face the end of his life. His late years were integral to his life adventure. My impression is that he grew happier as he was getting older. The many battles of his working life were over; his job had been done and had been appreciated; he was satisfied that he had delivered his message.

Bowlby told me that life after 80 is a gift. He did not enter into any discussion about what may or may not happen after death. But he conveyed to me a sense of connection and continuity with future generations through his children, grandchildren, colleagues, students and patients: a connection with life.

From the close contact I had with Bowlby, I am more able to appreciate that old age is not an isolated terminal phase of life but an integral part of our development, where earlier stages can be recreated, reconstructed and worked through. The idea that we all need, for our whole life, to love and to be loved was one of the essentials of his teaching. He encouraged me to persevere in this.

So active and dependable was Bowlby in his late years that John Byng-Hall (1991b, p. 267) felt prompted to say: "I have images of him, even last winter [Bowlby was 82], shaking the rain off his green mackintosh and hat as he arrived on time for some evening meeting, while others sent their apologies". He was immensely loyal and supportive to his colleagues, as well as a very committed family man – fond of outdoor and indoor pursuits.

Bowlby rarely created fun, but was quick to respond to it with humour. Despite his at times severe and restrained countenance, Tirril Harris told me that he would readily loosen up and be fun at Christmas parties, like those of his Tavistock Research Unit that he enthusiastically joined every year.

Sophie Barnard, one of Bowlby's grandchildren, intimated to me on 17 December 2014 that her grandfather was unassuming and never talked to her about his achievements. She first realised that he was world-renowned when in her late teens she was invited to his 80th birthday international conference. She also recalled having fun with him at Christmas. She added that he showed deep affection for all his grandchildren and was very sensitive about their interests.

Barnard elaborated on this. She has always liked art and ballet; so Bowlby often took her to art galleries and, each year, gave to her a ticket for a first ballet performance at the Royal Opera House as a Christmas present. Her brother Ben has loved natural life and motor-racing; so Bowlby often took him for a walk in Hampstead Heath or in the wilds of Skye during the family summer holidays, and also developed a keen interest in motor-racing in order to communicate with him better. Bowlby indeed lived life like a fast train.

The journey is coming to an end. Bowlby was waiting for me in his garden at home, where he was now supervising me…. [Carlos Durán was to tell me that his father-in-law loved gardening, had an encyclopaedic knowledge of plants and trees, and that working with him in the garden was a real great pleasure.]

Bowlby greeted me with a lively, cheerful smile – denoting warmth and pleasure. It was Thursday, 26 July 1990, a bright, pleasant, sunny day – with an unusually cloudless blue sky. I felt at home. We sat at an old wooden table…. It was our last time together.

John Bowlby's local newspaper in Hampstead, the *Ham and High*, published on 7 September 1990 an obituary with excerpts from his last interview:

> I've always run in front of the hounds, sketching out the territory. It's been a fight sometimes but I've tried to keep controversy at a low level. I'm a one-note man….
>
> I haven't attempted to deal with the universe – just certain fundamentals.

FIGURE 12.1 John Bowlby in his late golden years.

APPENDIX

The literature on attachment theory has extensively developed since Bowlby's death. There are now thousands of publications. Howe (2011) gives a helpful introduction; Cassidy and Shaver (2008) provide a comprehensive account of attachment across the life cycle, including the adult attachment interview, assessment and applications; Clulow (2001) explores attachment in adult romantic relationships. However, I leave it up to the interested reader to find their way into current attachment research, something that is beyond the scope of this book. My main focus has been, indeed, John Bowlby: his life and work, through which the genesis and early development of attachment theory can be spelled out.

A number of authors have written about Bowlby's journey: Ainsworth, 1990; King, 1991; Rayner, 1991; Byng-Hall, 1991a, 1991b; Bretherton, 1991, 1992; Holmes, 1993, 2001; Karen, 1994, 1998; Parkes, 1995; Grossman, 1995; Heard & Lake, 1997; Marrone, 1998; Van Dijken, 1998; Coates, 2004, Issroff, 2005; Hauptman 2005; Kraemer, Steele & Holmes, 2007; Rustin, 2007; Stevenson-Hinde, 2007; Van der Horst et al., 2007; Van der Horst, 2011. The list is not exhaustive; but agglutinates a range of key contributions, from which I have extracted the following abridged chronology of Edward John Mostyn Bowlby:

1907	Born in London, 26 February. Fourth child and second son of Sir Anthony and Lady Mary (May) Bowlby.
1911	Minnie, his nursemaid and primary attachment figure, leaves.
1914–1919	Father away at the Front, First World War.
1917–1921	At Lindisfarne preparatory boarding school.
1921–1924	At Royal Naval College, Dartmouth.
1924–1925	At sea on HMS Royal Oak.

1925–1928	Reads natural sciences at Trinity College, Cambridge. Becomes interested in developmental psychology and reads psychology in the final year.
1928–1929	Works at two progressive schools: Bedales Junior, in Petersfield, and Priory Gate, in Norfolk.
1929	Father dies.
1929	Starts Medical School at University College Hospital, London, and personal analysis with Joan Riviere.
1933	Qualifies as a medical doctor.
1933–1936	Trains in adult psychiatry at the Maudsley Hospital with Aubrey Lewis.
1937–1940	Trains and works at the London Child Guidance Clinic.
1937	Becomes associate member of the British Psychoanalytical Society.
1938	Marries Ursula Longstaff.
1938–1939	Trains in child analysis, supervised by Melanie Klein.
1939	Mary Ignatia Bowlby is born.
1939	Publication of *Personal Aggressiveness and War*, with Evan Durbin.
1939	Elected full member of the British Psychoanalytical Society, following his dissertation "The Influence of Early Environment in the Development of Neurosis and Neurotic Character". Personal analysis ends.
1940–1945	Works at Royal Army Medical Corps with a group of psychiatrists from the London Tavistock Clinic, mainly involved with War Office Selection Boards.
1940	Anthony (Tony) Bowlby is born.
1941	Richard Bowlby is born.
1944	Publication of "Forty-four Juvenile Thieves: Their Characters and Home Life" in the *International Journal of Psychoanalysis* (first psychoanalytic paper to include statistical analysis).
1944–1961	Plays several roles at the British Psychoanalytical Society. Training Secretary (1944–1947). Member of Council (1944–1948; 1951–1954; 1956–1957; and 1958–1961). Deputy President (1956–1957; and 1958–1961).
1945	Pia Bowlby is born.
1946	Publication of *Forty-four Juvenile Thieves: Their Characters and Home Life* (the book).
1946–1990	Works at the Tavistock Clinic. Consultant child psychiatrist (1946–1972). Director of Children and Parents' Department (1946–1968). Deputy Director of the Tavistock Clinic (1947–1950). Chairman of the Staff Committee of Family Psychiatry and Community Mental Health (1968–1972). Honorary consultant (1972–1990). Creates Tavistock's child psychotherapy training in 1947 and separation research unit in 1948.
1948	Robert Bowlby is born.
1950–1972	Consultant in Mental Health, World Health Organization (WHO).

1951	Publication of *Maternal Care and Mental Health*.
1952	Organises research film 'A two-year-old goes to hospital', made by James Robertson.
1953	Publication of *Child Care and the Growth of Love*.
1953–1956	WHO study group on "The Psychobiology of the Child".
1957	Mother dies.
1957–1959	Presents a series of controversial papers to the British Psychoanalytical Society: "The Nature of the Child's Tie to his Mother", "Separation Anxiety", "Grief and Mourning in Infancy and Childhood".
1957–1958	Fellow at the Center for Advanced Study in the Behavioral Sciences, Stanford University, California.
1958	Publication of "The Nature of the Child's Tie to his Mother", blueprint of Attachment Theory.
1958–1965	Collaboration with Harry Harlow, Robert Hinde and other ethologists.
1958–1963	Consultant, National Institute of Mental Health, USA.
1960–1961	Chairman, Association for Child Psychology and Psychiatry.
1962–1966	President, International Association for Child Psychiatry and Allied Professions.
1963–1972	Member of External Scientific Staff, Medical Research Council.
1964	Fellow, Royal College of Physicians.
1967	Welcomes Mary Ainsworth's introduction of the concept of a 'secure base'.
1968	Visiting Professor in Psychiatry, Stanford University, California.
1969	Publication of *Attachment and Loss Volume 1: Attachment*.
1970–1976	Member of Council, Royal College of Psychiatrists.
1971	Honorary Doctor of Science, Leicester University.
1971	Foundation Fellow, Royal College of Psychiatrists.
1972	Commander of the British Empire.
1973	Publication of *Attachment and Loss Volume 2: Separation, Anxiety and Anger*.
1973	Travelling Professor, Australian and New Zealand College of Psychiatrists.
1974	Honorary member, British Paediatric Association.
1974	Stanley Hall Medal, American Psychological Association.
1974	Sir James Spence Medal, British Paediatric Association.
1977	Honorary Doctorate of Science, Cambridge University.
1979	Publication of *The Making and Breaking of Affectional Bonds*.
1980	Publication of *Attachment and Loss Volume 3: Loss, Sadness and Depression*.
1980	Honorary Fellow, Royal College of Psychiatrists.
1980	Visiting Professor of Psychiatry, University of Southern California, Los Angeles.

1981	Foreign Honorary Member, American Academy of Arts and Sciences.
1981	Freud Memorial Visiting Professor of Psychoanalysis, University College London.
1981	Distinguished Scientific Contribution Award, Society for Research in Child Development.
1982	Honorary Member, Royal Society of Medicine.
1984	Salmon Medal, New York Academy of Medicine.
1986	Honorary Member, American Academy of Child Psychiatry.
1986	William Schoenfeld Award, American Society for Adolescent Psychiatry.
1987	Honorary Fellow, Royal Society of Medicine.
1987	Celebration of his 80th birthday with an international conference, 'Fruits of Attachment Theory: Findings and Applications across the Life Cycle', organised by the Tavistock Clinic, at London Regent's College.
1988	Publication of *A Secure Base: Clinical Applications of Attachment Theory*.
1989	Fellow, American Psychological Society.
1989	Fellow, British Academy.
1989	Distinguished Scientific Contribution Award, American Psychological Association.
1990	Publication of *Charles Darwin: A New Biography*.
1990	Dies in Skye, 2 September.

REFERENCES

Adshead, G. (1998). Psychiatric staff as attachment figures. *British Journal of Psychiatry*, 172, 64–69.

Adshead, G., & Aiyegbusi, A. (2014). Four pillars of security: attachment theory and practice in forensic mental health care. In A. N. Danquad & K. Berry (Eds.), *Attachment Theory in Adult Mental Health: A Guide to Clinical Practice* (pp. 199–212). London, UK, and New York, NY: Routledge.

Ahrenfeldt, R. H. (1958). *Psychiatry in the British Army in the Second World War*. London, UK: Routledge & Kegan Paul.

Ainsworth, M. D. S. (1967). *Infancy in Uganda: Infant Care and the Growth of Attachment*. Baltimore, MD: The Johns Hopkins University Press.

Ainsworth, M. D. S. (1983). A sketch of a career. In A. N. O'Connell & N. F. Russo (Eds.), *Models of Achievement: Reflections of Eminent Women in Psychology* (pp. 200–219). New York, NY: Columbia University Press.

Ainsworth, M. D. S. (1990). Remembrances of John Bowlby. *Journal of The Institute for Self Analysis*, 4(1), 12–14.

Ainsworth, M. D. S. (1991). Attachment and other affectional bonds across the life cycle. In C. M. Parkes, J. Stevenson-Hinde, & P. Marris (Eds.), *Attachment Across the Life Cycle* (pp. 33–51). London, UK, and New York, NY: Tavistock/Routledge.

Akhtar, S., & Kramer, S. (1999). Beyond the parental orbit: Brothers, sisters and others. In S. Akhtar & S. Kramer (Eds.), *Brothers and Sisters: Developmental, Dynamic, and Technical Aspects of the Sibling Relationship* (pp. 3–24). North Bergen, NJ: Jason Aronson.

Allen, J. P., & Miga, E. M. (2010). Attachment in adolescence: A move to the level of emotional regulation. *Journal of Social Personal Relationships*, 27(2), 181–190.

Anthony, E. J. (1965). Group analytic psychotherapy with children and adolescents. In E. J. Anthony & S. H. Foulkes (Eds.), *Group Psychotherapy: The Psychoanalytic Approach* (pp. 186–232). London, UK: Maresfield.

Antonucci, T. C. (1986). A hierarchical mapping technique. *Generations*, 10(4), 10–12.

Appignanesi, L., & Forrester, J. (1992). *Freud's Women*. New York, NY: Basic Books.

Atger, F. (2007). L'attachement a l'adolescence. *Dialogue*, 175, 73–86.

Axline, V. M. (1947). *Play Therapy*. Boston, MA: Houghton Mifflin.

Axline, V. M. (1950). Entering the child's world via play experiences. *Progressive Education*, 27, 68–75.

Bakman, N. (2008). She can be put to work: Joan Riviere as translator between Freud and Jones. *Psychoanalysis and History*, 10(1), 21–36.

Balint, M. (1937). Early developmental stages of the ego: Primary object love. In *Primary Love and Psycho-Analytic Technique* (1965 edition, pp. 234–267). London, UK: Tavistock.

Balint, M. (1952). On love and hate. *International Journal of Psychoanalysis*, 33, 355–362.

Bamber, J. H. (1988). Group analysis with children and adolescents. *Group Analysis*, 21(2), 99–102.

Bank, S., & Kahn, M. (1997). *The Sibling Bond*. New York, NY: Basic Books.

Bartlett, F. C. (1961). Frederic Charles Bartlett. In C. Murchinson (Ed.), *A History of Psychology in Autobiography: Vol. 3* (pp. 39–52). New York, NY: Russell and Russell.

Behr, H. (1988). Group analysis with early adolescents: Some clinical issues. *Group Analysis*, 21(2), 119–133.

Behr, H., & Hearst, L. (2005). Groups for children and adolescents. In H. Behr & L. Hearst (Eds.), *Group-Analytic Psychotherapy: A Meeting of Minds* (pp. 203–219). London, UK: Whurr.

Benedeck, T. (1956). Toward the biology of the depressive constellation. *Journal of the American Psychoanalytic Association*, 4, 389–427.

Berkovitz, I. H. (Ed.). (1995). *Adolescents Grow in Groups. Experiences in Adolescent Group Psychotherapy*. New York, NY: Jason Aronson.

Bertalanffy, L. von (1956). General Systems Theory. *General Systems Yearbook*, 1, 1–10.

Bettelheim, B. (1976). *The Uses on Enchantment: The Meaning and Importance of Fairy Tales*. New York, NY: Vintage Books.

Bettelheim, B. (1984). *Freud and Man's Soul: An Important Re-interpretation of Freudian Theory*. New York, USA: Vintage Books.

Bion, W. R. (1946). The Leaderless Group Project. *Bulletin of the Menninger Clinic*, 10, 77–81.

Bion, W. R. (1961). *Experiences in Groups*. London, UK: Tavistock.

Bion, W. R. (1962). *Learning from Experience*. London, UK: Heinemann.

Bion, W. R. (1967a). Notes on memory and desire. *Psychoanalytic Forum*, 2, 271–280.

Bion, W. R. (1967b). *Second Thoughts*. New York, NY: Aronson.

Bion, W. R. (1974). *Brazilian Lectures: Vol. 1*. Rio de Janeiro, Brazil:Imago Editora.

Bion, W. R. (1980). *Bion in New York and Sao Paulo*. (Edited by F. Bion). Perthshire, UK: Clunie Press.

Bion, W. R., & Rickman, J. (1943). Intra-group tensions in therapy. *The Lancet*, 1943(2), 678–681.

Blatz, W. (1940). *Hostages to Peace: Parents and the Children of Democracy*. New York, NY: Morrow.

Bléandonu, G. (1994). *Wilfred Bion: His Life and Works 1897–1979*. London, UK: Free Association Books.

Blos, P. (1962). *On Adolescence: A Psychoanalytic Interpretation*. New York, NY: The Free Press of Glencoe.

Bourne, S., & Lewis, E. (1984). Pregnancy after stillbirth and neonatal birth: Psychological risks and management. *The Lancet*, 324(7 July), 31–33.

Bourne, S., & Lewis, E. (1991a). Perinatal bereavement: A milestone and some new dangers. *British Medical Journal*, 302 (18 May), 1167–1168.

Bourne, S., & Lewis, E. (1991b). *Annotated Bibliography on the Psychological Aspects of Perinatal Death*. London, UK: Tavistock Clinic.

Bowlby, J. (1938). The abnormally aggressive child. *Human Relations*, 19, 230–234.

Bowlby, J. (1939). Jealous and spiteful children. *Home and School*, 4(5), 83–85.

Bowlby, J. (1940). The influence of early environment in the development of neurosis and neurotic character. *International Journal of Psychoanalysis*, 21, 154–178.

Bowlby, J. (1944). Forty-four juvenile thieves: Their characters and home life. *International Journal of Psychoanalysis*, 25, 107–128.

Bowlby, J. (1946a). Psychology and democracy. *Political Quarterly*, 17, 61–76.

Bowlby, J. (1946b). *Forty-four Juvenile Thieves: Their Characters and Home Life*. London, UK: Bailliere, Tindall, & Cox.

Bowlby, J. (1947). The therapeutic approach in sociology. *The Sociological Review*, 2, 123–128.

Bowlby, J. (1949). The study and reduction of group tensions in the family. *Human Relations*, 2, 123–128.

Bowlby, J. (1951). *Maternal Care and Mental Health*. Geneva, Switzerland: World Health Organization.

Bowlby, J. (1953a). *Child Care and the Growth of Love*. Harmondsworth, UK: Penguin Books.

Bowlby, J. (1953b). The contribution of studies of Anim Behav. In J. M. Tanner (Ed.), *Prospects in Psychiatric Research: The Proceedings of the Oxford Conference of the Mental Health Research Fund* (pp. 80–108). Oxford, UK: Blackwell Scientific Publications.

Bowlby, J. (1953c). Critical phases in the development of social responses in man and other animals. In M. L. Johnson & M. Abercrombie (Eds.), *New Biology* (pp. 25–32). Harmondsworth, UK: Penguin Books.

Bowlby, J. (1957). An ethological approach to research in child development. *British Journal of Medical Psychology*, 30, 230–240.

Bowlby, J. (1958a). The nature of the child's tie to his mother. *International Journal of Psychoanalysis*, 39, 350–373.

Bowlby, J. (1958b). *Can I leave my baby?* London, UK: The National Association for Mental Health.

Bowlby, J. (1958c). Psychoanalysis and child care. In J. D. Sutherland (Ed.), *Psychoanalysis and Contemporary Thought* (pp. 33–57). London, UK: The Hogarth Press.

Bowlby, J. (1959). The roots of human personality. In P. Halmos & A. Iliffe (Eds.), *Readings in General Psychology* (pp. 108–129). London, UK: Routledge & Kegan Paul.

Bowlby, J. (1960a). Separation anxiety. *The International Journal of Psychoanalysis*, 41, 89–113.

Bowlby, J. (1960b). Grief and mourning in infancy and early childhood. *Psychoanalytic Study of the Child*, 15, 9–52.

Bowlby, J. (1960c). Symposium on 'psychoanalysis and ethology' II: Ethology and the development of object relations. *International Journal of Psychoanalysis*, 41, 313–317.

Bowlby, J. (1961a). Separation anxiety: A critical review of the literature. *Journal of Child Psychology and Psychiatry*, 1, 251–269.

Bowlby, J. (1961b). Processes of mourning. *The International Journal of Psychoanalysis*, 42, 317–340.

Bowlby, J. (1961c). The Adolf Meyer Lecture: Childhood mourning and its implications for psychiatry. *American Journal of Psychiatry*, 118, 481–498.

Bowlby, J. (1969). *Attachment and Loss: Vol. 1. Attachment* (1991 edition). London, UK: Penguin Books.

Bowlby, J. (1973). *Attachment and Loss: Vol. 2. Separation, Anxiety and Anger* (1991 edition). London, UK: Penguin Books.

Bowlby, J. (1974). Problems of marrying research with clinical and social needs. In K. Connolly & J. Bruner (Eds.), *The Growth of Competence* (pp. 303–307). London, UK: Academic Press.

Bowlby, J. (1977). The making and breaking of affectional bonds. *British Journal of Psychiatry*, 130, 201–210.

Bowlby, J. (1978). Attachment Theory and its therapeutic implications. In S. C. Feinstein & P. L. Giovacchini (Eds.), *Adolescent Psychiatry: Developmental and Clinical Studies, Vol. VI* (pp. 5–33). Chicago, IL: University of Chicago Press.

Bowlby, J. (1979a). *The Making and Breaking of Affectional Bonds*. London, UK: Routledge.

Bowlby, J. (1979b). On knowing what you are not supposed to know and feeling what you are not supposed to feel. *Canadian Journal of Psychiatry*, 24, 403–408.

Bowlby, J. (1980). *Attachment and Loss: Vol. 3. Loss, Sadness and Depression* (1991 edition). London, UK: Penguin Books.

Bowlby, J. (1981). Perspective: A contribution. *Bulletin of the Royal College of Psychiatrists*, 5, 2–4.

Bowlby, J. (1984). Violence in the family as a disorder of the attachment and care-giving systems. *The American Journal of Psychoanalysis*, 44, 9–27.

Bowlby, J. (1988a). *A Secure Base: Clinical Applications of Attachment Theory*. London, UK: Routledge.

Bowlby, J. (1988b). Developmental Psychiatry Comes of Age. *American Journal of Psychiatry*, 145, 1–10.

Bowlby, J. (1990). *Charles Darwin: A New Biography*. London, UK: Hutchinson.

Bowlby, J. (1991a). The role of the psychotherapist's personal resources in the treatment situation. *Bulletin of the British Psychoanalytical Society*, 27(11), 26–30.

Bowlby, J. (1991b). Postscript. In C. M. Parkes, J. Stevenson-Hinde, & P. Marris (Eds.), *Attachment Across the Life Cycle* (pp. 293–297). London, UK, and New York, NY: Tavistock/Routledge.

Bowlby, J., & Durbin, E. F. (1939). *Personal Aggressiveness and War*. London, UK: Routledge & Kegan Paul.

Bowlby, J., Miller, E., & Winnicott, D. (1939). Letter. *British Medical Journal*, 2(4119), 1202–1203.

Bowlby, J., & Caplan, G. (1948). The aims and methods of child guidance. *Health Education Journal*, 6, 1–8.

Bowlby, J., et al. (1948). Diagnosis and treatment of psychological disorders in childhood. *Medical Press*, 220, 1–10.

Bowlby, J., & Robertson, J. (1952a). A two-year-old goes to hospital: A scientific film. *Proceedings of the Royal Society of Medicine*, 46, 425–427.

Bowlby, J., & Robertson, J. (1952b). Recent trends in the care of deprived children in the UK. *Bulletin of the World Federation for Mental Health*, 4(3), 131–139.

Bowlby, J., Figlio, K., & Young, R. M. (1986). An interview with John Bowlby on the origins and reception of his work. *Free Associations*, 6, 36–64.

Brave, A., & Ferid, H. (1990). John Bowlby and feminism. *Journal of the Institute for Self Analysis*, 4(1), 30–35.

Brearley, M. (2014). The roots of sport. *The Institute of Psychoanalysis: News and Events* [annual issue], 1–3.

Breger, L. (2009). *A Dream of Undying Fame: How Freud Betrayed His Mentor and Invented Psychoanalysis*. New York, NY: Basic Books.

Bretherton, I. (1991). The roots and growing points of attachment theory. In C. M. Parkes, J. Stevenson-Hinde, & P. Marris (Eds.), *Attachment Across the Life Cycle* (pp. 9–32). London, UK, and New York, NY: Tavistock/Routledge.

Bretherton, I. (1992). The origins of attachment theory: John Bowlby and Mary Ainsworth. *Developmental Psychology*, 28, 759–775.

Bridger, H. (1946). The Northfield Experiment. *Bulletin of the Menninger Clinic*, 10(3), 71–76.

Bridger, H. (1985). Northfield revisited. In M. Pines (Ed.), *Bion and Group Psychotherapy* (pp. 87–107). London, UK: Routledge & Kegan Paul.

Bridger, H. (1990). The discovery of the therapeutic community. In E. Trist & H. Murray (Eds.), *The Social Engagement of Social Science: A Tavistock Anthology, Vol I. The Socio-Psychological Perspective* (pp. 68–87). London, UK: Free Association Books.

Briggs, S. (2002). *Working with Adolescents: A Contemporary Psychodynamic Approach*. New York, NY: Palgrave MacMillan.

Bruggen, P. (1979). Authority in work with younger adolescents: A personal review. *Journal of Adolescence*, 2, 345–354.

Bruggen, P. (1997). *Who Cares? True Stories of the NHS Reforms*. Charlbury, UK: John Carpenter.

Bruggen, P. (2006). Castaway's corner. *Clinical Child Psychology and Psychiatry*, 11(2), 307–311.

Bruggen, P., & Pitt-Aikens, T. (1975). Authority as a key factor in adolescent disturbance. *British Journal of Medical Psychology*, 48(2), 153–159.

Bruggen, P., Dunn, C., & O'Brian, C. (1981). Daily meetings chaired by an adolescent in a psychiatric ward. *Bulletin of the Royal College of Psychiatrists*, 5(2), 20–22.

Bruggen, P., & O'Brian, C. (1986). *Surviving Adolescence: A Handbook for Adolescents and Their Parents*. London, UK: Faber and Faber.

Bruggen, P., & O'Brian, C. (1987). *Helping Families: Systems, Residential and Agency Responsibility*. London, UK: Faber and Faber.

Burlingame, G. M., Fuhriman, A., & Mosier, J. (2003). The differential effectiveness of group psychotherapy: A meta-analytic perspective. *Group Dynamics: Theory Research and Practice*, 7(1), 3–12.

Bush, E. W. (1935). *How to Become a Naval Officer*. London, UK: Gieves.

Byng-Hall, J. (1987). *Interview with John Bowlby*. Contemporary Medical Archives Centre, PP/BOW/A.5/17.

Byng-Hall, J. (1991a). An appreciation of John Bowlby: His significance for family therapy. *Journal of Family Therapy*, 13, 5–16.

Byng-Hall, J. (1991b). Address at John Bowlby Memorial Service. *Infant Mental Health Journal*, 12, 267–268.

Camus, A. (1983). *The Outsider*. London: Penguin Books.

Camus, A. (1996). *The First Man*. London: Penguin Books

Caparrós, N. (Ed.). (2004). *Y el Grupo Creo al Hombre*. Madrid, Spain: Biblioteca Nueva.

Casement, P. (1986). *On Learning from the Patient*. London, UK, and New York, NY: Tavistock Publications.

Cassidy, J., & Shaver, P. R. (Eds.). (2008). *Handbook of Attachment: Theory, Research, and Clinical Applications* (second edition). New York, NY: The Guilford Press.

Clulow, C. (2001). *Adult Attachment and Couple Psychotherapy*. London, UK: Brunner-Routledge.

Coates, S. W. (2004). John Bowlby and Margaret Mahler: Their lives and theories. *Journal of American Psychoanalytic Association*, 52(2), 571–601.

Coleman, J. C. (1985). *Psicología de la Adolescencia*. Madrid, Spain: Morata.

Coles, P. (2003). *The Importance of Sibling Relationships in Psychoanalysis*. London, UK: Karnac.

Coles, P. (2013). *The Uninvited Guest from the Unremembered Past: An Exploration of the Unconscious Transmission of Trauma*. London, UK: Karnac.

Cousteau, V. (1987). How to swim with sharks: A primer. *Perspectives in Biology and Medicine*, 30(4), 486–489.

Cundy, L. (Ed.). (2015). *Love in the Age of the Internet: Attachment in the Digital Era*. London, UK: Karnac.

Dalal, F. (1998). *Taking the Group Seriously: Towards a Post-Foulkesian Group-Analytic Theory*. London, UK: Karnac.

Dalal, F. (2011). *Thought Paralysis: The Virtues of Discrimination (The Exploring Psycho-Social Studies Series)*. London, UK: Karnac.

Dicks, H. V. (1970). *Fifty Years of the Tavistock Clinic.* London, UK: Routledge & Kegan Paul.

Dillon, J. (2010a). The tale of an ordinary little girl. *Psychosis,* 2(1), 79–83.

Dillon, J. (2010b). *The Personal is Political, Telling Stories? Attachment-Based Approaches to the Treatment of Psychosis.* London, UK: Karnac.

Dillon, J. (2012). Recovery from 'psychosis'. In J. Geekie, P. Randal, D. Lampshire, & J. Read (Eds.), *Experiencing Psychosis: Personal and Professional Experiences* (pp. 17–22). London, UK, and New York, NY: Routledge.

Dillon, J., & Hornstein, G. A. (2013). Hearing voices peer support groups: A powerful alternative for people in distress. *Psychosis,* 5(3), 286–295.

Dillon, J., Bullimore, P., Lampshire, D., & Chamberlin, J. (2013). The work of experience-based experts. In J. Rend & J. Dillon (Eds.), *Models of Madness: Psychological, Social and Biological Approaches to Psychosis* (pp. 305–318). London, UK, and New York, NY: Routledge.

Dubois-Comtois, K., Cyr, C., Pascuzzo, K., Lessard, M., & Poulin, C. (2013). Attachment theory in clinical work with adolescents. *Journal of Child and Adolescent Behavior* [http://dx. doi.org/10.4172/jcalb.1000111], 1(3).

Dunn, J. (2014). Siblings relationships across the life-span. In D. Hindle & S. Sherwin-White (Eds.), *Sibling Matters: A Psychoanalytic, Developmental and Systemic Approach* (pp. 69–81). London, UK: Karnac.

Dunn, J., & Kendrick, C. (1982). *Siblings: Love, Envy and Understanding.* London, UK: Grant McIntyre.

Dunn, J., & McGuire, S. (1992). Sibling and peer relationships in childhood. *Journal of Child Psychology and Psychiatry,* 33(1), 67–105.

Dupont, J. (Ed.). (1988). *The Clinical Diary of Sandor Ferenczi.* Cambridge, MA: Harvard University Press.

Dwivedi, K. N. (Ed.). (1998). *Group Work with Children and Adolescents: A Handbook.* London, UK: Jessica Kingsley.

Erikson, E. H. (1950). *Childhood and Society.* New York, NY: Norton.

Erikson, E. H. (1971). *Identity: Youth and Crisis.* London, UK: Faber and Faber.

Evans, J. (1988). Research findings and critical practice with adolescents. *Group Analysis,* 22(2), 103–114.

Evans, J. (1998). *Active Analytic Group Therapy for Adolescents.* London, UK: Jessica Kingsley.

Evans, J. (2000). Adolescent group therapy and its contribution to the understanding of adult groups. In M. Pines (Ed.), *The Evolution of Group Analysis* (pp. 98–108). London, UK: Jessica Kingsley.

Ezquerro, A. (1989). Group psychotherapy with the pre-elderly. *Group Analysis,* 22(3), 299–308.

Ezquerro, A. (1991). *Attachment and its Circumstances: Does it Relate to Group Analysis?* Theoretical dissertation for membership of the Institute of Group Analysis, December 1991. Archives Institute of Group Analysis Library, London, UK.

Ezquerro, A. (1995). Group therapy within the NHS III: Should we invest in group Psychotherapy? A Personal Account. *Group Analysis,* 28(4), 453–457.

Ezquerro, A. (1996a). The Tavistock and Group-Analytic Approaches to Group psychotherapy: A trainee's perspective. *Psychoanalytic Psychotherapy,* 10(2), 155–170.

Ezquerro, A. (1996b). Bion y Foulkes: Una Narrativa Grupo-Analítica en los Albores de un Nuevo Siglo y Milenio. *Boletín Sociedad Española de Psicoterapia y Técnicas de Grupo,* 4(10), 73–84.

Ezquerro, A. (1997a). Tradición Institucional y Cambio. *Boletín Sociedad Española de Psicoterapia y Técnicas de Grupo,* 4(11), 183–190.

Ezquerro, A. (1997b). Texto y Contexto en Dos Instituciones Terapéuticas. *Boletín Sociedad Española de Psicoterapia y Técnicas de Grupo,* 4(12), 147–153.

Ezquerro, A. (1998a). Abuso Sexual Infantil. *Boletín Sociedad Española de Psicoterapia y Técnicas de Grupo*, 4 (13), 139–140.

Ezquerro, A. (1998b). Gli Approcci Tavistock e Gruppoanalitico alla Psycoterapia di Gruppo. *Rivista Italiana di Gruppoanalisi*, 13(1), 41–57.

Ezquerro, A. (1998c). Los Modelos Tavistock y Grupo-Analitico: ¿Antagonistas o Complementarios? *Clínica y Analisis Grupal*, 20(1), 39–62.

Ezquerro, A. (1999). Abuso Sexual Infantil: De la Negación a la Evidencia Terapéutica. *Boletín Sociedad Española de Psicoterapia y Técnicas de Grupo*, 4(16), 129–138.

Ezquerro, A. (2000a). Avoidant group life: The roots of insecure attachment. *Bulletin Oxford Psychotherapy Society*, 32, 37–41.

Ezquerro, A. (2000b). Entramado Vincular en un Grupo de Jubilados. *Clínica y Análisis Grupal*, 22(3), 47–56.

Ezquerro, A. (2004a). El Grupo en la Clínica Primera Parte: Aspectos Históricos. In N. Caparros (Ed.), *Y el Grupo Creo al Hombre* (pp. 193–211). Madrid, Spain: Biblioteca Nueva.

Ezquerro, A. (2004b). El Grupo en la Clínica Segunda Parte: Enfoques Grupo-Analíticos. In N. Caparros (Ed.), *Y el Grupo Creo al Hombre* (pp. 212–227). Madrid, Spain: Biblioteca Nueva.

Ezquerro, A. (2010). Cohesion and coherency in group analysis. *Group Analysis*, 43(4), 496–504.

Ezquerro, A. (2015). John Bowlby: The timeless supervisor. *Attachment: New Directions in Psychotherapy and Relational Psychoanalysis*, 9(2), 165–175.

Ezquerro, A., & Bajaj, P. (2007). Combining individual and group-analytic psychotherapy: When the group is not enough or is it? *Group*, 31, (1–2), 5–16.

Ezquerro, A., & Canete, M. (1999). Group-analytic psychotherapy of psychosis. *Group Analysis*, 32(4), 507–514.

Ezquerro, A., & Canete, M. (2000). Group-analytic psychotherapy with the elderly. *Bulletin Oxford Psychotherapy Society*, 32, 26–29.

Ezquerro, A., & Canete, M. (2004). Gruppenanalytishe Psychotherapie der Pychose. In M. Hayne & D. Kunzke (Eds.), *Moderne Gruppenanalyse* (pp. 253–261). Giessen, Germany: Psychosozial-Verlag.

Ezquerro, A., & Canete, M. (2012). Bipolar affective disorders and group analysis. *Group Analysis*, 45(2), 203–217.

Ezquerro, A., Canete, M., & Stormont, F. (2000). Group-Analytic psychotherapy with the elderly. *British Journal of Psychotherapy*, 17(1), 94–105.

Ezquerro, A., Canete, M., and Stormont, F. (2004). Gruppenanalytishe Psychotherapie mit Alteren, In M. Hayne & D. Kunzke (Eds.), *Moderne Gruppenanalyse* (pp. 262–280). Giessen, Germany: Psychosozial-Verlag.

Fairbairn, W. R. D. (1943). The war neuroses, their nature and significance. In *Psychoanalytic Studies of the Personality* (1952 edition, pp. 256–288). London, UK: Routledge & Kegan Paul.

Fairbairn, W. R. D. (1952). *Psychoanalytic Studies of the Personality*. London, UK: Routledge & Kegan Paul.

Feinstein, A. (2010). *A History of Autism: Conversations with the Pioneers*. Chichester, UK: Wiley-Blackwell.

Ferenczi, S. (1932). Confusion of the tongues between the adults and the child: The language of tenderness and passion. In M. Balint (Ed.), *Final Contributions to the Problems and Methods of Psychoanalysis* (1960 edition, pp. 156–167). London, UK: Karnac.

Ferenczi, S. (1949). Confusion of the tongues between the adults and the child: The language of tenderness and passion. *International Journal of Psycho-Analysis*, 30, 225–230.

Festic, F. (2009). *The Body of the Postmodernist Narrator: Between Violence and Artistry*. Newcastle upon Tyne, UK: Cambridge Scholars Publishing.

Fitzpatrick, G. (1945). War Officer Selection Boards and the role of the psychiatrist in them. *Journal of the Royal Army Medical Corps*, 84, 75–78.

Flaherty, S. C., & Sadler, L. S. (2011). A review of attachment theory in the context of adolescent parenting. *Journal of Paediatric Health Care*, 25(2), 114–121.

Fonagy, P. (2001). *Attachment Theory and Psychoanalysis*. New York, NY: Other Press.

Fonagy, P., & Target, M. (1996). Playing with reality, I: Theory of mind and the normal development of psychic reality. *International Journal of Psycho-Analysis*, 77, 217–233.

Fonagy, P., & Target, M. (2007). The rooting of the mind in the body: New links between attachment theory and psychoanalytic thought. *Journal of the American Psychoanalytic Association*, 55(2), 411–456.

Foulkes, S. H. (1946). Group analysis in a military neurosis centre. *Lancet*, 1946(1), 303–313.

Foulkes, S. H. (1948). *Introduction to Group Analytic Psychotherapy*. London, UK: Heinemann.

Foulkes, S. H. (1964). *Therapeutic Group Analysis*. London, UK: George Allen & Unwin.

Foulkes, S. H. (1975). *Group Analytic Psychotherapy: Method and Principles*. London, UK: Gordon & Breach.

Fraiberg, S., Anderson, E., & Shapiro, V. (1975). Ghosts in the nursery: A psychoanalytic approach to the problems of impaired infant–mother relationships. *Journal of the American Academy of Child Psychiatry*, 14, 387–421.

Frankel, R. (1998). *The Adolescent Psyche. Jungian and Winnicottian Perspectives*. London, UK and New York, NY: Routledge.

Freud, A., & Burlingham, D. (1944). *Infants without Families*. London, UK: Allen & Unwin.

Freud, A., & Dann, S. (1951). An experiment in group upbringing. *Psychoanalytic Study of the Child*, 6, 127–168. Reprinted as: Freud, A., & Dann, S. (1967). An experiment in group upbringing. In Y. Brackbill & G. Thompson (Eds.), *Behaviour in Infancy and Early Childhood* (pp. 127–168). New York, NY: Free Press.

Freud, S. (1896). The aetiology of hysteria. In *Standard Edition: Vol. 3. The Complete Works of Sigmund Freud* (1953 edition). London, UK: Hogarth Press.

Freud, S. (1900). Interpretation of dreams. In *Standard Edition: Vols. 4 and 5. The Complete Works of Sigmund Freud* (1953 edition). London, UK: Hogarth Press.

Freud, S. (1905). Three essays on the theory of sexuality. In *Standard Edition: Vol. 7. The Complete Works of Sigmund Freud* (1953 edition). London, UK: Hogarth Press.

Gabbard, G. O. (1994). Psychotherapists who transgress sexual boundaries. *Bulletin of the Menninger Clinic*, 58, 124–135.

Gabbard, G. O. (1995). The early history of boundary violations in psychoanalysis. *Journal of the American Psychoanalytic Association*, 43, 1115–1136.

Gabbard, G. O. (1996). Lessons to be learned from the study of boundary violations. *American Journal of Psychotherapy*, 50, 311–321.

Gabbard, G. O., & Lester, E. (1996). *Boundaries and Boundary Violations in Psychoanalysis*. New York, NY: Basic Books.

Garelick, A. (2012). Doctors' health: stigma and the professional discomfort in seeking help. *The Psychiatrist*, 36, 81–84.

Garland, C. (1998). *Understanding Trauma: A Psychoanalytical Approach*. London, UK: Duckworth.

Garland, C. (2010). *The Groups Book. Psychoanalytic Group Therapy: Principles and Practice*. London, UK: Karnac.

Garvey, C. (1977). *The Developing Child*. Cambridge, MA: Harvard University Press.

Gay, P. (2006). *Freud: A Life for Our Time*. New York, NY, and London, UK: W. W. Norton & Company.

Gerhardt, S. (2010). *The Selfish Society: How We All Forgot to Love One Another and Made Money Instead*. London, UK: Simon & Schuster.

Geyskens, T. (2003). Imre Hermann's Freudian theory of attachment. *International Journal of Psychoanalysis*, 84(6), 1517–1529.

Ginott, H. (1961). *Group Psychotherapy with Children*. New York, NY: McGraw-Hill.

Glenn, L. (1987). Attachment theory and group analysis: The group matrix as a secure base. *Group Analysis*, 20(2), 109–126.

Glover, E. (1966). Psychoanalysis in England. In F. Alexander, S. Eisenstein, & M. Grotjahn (Eds.), *Psychoanalytic Pioneers* (pp. 534–545). New York, NY: Basic Books.

Golding, M. (2006). *The hitch hiker's guide to autism: An educator's unique account of the history of autism and the development of a relevant and empowering curriculum 1959–2005*. Address to the Second World Autism Congress (October 2006). Cape Town, South Africa.

Grosskurth, P. (1986). *Melanie Klein: Her World and Her Work*. London, UK: Maresfield Library.

Grossmann, K. E. (1995). The evolution and history of attachment theory. In S. Goldberg, R. Muir, & J. Kerr (Eds.), *Attachment Theory: Social, Developmental and Clinical Perspectives* (pp. 85–121). Hillsdale, NJ: The Analytic Press.

Grunebaum, H., & Solomon, L. (1980). Toward a peer theory of group psychotherapy, I: On the developmental significance of peers and play. *International Journal of Group Psychotherapy*, 30(1), 23–49.

Grunebaum, H., & Solomon, L. (1982). Toward a theory of peer relationships, II: On the stages of social development and their relationship to group psychotherapy. *International Journal of Group Psychotherapy*, 32(3), 283–307.

Guntrip, H. (1975). My experience of analysis with Fairbairn and Winnicott. *International Review of Psychoanalysis*, 2, 145–156.

Harlow, H. F. (1958). The nature of love. *American Psychologist*, 13, 673–685.

Harlow, H. F., & Zimmermann, R. R. (1958). The development of affectional responses in infant monkeys. *Proceedings of the American Philosophical Society*, 102, 501–509.

Harlow, H. F., & Zimmermann, R. R. (1959). Affectional responses in the infant monkey. *Science*, 130, 421–432.

Harris, T. (1990). Obituary: John Bowlby (1907–1990). *British Journal of Medical Psychology*, 63, 305–309.

Harrison, T. (2000). *Bion, Rickman, Foulkes and the Northfield Experiments*. London, UK: Jessica Kingsley.

Harter, S., Bresnick, S., Bouchey, H. A., & Whitesell, N. R. (1997). The development of multiple role-related selves during adolescence. *Developmental Psychopathology*, 9, 835–853.

Hartmann, N. (1912). *Philosophische Grundfragen der Biologie*. Göttingen, Germany: Vandenhoeck & Ruprecht.

Hauptman, B. (2005). Reflections on Donald Winnicott and John Bowlby. In J. Issroff (Ed.), *Winnicott and Bowlby: Personal and Professional Perspectives* (pp. 101–114). London, UK: Karnac.

Haynal, A., & Falzender, E. (1993). Slaying the dragons of the past or cooking the hare in the present: A historical view on affects in the psychoanalytic encounter. *Psychoanalytic Enquiry*, 13(4), 357–371.

Hazel, J. (1996). *H. J. S. Guntrip: A Psychoanalytical Biography*. London, UK and New York, NY: Free Association Books.

Heard, D., & Lake, B. (1997). *The Challenge of Attachment for Caregiving*. London, UK, and New York, NY: Routledge.

Herman, J. L. (1992). *Trauma and Recovery*. New York, NY: Basic Books.

Hermann, I. (1923). Zur Psychologie der Chimpanzen. *Internationale Zeitschrift für Psychoanalyse*, 9, 80–87.

Hermann, I. (1972). *L' Instinct Filial*. Paris, France: Denoel.

Hoag, M. J., & Burlingame, G. M. (1997). Evaluating the effectiveness of child and adolescent group treatment: A meta-analytic review. *Journal of Clinical Child Psychology*, 26, 234–246.

Holden, H. M. (2009). *The war time residential nurseries at Dyrham Park*. London, UK: Final Report to the National Trust.

Holden, K. (2013). *Nanny Knows Best: The History of the British Nanny*. Stroud, UK: History Press.

Holmes, J. (1993). *John Bowlby and Attachment Theory*. London, UK, and New York, NY: Routledge.

Holmes, J. (2001). *The Search for the Secure Base: Attachment Theory and Psychotherapy*. London, UK: Routledge.

Holmes, J. (2010). *Exploring in Security: Towards an Attachment-Informed Psychoanalytic Psychotherapy*. Hove, UK, and New York, NY: Routledge.

Hopkins, J. (1990). The observed infant of attachment theory. *Journal of the Institute for Self Analysis*, 4(1), 16–29.

Hopper, E. (2003). The problem of context in group-analytic psychotherapy: A clinical illustration and a brief theoretical discussion. In E. Hopper (Ed.), *The Social Unconscious: Selected Papers* (pp. 103–125). London, UK, and Philadelphia, PA: Jessica Kingsley Publishers.

Howe, D. (2011). *Attachment Across the Lifecourse: A Brief Introduction*. Basingstoke, UK: Palgrave MacMillan.

Hunter, V. (1991). John Bowlby: An interview. *Psychoanalytic Review*, 78, 159–175.

Hunter, V. (2015). John Bowlby: An interview by Virginia Hunter. *Attachment: New Directions in Psychotherapy and Relational Psychoanalysis*, 9(2), 138–157.

Huxley, A. (1954). *The Doors of Perception: On the Author's Sensations Under the Influence of Mescaline*. London, UK: Chatto and Windus.

Hynes, S. (1990). *A War Imagined: The First World War and English Culture*. London, UK: The Bodley Head.

Inglis, R. (1990). *The Children's War: Evacuation 1939–1945*. Glasgow, UK: Fontana/Collins.

Isaacs, S. (Ed.). (1941). *The Cambridge Evacuation Survey: A War-time Study in Social Welfare and Education*. London, UK: Methuen.

Issroff, J. (2005). Winnicott and Bowlby: Personal reminiscences. In J. Issroff (Ed.), *Winnicott and Bowlby: Personal and Professional Perspectives* (pp. 13–70). London, UK: Karnac.

Jacobsson, G. (2005). *On the Threshold of Adulthood: Recurrent Phenomena and Developmental Tasks during the Period of Young Adulthood* [Doctoral Thesis Monograph]. Stockholm, Sweden: Pedagogiska Institutionen.

Jaffa, T. (1987). Supervision of the community meeting: Experience in an adolescent unit. *Bulletin of the Royal College of Psychiatrists*, 11(2), 57–58.

Johns, M. (2002). Identification and dis-identification in the development of sexual identity. In J. Trowell & A. Etchegoyen (Eds.), *The Importance of Fathers: A Psychoanalytic Re-evaluation* (pp. 167–181). Hove, UK: Brunner-Routledge.

Jones, E. (1957). *The Life and Work of Sigmund Freud: Vol. 3. The Last Phase, 1919–1939*. New York, NY: Basic Books.

Kahan, B. (1990). John Bowlby's obituary: Man of integrity. *Community Care*, 20 September.

Kahr, B. (2012). Reminiscences by John Bowlby: Portraits of colleagues, 1935–1945 (previously unpublished). *Attachment: New Directions in Psychotherapy and Relational Psychoanalysis*, 6(1), 27–49.

Kaplan, E. (1976). Manifestations of aggression in latency and preadolescent girls. *The Psychoanalytic Study of the Child*, 31, 63–79.

Kaplan, T. (2002). From a short-life project to a mainstream service: Convincing commissioners to fund a community mental health team. *Child and Adolescent Mental Health*, 7(3), 114–120.

Kaplan, T., & Racussen, L. (2012). A crisis recovery model for adolescents with severe mental health problems. *Clinical Child Psychology and Psychiatry*, 18(2), 246–259.

Karen, R. (1994). *Becoming Attached: Unfolding the Mystery of the Infant–Mother Bond and its Impact on Later Life*. New York, NY: Warner Books.

Karen, R. (1998). *Becoming Attached: First Relationships and How They Shape our Capacity to Love*. Oxford, UK, and New York, NY: Oxford University Press.

King, P. (1989). Activities of British psychoanalysts during the Second World War and the influence of their inter-disciplinary collaboration on the development of psychoanalysis in Great Britain. *International Review of Psychoanalysis*, 16, 15–33.

King, P. (1991). John Bowlby's contributions to the British Psychoanalytical Society. *Bulletin of the British Psychoanalytical Society*, 27(11), 26–30.

Kinsey, A., Pomeroy, W., Martin, C., & Gebhard, P. (1953). *Sexual Behavior in the Human Female*. Philadelphia, PA: Saunders.

Klein, M. (1952). The origins of transference. *International Journal of Psychoanalysis*, 33(4), 433–438.

Kohon, G. (1986). Introduction. In G. Kohon (Ed.), *The British School of Psychoanalysis: The Independent Tradition* (pp. 19–80). New Haven, CT: Yale University Press.

Kraemer, S. (2011). 'The dangers of this atmosphere': A Quaker connection in the Tavistock Clinic's development. *History of the Human Sciences*, 24(2), 82–102.

Kraemer, S. (2015). Anxiety at the front line. In D. Armstrong & M. Rustin (Eds.), *Social Defences against Anxiety: Explorations in a Paradigm* (pp. 144–160). London, UK: Karnac.

Kraemer, S., & Roberts, J. (Eds.) (1996). *The Politics of Attachment: Towards a Secure Society*. London, UK: Free Association Books.

Kraemer, S., Steele, H., & Holmes, J. (2007). A tribute to the legacy of John Bowlby at the centenary of his birth. *Attachment and Human Development*, 9(4), 303–306.

Kriss, A., Steele, M., & Steele, H. (2014). Sibling relationships: an attachment perspective. In D. Hindle & S. Sherwin-White (Eds.), *Sibling Matters: A Psychoanalytic, Developmental and Systemic Approach* (pp. 82–95). London, UK: Karnac.

Krull, M. (1979). *Freud and His Father*. London, UK: Hutchinson.

Kuhn, T. S. (1962). *The Structure of Scientific Revolutions*. Chicago, IL: University of Chicago Press.

Kymissis, P. (1996). Developmental approach to socialization and group formation. In P. Kymissis & D. A. Halperin (Eds.), *Group Therapy with Children and Adolescents* (pp. 35–54). Washington, DC: American Psychiatric Press.

Lorenz, K. (1952). *King Solomon's Ring*. London, UK: Methuen.

Lucas, T. (1988). Holding and holding-on: Using Winnicott's ideas in group psychotherapy with twelve-to-thirteen-year-olds. *Group Analysis*, 21(2), 135–151.

MacLennan, B. W., & Dies, K. R. (1992). *Group Counselling and Psychotherapy with Adolescents*. New York, NY: Columbia University Press.

Magagna, J., & Jackson, M. (2015). Conclusion. In J. Magagna (Ed.), *Creativity and Psychotic States in Exceptional People: The Work of Murray Jackson* (pp. 114–126). London, UK, and New York, NY: Routledge.

Main, M. (1991). Metacognitive knowledge, metacognitive monitoring, and singular (coherent) vs. multiple (incoherent) models of attachment. In C. M. Parkes, J. Stevenson-Hinde, & P. Marris (Eds.), *Attachment Across the Life Cycle* (pp. 127–159). London, UK, and New York, NY: Tavistock/Routledge.

Main, M., & Weston, D. (1982). Avoidance of the attachment figure in infancy: Descriptions and interpretations. In C. M. Parkes & J. Stevenson-Hinde (Eds.), *The Place of Attachment in Human Behaviour* (pp. 31–59). New York, NY: Basic Books.

Main, T. (1946). The hospital as a therapeutic institution. *Bulletin of the Menninger Clinic*, 10(3), 66–70.

Makari, G. (2008). *Revolution in Mind*. London: Duckworth.

Mandela, N. (1994). *Long Walk to Freedom: The Autobiography of Nelson Mandela*. London, UK: Little Brown and Company.

Marcel, M. (2005). *Freud's Traumatic Memory: Reclaiming Seduction Theory and Revisiting Oedipus*. Pittsburgh, PA: Duquesne University Press.

Markiewicz, D., Lawford, H., Doyle, A. B., & Haggart, N. (2006). Developmental differences in adolescents and young adults' use of mothers, fathers, best friends, and romantic partners to fulfil attachment needs. *Journal of Youth and Adolescence*, 35, 127–140.

Marris, P. (1996). The management of uncertainty. In S. Kraemer & J. Roberts (Eds.), *The Politics of Attachment: Towards a Secure Society* (pp. 192–199). London, UK: Free Association Books.

Marrone, M. (1998). *Attachment and Interaction*. London, UK, and Philadelphia, PA: Jessica Kingsley.

Martin, F. E. (1991). John Bowlby, 1907–1990: A tribute and personal appreciation. *Journal of Melanie Klein and Object Relations*, 9, 63–69.

Masson, J. M. (1985). *The Assault on Truth: Freud's Suppression of the Seduction Theory*. New York, NY: Penguin.

Matte-Blanco, I. (1971). Book review: Attachment and Loss, Vol. 1. *International Journal of Psycho-Analysis*, 52, 197–199.

Mayhew, B. (2006). Between love and aggression: The politics of John Bowlby. *History of the Human Sciences*, 19(1), 19–35.

McCartney, J. L. (1966). Overt transference. *Journal of Sexual Research*, 2, 227–237.

McCluskey, U. (2002). The dynamics of attachment in systems-centred group. *Psychotherapy, Group Dynamics: Theory, Research and Practice*, 6, 131–142.

McRoberts, C. Burlingame, G. M., & Hoag, M. J. (1998). Comparative efficacy of individual and group psychotherapy: A meta-analytic perspective. *Group Dynamics: Theory Research and Practice*, 2(2), 101–117.

McGuire, W. (Ed.). (1974). *The Freud/Jung Letters: The Correspondence Between Sigmund Freud and C. G. Jung*. Princeton, NJ: Princeton University Press.

Meng, H., & Freud, E. L. (1963). *Psychoanalysis and Faith: The Letters of Sigmund Freud and Oskar Pfister*. New York, NY: Basic Books.

Miller, D. (1974). *Adolescence: Psychology, Psychopathology and Psychotherapy*. New York, NY: Jacob Aronson.

Moreno, J. L. (1946). *Psychodrama: Vol. I*. New York, NY: Beacon House.

Moretti, M. M., & Holland, R. (2003). Navigating the journey of adolescence: Parental attachment and the self from a systemic perspective. In S. Johnson & V. Whiffen (Eds.), *Clinical Applications of Attachment Theory* (pp. 41–56). New York, NY: Guilford.

Moretti, M. M., & Peled, M. (2004). Adolescent-parent attachment: Bonds that support healthy development. *Paediatric Child Health*, 9(8), 551–555.

Music, G. (2014). *The Good Life: Wellbeing and the New Science of Altruism, Selfishness and Immorality*. Hove, UK, and New York, NY: Routledge.

Newcombe, N., & Lerner, J. C. (1982). Britain between the wars: The historical context of Bowlby's theory of attachment. *Psychiatry*, 45, 1–12.

Nietzsche, F. (2000). *Basic Writings of Nietzsche*. New York, NY: Random House Inc.

Nitsun, M. (1996). *The Anti-Group: Destructive Forces in the Group and their Creative Potential*. London, UK: Routledge.

Nitsun, M. (2006). *The Group as an Object of Desire: Exploring Sexuality in Group Therapy*. London, UK, and New York, NY: Routledge.

Nitsun, M. (2015). *Beyond the Anti-Group: Survival and Transformation*. London, UK, and New York, NY: Routledge.

Oakley, C. (2007). *Football Delirium*. London, UK: Karnac.

Obholzer, A., & Roberts, V. Z. (Eds.). (1994). *The Unconscious at Work: Individual and Organizational Stress in the Human Services*. London, UK: Routledge.

Obholzer, A. (2001). Security and creativity at work. In C. Clulow (Ed.), *Adult Attachment and Couple Psychotherapy: The 'Secure Base' in Practice and Research* (pp. 185–193). Hove, UK: Brunner-Routledge.

O'Connell, B. A. (1979). Normal adolescence. *Journal of the Irish Medical Association*, 72(9), 359–365.

Palazzoli, M., Boscolo, L., Cecchin, G., & Prata, G. (1978). *Paradox and Counterparadox*. London, UK: Jason Aronson.

Papini, D. R., & Roggman, L. A. (1992). Adolescent perceived attachment to parents in relation to competence, depression, and anxiety: A longitudinal study. *Journal of Early Adolescence*, 12, 420–440.

Parkes, C. M. (1978). *Bereavement: Studies of Grief in Adult Life*. Harmondsworth, UK: Penguin Books.

Parkes, C. M. (1995). Edward John Mostyn Bowlby 1907–1990. *Proceedings of the British Academy*, 87, 247–261.

Parkes, C. M., & Stevenson-Hinde, J. (Eds.). (1982). *The Place of Attachment in Human Behaviour*. London, UK: Tavistock Publications.

Parkes, C. M., Stevenson-Hinde, J., & Marris, P. (Eds.). (1991). *Attachment Across the Life Cycle*. London, UK: Routledge.

Partridge, S. (2014). The hidden neglect and sexual abuse of infant Sigmund Freud. *Attachment: New Directions in Psychotherapy and Relational Psychoanalysis*, 8(2), 139–150.

Paskauskas, R. A. (Ed.). (1993). *The Complete Correspondence of Sigmund Freud and Ernest Jones 1908–1939*. Cambridge, MA: Belknap Press & Harvard University Press.

Perry, A. (Ed.). (2009). *Teenagers and Attachment: Helping Adolescents Engage with Life and Learning*. London, UK: Worth Publishing.

Piaget, J. (1951). *Play, Dreams and Imitation in Childhood*. New York, NY: Norton.

Piaget, J. (1953). *The Origins of Intelligence in the Child*. New York, NY: International Universities Press.

Piaget, J. (1954). *The Child's Construction of Reality*. New York, NY: Basic Books.

Pietromonaco, P. R., & Barrett, L. F. (2000). The Internal Working Models concept: What do we really know about the self in relation to others? *Review of General Psychology*, 4(2), 155–175.

Pines, M. (1991). A history of psychodynamic psychiatry in Britain. In J. Homes (Ed.), *Textbook of Psychotherapy in Psychiatric Practice* (pp. 282–311). Edinburgh, UK: Churchill Livingston.

Pines, M. (1998). *Circular Reflections: Selected Papers on Group Analysis and Psychoanalysis*. London, UK, and Philadelphia, PA: Jessica Kingsley.

Pines, M. (2000). Reflections of a group analyst. In J. J. Shay & J. Wheelis (Eds.), *Odysseys in Psychotherapy* (pp. 282–311). New York, NY: Ardent Media.

Pollock, G. (2010). Aesthetic wit(h)nessing in the era of trauma. *EurAmerica*, 40, 829–886.

Randall, P. (2001). *Bullying in Adulthood: Assessing the Bullies and their Victims*. Hove, UK: Brunner-Routledge.

Rayner, E. (1990). *The Independent Mind in British Psychoanalysis*. London, UK: Free Association Books.

Rayner, E. (1991). John Bowlby's contributions: A brief summary. *Bulletin of the British Psychoanalytical Society*, 27(11), 20–23.

Redl, F. (1966). *When We Deal with Children*. New York, NY: Free Press.

Rees, J. R. (1947). *Mental Health and the Offender*. London, UK: The Clarke Hall Fellowship.

Reid, S., & Kolvin, I. (1993). Group psychotherapy for children and adolescents. *Archives of Disease in Childhood*, 69, 244–250.

Ribble, M. A. (1944). Infantile experiences in relation to personality development. In J. Hunt (Ed.), *Personality and the Behaviour Disorders* (pp. 621–651). New York, NY: Ronald Press.

Richardson, S. (2011). Will you sit by her side? An attachment-based approach to working with dissociative conditions. In V. Sinason (Ed.), *Attachment, Trauma and Multiplicity: Working with Dissociative Identity Disorder* (second edition, pp. 150–165). London, UK, and New York, NY: Routledge.

Richardson, S. (2013). Emerging narratives of historic abuse: Is this a watershed moment? *Attachment: New Directions in Psychotherapy and Relational Psychoanalysis*, 7(2), i–x.

Riviere, J. (1927). Symposium on Child Analysis. *International Journal of Psychoanalysis*, 8, 370–377.

Riviere, J. (1952). The unconscious phantasy of an inner world reflected in examples from literature. *International Journal of Psychoanalysis*, 33, 160–172.

Robertson, J., & Robertson, J. (1989). *Separation and the Very Young*. London, UK: Free Association Books.

Robinson, M. (1980). Systems theory for the beginning therapist. *Australian Journal of Family Therapy*, 1(4), 183–194.

Rose, S. R. (1998). *Group Work with Children and Adolescents*. Thousand Oaks, CA: Sage.

Rosenstein, D. S., & Horowitz, H. A. (1996). Adolescent attachment and psychopathology. *Journal of Consulting and Clinical Psychology*, 64, 244–253.

Rustin, M. (2007). John Bowlby at the Tavistock. *Attachment and Human Development*, 9(4), 355–359.

Rustin, M. (2009). Esther Bick's legacy of infant observation at the Tavistock: Some reflections 60 years on. *Infant Observation: The International Journal of Infant Observation and its Applications*, 12(1), 29–41.

Rutter, M. (1980). Attachment and the development of social relationships. In M. Rutter (Ed.), *Scientific Foundations of Developmental Psychiatry* (pp. 267–279). London, UK: Heinemann Medical.

Sanders, R. (2004). *Sibling Relationships: Theory and Issues for Practice*. New York, NY: Palgrave MacMillan.

Scarf, M. (1976). *Body, Mind, Behaviour*. New York, NY: Dell.

Schaefer, C. E. (Ed.). (1999). *Short-term Psychotherapy Groups for Children: Adapting Group Processes for Specific Problems*. Northvale, NJ: Aronson.

Schlapobersky, J. (2016). *From the Couch to the Circle: Group-Analytic Psychotherapy in Practice*. London, UK, and New York, NY: Routledge.

Shechtman, Z., & Ben-David, M. (1999). Group and individual treatment of childhood aggression: A comparison of outcome and process. *Group Dynamics: Theory Research and Practice*, 3(4), 1–12.

Shepard, M. (1971). *The Love Treatment: Sexual Intimacy between Patients and Psychotherapists*. New York, NY: Wyden.

Simon, H. A. (1996). *The Sciences of the Artificial*. Cambridge, MA: MIT Press.

Sinason, V. (Ed.). (2002). *Attachment, Trauma and Multiplicity: Working with Dissociative Identity Disorder*. London, UK, and New York, NY: Routledge.

Sinason, V. (2011). Introduction. In V. Sinason (Ed.), *Attachment, Trauma and Multiplicity: Working with Dissociative Identity Disorder* (second edition, pp. 3–20). London, UK, and New York, NY: Routledge.

Slavson, S. R. (1940). Foundations of group therapy with children. In M. Schiffer (Ed.), *Dynamics of Group Psychotherapy* (1979 edition, pp. 523–537). New York, NY: Jason Aronson.

Slavson, S. R., & Schiffer, M. (1975). *Group Psychotherapies for Children*. New York, NY: Free Press.

Smuts, A. (1977). *Interview with Dr John Bowlby in London on 6th June and 23rd July 1977; and additional written material sent by Dr Bowlby in September and October 1979*. Unpublished. Archives Tavistock & Portman Joint Library, London, UK.

Southern, D. (1990). Remembrances of John Bowlby. *Journal of the Institute for Self Analysis*, 4(1), 14–15.

Southgate, J. (1990). John Bowlby as a supervisor. *Journal of the Institute for Self Analysis*, 4(1), 8–12.

Southgate, J. (2011). A theoretical framework for understanding multiplicity and dissociation. In Sinason (Ed.), *Attachment, Trauma and Multiplicity: Working with Dissociative Identity Disorder* (pp. 83–95). London, UK, and New York, NY: Routledge.

Spitz, R. A. (1945). Hospitalism: An inquiry into the genesis of psychiatric conditions in early childhood. *The Psychoanalytic Study of the Child*, 1, 53–74.

Spitz, R. A. (1947). *Grief: A peril in infancy* [Film]. University Park, PA: Penn State Audio Visual Services.

Spitz, R. A. (1957). *No and Yes*. New York, NY: International University Press.

Sroufe, L. A. (1979). Socioemotional development. In J. Osofsky (Ed.), *Handbook of Infant Development* (pp. 462–515). New York, NY: John Wiley.

Steinberg, D. (1983). *The Clinical Psychiatry of Adolescence*. Chichester, UK: John Wiley.

Steiner, J. (1993). *Psychic Retreats. Pathological Organizations in Psychotic, Neurotic and Borderline Patients*. London, UK, and New York, NY: Routledge.

Steiner, R. (1985). Some thoughts about tradition and change arising from an examination of the British Psychoanalytical Society's controversial discussions (1943–1944). *International Review of Psycho-Analysis*, 12, 27–71.

Stern, D. N. (1985). *The Interpersonal World of the Infant*. New York, NY: Basic Books.

Stevenson-Hinde, J. (2007). Attachment Theory and John Bowlby: Some reflections. *Attachment and Human Development*, 9(3), 337–342.

Stringer, L. (1971). *The Sense of the Self*. Philadelphia, PA: Temple University Press.

Sullivan, H. S. (1953). *The Collected Works of Harry Stack Sullivan: Vol. I*. In H. S. Perry & M. L. Gavel (Eds.). New York, NY: Norton.

Sullivan, H. S. (1955). *The Interpersonal Theory of Psychiatry*. London, UK: Tavistock.

Suomi, S. J. (1995). Influence of attachment theory on ethological studies of bio-behavioral development in nonhuman primates. In S. Goldberg, R. Muir, & J. Kerr (Eds.), *Attachment Theory: Social, Developmental, and Clinical Perspectives* (pp. 185–201). Hillsdale, NJ: Analytic Press.

Sutherland, J. (1990). John Bowlby: Some personal reminiscences. *The Tavistock Gazette*, 29, 13–16.

Suttie, I. D. (1935). *The Origins of Love and Hate*. London, UK: Kegan Paul.

Swan, J. (1974). Mater and Nannie: Freud's two mothers and the discovery of the Oedipus complex. *American Imago*, 31(1), 1–64.

Tanner, J. M., & Inhelder, B. (Eds.). (1971). *Discussions on Child Development: A Consideration of Biological, Psychological and Cultural Approaches to the Understanding of Human Development and Behaviour. The Proceedings of the Meetings of the World Health Organization Study Group 1953–1956* [four volumes]. New York, USA: International University Press.

Tijhuis, L. (1997). Transition and conflict in the development of individuals and the group in group psychotherapy with adolescents. *International Journal of Adolescent Medicine and Health*, 9(2), 135–149.

Tijhuis, L. (1998). Peers as the guardian angels of individuation in the therapy group: Ego supportive group therapy for children and adolescents. *Group Analysis*, 31(4), 547–563.

Tinbergen, N. (1951). *The Study of Instinct*. Oxford, UK: Clarendon Press.

Tondo, L. (2012). Interview with John Bowlby. *Attachment: New Directions in Psychotherapy and Relational Psychoanalysis*, 6(1), 1–26.

Trist, E. (1985). Working with Bion in the 1940s: The group decade. In M. Pines (Ed.), *Bion and Group Psychotherapy* (pp. 1–38). London, UK: Routledge & Kegan Paul.

Tschan, W. (2014). *Professional Sexual Misconduct in Institutions: Causes, Consequences, Prevention and Intervention*. Gottingen, Germany, and Boston, MA: Hogrefe.

Van der Horst, F. C. P. (2011). *John Bowlby: From Psychoanalysis to Ethology*. Chichester, UK: Wiley-Blackwell.

Van der Horst, F. C. P., Van der Veer, R., & Van Ijzendoom, M. H. (2007). John Bowlby and ethology: An annotated interview with Robert Hinde. *Attachment and Human Development*, 9(4), 321–335.

Van der Horst, F. C. P., LeRoy, H. A., & Van der Veer, R. (2008). When strangers meet: John Bowlby and Harry Harlow on attachment behavior. *Integrative Psychological and Behavioral Science*, 42(4), 370–388.

Van Dijken, S. (1998). *John Bowlby: His Early Life. A Biographical Journey into the Roots of Attachment Theory*. London, UK, and New York, NY: Free Association Books.

Vandell, D. L., & Mueller, E. C. (1980). Peer play and friendships during the first two years. In H. Foot, T. Chapman, & J. Smith (Eds.), *Friendship and Childhood Relationships* (pp. 181–209). London, UK: Wiley.

Vernon, P. E., & Parry, J. B. (1949). *Personnel Selection in the British Forces*. London, UK: University of London Press.

Waddell, M. (2002). *Inside Lives: Psychoanalysis and the Growth of the Personality*. London, UK: Karnac.

Waddington, C. H. (1957). *The Strategy of the Genes*. London, UK: Allen & Unwin.

Watzlawick, P. (1983). *The Situation is Hopeless but not Serious: The Pursuit of Unhappiness*. London, UK: Norton.

Welsh, T. (2013). *The Child as Natural Phenomenologist: Primal and Primary Experience in Merleau-Ponty's Psychology*. Evanston, IL: North-Western University Press.

White, K., & Schwartz, J. (Eds.). (2005). *Sexuality and Attachment in Clinical Practice*. London, UK: Karnac.

Widlocher, D. (Ed.). (2002). *Infantile Sexuality and Attachment*. London, UK: Karnac.

Wiener, N. (1948). *Cybernetics, or Control and Communication in the Animal and the Machine*. Cambridge, MA: MIT Press.

Winnicott, D. W. (1945). Primitive emotional development. In *Collected Papers: Through Paediatrics to Psychoanalysis* (1984 edition, pp. 145–156). London, UK: Karnac.

Winnicott, D. W. (1949). Hate in the countertransference. *International Journal of Psychoanalysis*, 30, 69–74.

Winnicott, D.W. (1965). *The Maturational Processes and the Facilitating Environment: Studies in the Theory of Emotional Development*. London, UK: The Hogarth Press and The Institute of Psychoanalysis.

Winnicott, D.W. (1969). Adolescent process and the need for personal confrontation. *Paediatrics*, 44, 752–756.

Winnicott, D. W. (1971). *Playing and Reality*. London, UK: Tavistock Publications.

Winnicott, D. W. (1990). *Deprivation and Delinquency*. New York, USA, and London, UK: Routledge.

World Health Organization (2003). *Guidelines for Medico-legal Care for Victims of Sexual Violence*. Geneva, Switzerland: WHO.

World Psychiatric Association (1996). *Madrid Declaration on Ethical Standards of Psychiatric Practice*. Approved by the WPA General Assembly in Madrid Spain on 25th August. Retrieved from http://www.wpanet.org/detail.php?section_id=5&content_id=48.

Woods, J. (1993). Limits and structure in child group psychotherapy. *Journal of Child Psychotherapy*, 19(1), 63–78.

Woods, J. W. (2003). *Boys Who Have Abused*. London, UK: Jessica Kingsley.

Yalom, I. (1985). *The Theory and Practice of Group Psychotherapy* (third edition). New York, NY: Basic Books.

Zulueta, F. de (1993). *From Pain to Violence: The Traumatic Roots of Destructiveness*. London, UK: Whurr Publishers.

AUTHOR INDEX

SUBJECT INDEX

 Taylor & Francis eBooks

Helping you to choose the right eBooks for your Library

Add Routledge titles to your library's digital collection today. Taylor and Francis ebooks contains over 50,000 titles in the Humanities, Social Sciences, Behavioural Sciences, Built Environment and Law.

Choose from a range of subject packages or create your own!

Benefits for you

» Free MARC records
» COUNTER-compliant usage statistics
» Flexible purchase and pricing options
» All titles DRM-free.

Benefits for your user

» Off-site, anytime access via Athens or referring URL
» Print or copy pages or chapters
» Full content search
» Bookmark, highlight and annotate text
» Access to thousands of pages of quality research at the click of a button.

REQUEST YOUR FREE INSTITUTIONAL TRIAL TODAY | **Free Trials Available**
We offer free trials to qualifying academic, corporate and government customers.

eCollections – Choose from over 30 subject eCollections, including:

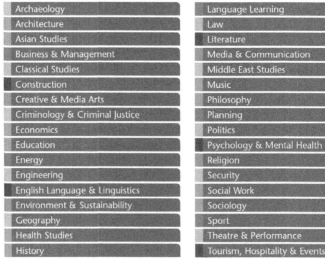

Archaeology	Language Learning
Architecture	Law
Asian Studies	Literature
Business & Management	Media & Communication
Classical Studies	Middle East Studies
Construction	Music
Creative & Media Arts	Philosophy
Criminology & Criminal Justice	Planning
Economics	Politics
Education	Psychology & Mental Health
Energy	Religion
Engineering	Security
English Language & Linguistics	Social Work
Environment & Sustainability	Sociology
Geography	Sport
Health Studies	Theatre & Performance
History	Tourism, Hospitality & Events

For more information, pricing enquiries or to order a free trial, please contact your local sales team:
www.tandfebooks.com/page/sales